T0382708

ROUTLEDGE LIBRARY EDITIONS:
INDUSTRIAL RELATIONS

Volume 6

CAPITALISM, THE STATE AND INDUSTRIAL RELATIONS

CAPITALISM,
THE STATE AND
INDUSTRIAL RELATIONS

DOMINIC STRINATI

Routledge
Taylor & Francis Group

LONDON AND NEW YORK

First published in 1982 by Croom Helm Ltd

This edition first published in 2025
by Routledge
4 Park Square, Milton Park, Abingdon, Oxon OX14 4RN

and by Routledge
605 Third Avenue, New York, NY 10158

Routledge is an imprint of the Taylor & Francis Group, an informa business

British Library Cataloguing in Publication Data
A catalogue record for this book is available from the British Library

ISBN: 978-1-032-81770-5 (Set)
ISBN: 978-1-032-80020-2 (Volume 6) (hbk)
ISBN: 978-1-032-80051-6 (Volume 6) (pbk)
ISBN: 978-1-003-49517-8 (Volume 6) (ebk)

DOI: 10.4324/9781003495178

Publisher's Note
The publisher has gone to great lengths to ensure the quality of this reprint but
points out that some imperfections in the original copies may be apparent.

Disclaimer
The publisher has made every effort to trace copyright holders and would
welcome correspondence from those they have been unable to trace.

Capitalism, the State and Industrial Relations

DOMINIC STRINATI

CROOM HELM
London & Canberra

© 1982 Dominic Strinati
Croom Helm Ltd, 2-10 St John's Road, London SW11

British Library Cataloguing in Publication Data

Strinati, Dominic
     Capitalism, the state and industrial relations.
     1. Industrial relations – Great Britain
     I. Title
     331'.0941   HD8391

     ISBN 0-85664-996-1

Printed and bound in Great Britain by
Biddles Ltd, Guildford and King's Lynn

CONTENTS

FOR PENNY, ADAM AND JONATHAN

ACKNOWLEDGEMENTS

This book was originally approved as a Ph.D. thesis by the
University of London. I would like to thank the following for
their very helpful advice and criticisms regarding my study,
either in discussing its arguments or commenting upon various
drafts, though they cannot, of course, be held responsible for
what it contains: Peter Baehr, Kevin Bonnett, Colin Crouch,
Chris Dandeker, Bob Jessop, Terry Johnson, Frank Longstreth,
Roger Penn, Ali Rattansi and John Scott. I would like to thank
Richard Scase for inviting me to contribute to the Social
Analysis series and for his advice and encouragement with the
study. I would also like to thank David Croom for his patience
and for his assistance with the completion of the book. I am
particularly grateful to Anthony Giddens not only for agreeing
to act as external examiner for my thesis but also for providing constructive and challenging advice and criticisms both
regarding the thesis and its publication in book form. I have
benefitted very greatly from the unselfish, assiduous and
scholarly way in which Angus Stewart gave of his time and
ideas in supervising and assisting my research, subjecting it
to sharp and constructive criticisms, while never losing sight
of the need for intellectual encouragement. Above all, I wish
to thank Penny, who has lived with this work as much as I have;
what I owe her could never accurately be conveyed by words
alone.

ABBREVIATIONS

ABCC	Association of British Chambers of Commerce
ACAS	Advisory, Conciliation and Arbitration Service
ACTT	Association of Cinematograph and Television Technicians
AEU	Amalgamated Engineering Union (later AUEW)
AIB	Association of Independent Businesses
ASSET	Association of Supervisory Staffs, Executives and Technicians (later ASTMS)
ASTMS	Association of Supervisory, Technical and Managerial Staffs
AUEW	Amalgamated Union of Engineering Workers
BBA	British Bankers' Association
BEC	British Employers Confederation
CAC	Central Arbitration Committee
CBI	Confederation of British Industry
CIR	Commission on Industrial Relations
CSO	Central Statistical Office
DOE	Department of Employment
EDC	Economic Development Committee
EEF	Engineering Employers Federation
EETPU	Electrical, Electronic, Telecommunications, and Plumbing Union
EP Act	Employment Protection Act 1975
ETU	Electrical Trades Union (later EETPU)
FBI	Federation of British Industry
GMWU	General and Municipal Workers Union
ICCUS	Inns of Court Conservative and Unionist Society
IPC	International Publishing Corporation
IR Act	Industrial Relations Act 1971
ME	Minutes of Evidence
NABM	National Association of British Manufacturers
NALGO	National Association of Local Government Officers
NBPI	National Board for Prices and Incomes
NCEO	National Confederation of Employers' Organisations

NEDC	National Economic Development Council
NEDO	National Economic Development Office
NFBTE	National Federation of Building Trades Employers
NIRC	National Industrial Relations Court
NUBE	National Union of Bank Employees
NUDAW	National Union of Distributive and Allied Workers (later USDAW)
NUGMW	National Union of General and Municipal Workers (later GMWU)
NUR	National Union of Railwaymen
RC	Royal Commission
SBA	Small Businesses Association
SIM	Society of Independent Manufacturers
TGWU	Transport and General Workers Union
TUC	Trades Union Congress
TULR Act	Trade Union and Labour Relations Act 1974
TULR (A) Act	Trade Union and Labour Relations (Amendment) Act 1976
USDAW	Union of Shop, Distributive and Allied Workers
WE	Written Evidence

Chapter 1

THE STATE AS A THEORETICAL AND HISTORICAL PROBLEM

The main aim of this study[1] is to analyse the changing role
of the state in British industrial relations in the 1960s and
1970s in the context of the changing relationship between the
economy, class conflict and the state and to examine some of
the factors which have shaped the policies and interventions
of the state to restructure both work relations and the state
in order to meet the 'crisis' of industrial relations that
began to emerge from the late 1950s onwards. To undertake this
analysis it is necessary to develop theoretical principles and
conceptual guidelines for the subsequent empirical research
and this first chapter will be devoted to this task. Accordingly, I shall critically explore the existing literature to
see to what extent it can be used to provide an explanatory
framework for studying the role of the state.

THEORIES OF CAPITALISM, CLASS AND THE STATE:
SOME CRITICAL COMMENTS

The Autonomy of the State
The problem of explaining the state is associated with such
questions as 'How independent is the state?'; 'Is the state
subject to the determining influence of economic forces and
ruling class pressure?'; 'Is the state autonomous and, if so,
how autonomous?'; or 'Is the state entrusted with the task
of balancing and implementing the demands of all classes in
society?'. These questions raise the issues of whether the
state is subordinate to other socio-economic structures which
constrain its course of action, whether it can determine such
structures enjoying freedom from external constraint, or
whether this freedom or autonomy is more apparent than real,
being in itself relative and/or determined. A number of
theories have been offered which vary markedly in terms of
whether or not the autonomy of the state is emphasised, and
what constitutes and determines such autonomy. In dealing
with these theories of the state I will have two main aims

1

in view: to clarify some of the major propositions that have
been put forward; and to suggest some of the problems posed by
the discussion which this study could attempt to come to grips
with.

The theoretical approach to the study of the state's role
that I shall advance will owe something to schools of thought
outside the Marxist tradition, which assert the total autonomy
of the state. With the exception of Weber's ideas, however, I
regard such speculation as the reverse side of the intellectual
coin to that offered by crude and deterministic Marxist theories of the state. To argue that the state is a completely
free institution is as sociologically unenlightening and as
historically inaccurate as the argument that the state is a
consciously manipulated instrument of an omniscient and monolithic ruling class, or an epiphenomenon of the economy. I
shall therefore consider this line of argument in order to
demonstrate its failure to pose the problem of the relation
between class power and state power and to conceptualise the
structural character of the relative autonomy of the state.

I wish to exclude Weber from these strictures, particularly since he did not set out an explicit theory of the state.[2]
His work exhibits an awareness of the state's connections with
structures of class power; he notes, for example, 'the state's
end is to safeguard (or to change) the external and internal
distribution of power' (1970; 334), recognising also the
potential autonomy of the state. But it must be emphasised
that he did not endeavour to come to grips with such problems
in proffering a definite solution of them.

This feature of Weber's work is due, in large part, to
his over-riding concern with the development of the modern
state, together with bureaucratic organisation, as central
components of the process identified as the rationalisation
of the Western world, the advent and growth of the rational,
bureaucratic state, the capitalist economic order and rationa-
listic normative systems. The development of the state, for
Weber, while it preceded capitalist development, is closely
associated with economic processes. The distinction Weber
draws and attempts to maintain relates to his critique of
the Marxist concept of socialist society and the 'withering
away of the state'. If, according to Weber, it is the case
that Marxist socialism views the state as merely an instrument
of class rule which it is assumed will no longer be functionally necessary when the revolution has abolished classes, then
this is to ignore the state as a means of administratively
regulating society, which is as central to it as an institutional form as any class influence, and which will characterise, as a result of the socialisation of production,
socialist society more than contemporary capitalism (1970;
228-9 and 230. Cf. Giddens: 1973; 125, 181-2 and 234-8).
This emphasis conceived of by Weber in terms of the administrative functions of the state conforms with the proposition

I will advance in respect of the relative autonomy of the
state which locates this property in the creative organisational and mediatory role of the state; while the various
agencies of the state, including the bureaucracy, form the
mechanisms by which this role is articulated and the state
acts upon society. In explaining the state it is necessary
to come to terms with the relation between class power and
state power. And while this is a venture Weber does not pursue, his speculations upon the links between the state and
the distribution of power and the administrative influence
of the state are themes which are crucial and which I will
try to account for, particularly in extending the notion of
administrative agency to the mediatory role of the state.

Acute difficulties arise for theories of the state that
fail to assess the relation between class power and the state
since the failure to pose this problem can lead to rather
unsatisfactory notions of the autonomy of the state, on the
part of authors who go out of their way to assert the independence of the 'political'. Thus, Aron, in contrast to economic
determinist schools of Marxist thought, argues, 'It has not
been shown that political phenomena are solely determined by
the stages of economic growth ... it may be, as the ancients
believed, that political phenomena have their own rhythm,
that despotisms break down and that democracies become corrupt'
(1967; 242. Cf. Poggi: 1978. Bendix: 1969). Thus, authors like
Aron are quite correct to say that political changes are not
solely determined by economic changes, but to merely assert
the independence of the political becomes as much an article
of faith as the idea that politics are solely determined by
economic factors. To put the point quite simply, this argument
fails to specify what is claimed, namely how the autonomy of
the state is structured.

The critical points I have been making can be established
by considering Dahrendorf's discussion of the state. Basically
Dahrendorf provides a critique of Marxist political theory by
arguing that, while in Marx's time industrial control gave
rise to the monopolisation of political power, this theory
has been 'refuted by the first government of a labour party
in an industrial country' (1959; 142). His position is predicated upon the idea that political power resides in electoral
victories and holding governmental office (1959: 306-307).
Dahrendorf is therefore led to conclude that 'managerial or
capitalist elites may be extremely powerful groups in society,
they may even exert partial control over governments and
parliaments, but these very facts underline the significance
of governmental elites' (1959; 302).

Few would deny 'the significance of governmental elites',
but it may be contended that Dahrendorf makes use of an
extremely narrow and formalistic concept of power, locating
it in state institutions, and thereby minimising the importance of industrial class power as a potential determinant of,

and constraint upon, political power. Secondly, I must admit
to finding it rather unenlightening to merely affirm the
independence of the state. Dahrendorf states that the Marxist
theory he criticises does not possess the status of a 'general
law' (1959; 142) and this is true, but then neither does his
own assertion. The structure of the autonomy of the state must
be theoretically specified and empirically examined. Dahrendorf
does note that the structural links between industrial and
political power are 'a subject for empirical research' but
then insists paradoxically that 'the political state and
industrial production are two essentially independent associations in which power is exercised' (1959; 142). The latter
cannot be so if it is a subject for empirical research. Moreover the problem is reduced to one concerning the relationship
between elite groups rather than the role of the state within
a capitalist society.

While such an approach has value insofar as it emphasises
the administrative role of the state, its bureaucratic organisation and the possibility of the development of bureaucratic
self-interests on the part of the controllers of the state in
the perpetuation of state power, it is thus confronted by a
number of major difficulties. It does not specify how the
autonomy of the state is determined. It tends to assert such
autonomy without assessing the ways in which the state may be
linked to the economy and to the structure of class power and
how it may be influenced and constrained accordingly. And
though it does at times stress the influence of pressure group
bargaining upon the actions of the state, little attempt is
made to gauge the relative weight and power of different
interest groups and the constraints of the economy. It thus
provides few indications as to the possible relationships
between the state, the economy and class power. In this
respect it is necessary to turn to Marxist theory, though
the approach discussed above stands as a highly convincing
corrective and preferable alternative to much of what has
traditionally passed for the Marxist theory of the state.

The Marxist-Instrumentalist Theory of the State
This theoretical approach is often epitomised by Marx's axiom
in The Communist Manifesto: 'the executive of the modern state
is but a committee for managing the common affairs of the
whole bourgeoisie' (1968; 37. Cf. Lenin: 1951. Mandel: 1971).
This view argues that the state is an instrument which can be
used to further the interests of an economically dominant
class, that is, the class which owns and controls the means
of production, namely the bourgeoisie: the state is thus
manipulated by a closely knit and homogeneous class which
controls the economy and which, because it is capable of
running the state, is constituted as a ruling class.

Miliband has attempted to secure this form of interpretation by re-defining Marx's axiom in suggesting that the

4

state acts on behalf of, not at the behest of, the bourgeoisie, in order to 'manage the common (as opposed to particular) affairs of the whole (as opposed to separate elements) bourgeoisie' (1973b; 85n). It is not difficult, however, to see that this is just a re-statement of the instrumentalist problematic for it in no way questions the view that the state is a tool or instrument designed to further the purposes of a homogeneous and cohesive capitalist class. Indeed, the very tenour of the proposition underlines even more this latter view, while the fact that the state acts on behalf of rather than at the behest of, the bourgeoisie in no way qualifies its role as a 'committee'. Furthermore, Miliband does not endeavour to suggest why and how the relationship between capital and the state should be organised in the manner he stipulates.

If this is so then what precisely is wrong with the instrumentalist approach to studying the state? Firstly, it minimises the effects of class struggles on the state, tending to see capital through its manipulation of the state as an all-powerful force which always wins out in the final analysis. It, secondly, ignores the complexity of the structure of capital, its relative lack of homogeneity and cohesion and the existence of important divisions within capital which structure its relationship to the state. It tends thus to see capital as a whole as a collective actor capable of assuming a degree of purposive action, unconstrained by prevailing social-structural conditions. In treating the state as an instrument of a social class, it ignores the existence of the state as an institutional structure and the constraints that this and the actual structure and importance of political organisation and political representation can impose upon any attempt to use the state or, more generally, on types of state intervention, as well as the role they play in the process of class formation. It, in effect, neglects the 'specific effectivity' of politics and the state, providing no means of analysing the forms of the state itself, such as liberal democracy, corporatism or fascism, or the changing relationships between parts of the state, like parliament, government and the judiciary. It is also incapable of explaining the many instances in which particular types of state policy, from nationalisation and the welfare state to taxation and expenditure, appear to deviate very sharply from the expressed interests of capital. It is likewise very difficult to decide in any empirical case exactly what the interests of capital are and how they could be fulfilled adequately by the state, especially given the existence of fractions of capital. It is also a-historical, having very little to say about the changing phases of capitalist development. This class reductionism and essentialism is, however, by no means exhaustive of Marx's writings on the state.

Bonapartism and the Relative Autonomy of the State

Since it connotes the determination of the relative autonomy of the state by way of its functions to maintain class rule, Marx's analysis of Bonapartism becomes germane in this context.[3] In particular, there are two major points I wish to extract from this discussion: the influence wrought by class struggle upon the autonomy of the state; and the manner in which the autonomy of the state is affected by political conflicts within the ruling class.

Marx's notion of the Bonapartist state[4] appears to suggest that it represented an autonomous institutional force. Bonapartism, for Marx, constituted an executive power with 'an immense bureaucratic and military organization, an ingenious and broadly based state machinery, and an army of half a million officials alongside the actual army, which numbers a further half million' (1973; 237). While it had previously been perfected as an instrument of the ruling class, 'only under the second Bonaparte does the state seem to have attained a completely autonomous position' (1973; 238 and 236-7). But the state is not independent of class forces. According to Marx 'the state power does not hover in mid-air. Bonaparte represents a class, indeed he represents the most numerous class of French society, the small peasant proprietors' (1973; 238).[5] Thus, despite its apparent independence, Marx stresses the class nature of Bonapartism:

> Bonaparte is the executive authority which has attained power in its own right and as such he feels it to be his mission to safeguard 'bourgeois order'. But the strength of this bourgeois order lies in the middle class. He therefore sees himself as the representative of the middle class and he issues decrees in this sense. However, he is only where he is because he has broken the political power of this middle class, and breaks it again daily.... But by protecting its material power he recreates its political power (1973; 245).

But the mechanisms whereby this relationship determines the Bonapartist state are not made clear in the '18th Brumaire'. Some suggestive reasons are however provided in 'The Civil War in France', where Marx argues that the Bonapartist state 'was the only form of government possible at a time when the bourgeoisie had already lost, and the working class had not yet acquired, the faculty of ruling the nation' (1974; 208). What is implicitly suggested here is that the relative autonomy of the state is influenced by class conflict; that is to say, the balance of power between classes, such that the militant assertion of working class demands, if they make inroads upon ruling class prerogatives and thereby alter the balance of class power, enhances the autonomy of the state but only insofar as it is made freer to formulate its own programmes

6

to further dominant class interests and repress or accommodate subordinate class pressures according to the demands of capital accumulation.

This structural effect on the role of the state may be reinforced or mitigated by another influence upon the state, which Marx emphasises, namely the effect of divisions within the ruling class. He writes 'the restraints by which their own divisions ("the rival fractions and factions of the appropriating class") had under former regimes still checked the state power, were removed by their union; and in view of the threatening upheaval of the proletariat they now used that state power mercilessly and ostentatiously as the national war-engine of capital against labour' (1974; 207-208). Thus, in respect of the parliamentary republic, one of the political forms preceding the establishment of the Bonapartist state, Marx comments, it

> was more than the neutral territory on which the two factions of the French bourgeoisie, legitimists and orleanists, big landed property and industry, could live side by side with equal rights. It was the inescapable condition of their joint rule, the only form of state in which both the claims of these particular fractions and the claims of all other classes of society were subjected to the general interest of the bourgeois class (1973; 215).

This statement underlines the fact that Marx regarded the ruling class not as a homogeneous, united group but as a class always subject to potential divisions which affect its relationship to the state, and structurally determine the relative autonomy of the state.

While it remains essential to spell out the precise mechanisms whereby class and intra-dominant class conflicts constrain the role of the state, these two propositions constitute crucial qualifications to the 'vulgar' Marxist theory of the state (cf. Miliband: 1965; 283), as does the more implicit attempt to relate the use of state power to the course of capitalist development in France. Thus, these caveats, when read in conjunction with Marx's analysis of Bonapartism, qualify the reductionist and mechanical equation of political rule with class rule that is sometimes assumed to be characteristic of the Marxist theory of the state, whereby the state is regarded as a 'permanent executive of the bourgeoisie', and as the main agent of ruling class conspiracies (cf. Hall: 1977).

The major problems with this model arise from its failure to totally avoid reductionism, to develop adequate political concepts, and to specify fully the structural factors which link the state with the dominant class and yet, at the same time, secure its relative autonomy. What is needed in analyses of the state is for the link between it and dominant classes,

and for its relative autonomy to be conceptualised in terms of
the state's organisational role in mediating the demands of
all classes, and in selecting, cohering and giving expression
to dominant class interests, while the determination of the
relationship between state and capital needs to be related to
the overall shape of the balance of class forces and the logic
of capitalist production and accumulation. These points can be
developed by a critical evaluation of contemporary Marxist
work outside the instrumentalist framework.

Marxist-Functionalism and the State

This perspective sees the capitalist state as a reparative
agency, functionally necessary and responsive to the underlying laws of the dynamics of the capitalist economy rooted
in the process of value production. The state is a mechanism
charged with the function of automatically (or so it would
appear) reacting to and dealing with the contradictions and
crises thrown up by the process of capital accumulation, while
conversely being incapable of obviating effectively the de-
stabilising consequences of such contradictions and crises,
which come merely to be expressed in a different politicised
form reflected by the state.

    Characteristic of this theory is Poulantzas' conception
of 'the general function of the state': 'inside the structure
of several levels dislocated by uneven development, the state
has the particular function of constituting the factor of
cohesion between the levels of a social formation ... as the
regulating factor of its global equilibrium as a system' (1973;
44-5). It follows that since the state 'is a factor of cohesion
of a (social) formation's unity, it is also the structure in
which the contradictions of the various levels of a formation
are condensed' (Ibid.: 45). Accordingly, 'the global role of
the state is a political role', reproducing political class
domination precisely by virtue of ensuring the continuity of
capitalist social formations (Ibid.: 50-4. Cf. 123-37).
Another example of this kind of approach is to be found in
the work of Gamble and Walton who stipulate, without extensive
argument, that the state performs three main functions:
managing demand, socialising costs, and maintaining social
peace and political stability. The fulfilment of these functions gave rise to the long period of postwar prosperity but
the state cannot provide a permanent solution to crises, since
it is now the 'major barrier to accumulation' (1976; 163 and
162-70). They continue, 'the modern state sector is largely
unproductive for private capital - it produces no surplus
value directly .... But without it no surplus value would be
produced at all.... Once accumulation falters the state's
concern to revive it and maintain prosperity comes into conflict with it' (Ibid.: 173 and 162-74 and 180-206).
    A major problem with this line of argument is that it
tends to assume an unproblematic causal relationship between

8

capitalist production and state intervention such that the
latter is automatically guaranteed as a reparative response
determined by the historically specifiable laws governing the
former; i.e. economism. It is reductionist in that the state
is reduced to the functions it performs for the economy or to
functions which are determined by the laws of the economy. Its
causality is therefore teleological in character. It thus fails
to consider the institutional mechanisms which mediate and make
the relationship work and the differentiated structures and
processes embodied in and articulating the relationships
between the economy and the state. This is bound up with the
fundamental question that may be asked of this approach: why
should the state intervene to save capitalism? Certain implicit
suggestions are made, such as Mattick's contention that economic
crises have been insufficient without state assistance to ensure
the regeneration of capital accumulation (1971), but since the
question itself is generally regarded as being unproblematic
no clear theoretical exposition is provided. The only real
answer to emerge is one which asserts that the state is constrained by the dynamic of the law of value for the law of
value requires something outside of itself to regulate it.
But this is merely to revert to economic reductionism, to a
view of the state as an epiphenomenon determined by economic
laws. It cannot however avoid this for this is the only way it
can explain why the state functions to ensure the reproduction
of capitalist relations of production. Its functionalism does
not overcome but is heavily dependent upon economism in framing
an explanation of the role of the state. Its major errors
therefore lie in its tendency towards functionalism and economism and its failure to provide an adequate account of the
influence of class conflict upon state action and of the ways
this may be compatible with an analysis of the functions performed by the state for the capitalist economy.[6]

Marxist Conflict Theory and the State
While Gamble and Walton are aware of the relevance of class
struggle as is suggested by their notion of the state's function of ensuring consensus and stability, they reject it as a
major explanatory principle in favour of the opportunities for,
and barriers to, accumulation provided by the role of the state
(Ibid.; 189). But this is precisely what the class conflict
theory rejects. This approach is predicated upon the constraining influence that the class struggle, the capital-labour
conflict, is thought to exercise in shaping the role and functions of the state. It is said to be the task of the capitalist
state to manage and contain class struggle. This class struggle
is not always analysed as being 'emergent' out of production
relations but rather at the level of distribution relations,
the 'wages struggle' (the industrial wage and the 'social'
wage) and as this is reflected within the state and politics.
    One example[7] of this is Poulantzas's analysis of the

political class struggle which, to avoid crude functionalism, argues that the relative autonomy of the state vis a vis class struggle is determined by the double function it possesses regarding the management of such struggle, namely politically organising the dominant classes and politically disorganising the dominated classes. These functions are entailed in and pre-suppose one another. The dominant classes within capitalist social formations are divided and fragmented due to the con-crete co-existence of differing modes of production, and the existence of different fractions of the bourgeoisie itself, be they industrial, commercial or financial, and are thus unable to organise politically. The state thus becomes 'the factor of the political unity of the power bloc under the protection of the hegemonic class or fraction' (1973; 299). It is linked to the strictly political interests of the domi-nant classes and is so 'by being relatively autonomous from these classes' (Ibid.; 282). The state's representation of the political unity of the dominant class forms 'the condition of possibility of the state's relative autonomy vis-a-vis the dominant classes' (Ibid.). The dominant classes are unable, but need to, organise politically to realise their hegemony. This function falls to the state which must be relatively autonomous from the interests of the dominant classes for such political organisation potentially involves state intervention against the interests, both economic and political, long-term and short-term, of certain sections of the dominant classes (but not against those, presumably, of the hegemonic class or fraction). It is also necessary because the state has to ensure the political disorganisation of the dominated classes: to ensure, politically, the unity and hegemony of the dominant classes the state must 'function as the factor of political disorganization; i.e. its function of preventing the working class from organizing itself into an "autonomous" political party' (Ibid.; 287-8). This entails the arrangement of com-promises with the dominated classes, even 'genuine' concessions that impose real sacrifices upon the dominant classes, but always within the limits imposed by the structure of class domination.[8]

This perspective also tends to reject much of what it sees as the more deterministic elements of Marxism, viewing the class struggle as the process which combines the objective and subjective dimensions of social reality. Gough's analysis of state expenditure, which we can take as another example of this theory, argues, following Poulantzas, that 'the capitalist state is characterized by a relative autonomy from the economic structure and is responsive to the ongoing struggle between and within the dominant and dominated classes' (1975; 56).[9] This is based upon a rejection of functionalist theories of the state because they 'suffer from two related weaknesses: the lack of a historical approach and a mechanistic distinction between the economic base and the superstructure, between

10

objective and subjective factors' (Ibid.; 55 and 57). It is accepted by Gough that nomological material forces may shape state action but to remain at this level is to neglect the significance of the class struggle as the 'motor' of history and politics (cf. Glyn and Sutcliffe: 1972; 10).

Now this theoretical approach may provide a useful corrective to the functionalist theory, but the same formal stricture may also be applied for while it does not assume a direct mechanistic and mono-causal relationship between objective economic laws and the state it does posit a direct and mechanical relationship between class struggle and state action. State intervention is merely a consequence of the changing expression of class struggle rooted in distribution relations. The content has changed but the form of argument remains the same. As such the mediating institutional links between the economy, class conflict, and state intervention and the constraints imposed by political structures tend to be neglected. It is not denied that class conflict forms a significant influence upon state intervention but it is still necessary to analyse the nature and structure of state agencies concerned with dealing with the manifestations of political struggle as opposed to apparatuses concerned with other functions related to other aspects of state-economy relations. For it is a possible feature of theories which relate the state to the influence exercised by group or class conflict to conceive of the state as an instrument of power to be used by one side against the other in the course of the conflict. And this 'instrumentalist' inflexion can be seen in the analyses discussed in that the state is theorised as an institutional extension and guarantor of the power of the dominant class, in that it expresses such power, without the constraints exercised by the institutional structure of state power and its relationship to the economy being taken into consideration.

In this perspective there is also, firstly, a related tendency towards 'politicism', that is, towards viewing the relationship between social classes and the state almost solely in political terms, reducing explanation to political factors, ignoring the impact of specifically economic factors. This is the case with Poulantzas' location of the state in the 'field' of class struggle which is framed solely in political terms. The state's role in relation to class struggle is, for Poulantzas, a purely political role oriented solely to the political conditions of such struggle. Therefore the state's role in relation to economic struggle is conceptualised out of existence, save for the 'effect of isolation' which means that economic struggle is not experienced as class struggle (1973; 130-1, 135 and 257). But even if we accept this, it is still by no means clear that such economic conflict, assuming the form of competing, sectional and non-class interests, will not generate problems for capitalism and its continuity requiring state intervention that is not predicated upon the functions of political organisation and political dis-organisation. Rather, economic conflicts may engender state intervention and state policies realised as a consequence not of the state's role vis-a-vis political class struggle but as a consequence of the state's provision of conditions indispensable for the maintenance of capital accumulation.

Secondly, it may be argued that this approach, like functionalist theory, fails to analyse adequately the 'specific effectivity' of the structures of the state. Poulantzas appears to argue that class struggles will be reflected within the structures of the state without giving due weight to the constraints that these structures may impose upon conflicts, thereby, to varying extents, determining their form, character, sequence, and outcome at the level of the state. Thus, while Poulantzas usefully recognises the possibility of contradictions between state apparatuses (1976), he tends to disregard the existence of the state as an objective institutional structure, the framework of which, and the various agencies of which, exercise a specifically political influence upon, rather than merely reflecting and expressing, the conflicts associated with the elaboration of state action and state policies. In brief, the attempt to explain the state's role in terms of class conflict tends to be undermined by the problems associated with politicism and instrumentalism.

'Critical Sociology' and the State
A contemporaneous tradition within Marxist thought, drawing on much earlier attempts to combat economism within Marxist studies of politics and culture, namely 'Frankfurt Marxism' (see Held: 1980) has attempted to come to terms with some of these problems. In so doing it has explicitly or implicitly made use of Weber's work on bureaucracy and the state. I will consider as an example of this here, the work of Offe. Offe's analyses are important because they attempt to relate the role of the state to the specificity of capitalism in a non-reductionist manner, to account for historical changes in the forms of state intervention and, very importantly, to pose the problem of the mediating institutional links between economic processes and state policies, including an assessment of the significance of political structures.[10] However, it may also be pointed out at this juncture that Offe does not go far enough in moving away from economic determinism, does not adequately relate class relations or the state to production, and retains an ultimately functionalist theory of the state.

For Offe, the capitalist state is structured by its relation to the capital accumulation process. The state is <u>divorced</u> or excluded from production. But it must attempt to create and <u>maintain</u> the conditions for accumulation since it is <u>dependent</u> upon the resources created by this process, for the 'institutional self-interest of the state' in its own power requires that it maintain accumulation precisely because it is dependent

12

upon a 'healthy accumulation process'. The latter thus 'acts
as the most powerful constraint criterion, but not necessarily
as the determinant of content, of the policy making process'
(1975; 126). But it should be noted dependency and constraint
do not necessarily connote direct determination. The other
function of the state, legitimation, secures the reciprocal
co-existence of the factors of exclusion, maintenance and
dependency tied into the role of the state and obscures its
capitalist nature (Ibid.; 125-7).

On the basis of this general definition of the role of
the capitalist state Offe attempts to explain historical and
qualitative changes in modes of state intervention by locating
them in the context of the specificity of capitalism, the
accumulation process, and changes in the structure and requirements of this process. Two major historical forms of state
intervention are alluded to by Offe. The first mode of state
intervention is allocation whereby resources and powers
belonging to the state are allocated in order to maintain
accumulation by means of the constitutional and juridical
authority of the state as structured by political power
struggles (Ibid.; 127-9).

The development of capitalism, however, gives rise to
problems which the structure of the accumulation process
cannot in and of itself resolve. The fundamental problem is
one of insufficient supplies of productive in-put commodities,
variable and constant capital, which become too costly, subject
to risks and uncertainties, and their use cannot be appropr-
iated by any single capital. The essentially competitive
nature of capitalist accumulation prevents capital from providing such in-puts itself. These conditions, in this case
the productive in-put commodities which the accumulation
process requires but cannot thus provide, are provided by
the state. Such intervention as is required as a condition
for accumulation leads to the second major mode of state
activity, productive state functions, where 'the state responds to situations in which labour and/or capital fail to
operate in the accumulation process by producing material
conditions which allow the continuation of accumulation'
(Ibid.; 132 & 129-34). As such this mode of intervention
emerges and complements state allocative functions. But
since the resources required have to be produced by the state
and the competitive structure of capital pre-empts its economic
and political unity, the fulfilment of this activity demands
that the state devise appropriate organisational forms and
decision-making rules for the dispensation of productive
functions (Ibid.; 134-44. Cf. Idem.: 1975a; 103-4. Idem.:
1976: cf. J. Hirsch: 1978).

Offe and Ronge take this further by relating the role of
the state to the commodity form, to the commodity production
and exchange relations characteristic of capitalism. When
economic agents are prevented from existing as values in

commodity exchange relations, and accumulation is threatened, the state can 'do nothing', allowing for the operation of self-correcting market mechanisms which the state itself underpins, a feature characteristic of the liberal laissez-faire state. But in time such self-corrective mechanisms cease to be effective. Thus the state can attempt to subsidise economic units rendered incapable of entering commodity exchange relations by maintaining them as agents capable of being returned once conditions permit to the commodity form, a strategy characteristic of the welfare state - this, however, generates fiscal crises (cf. O'Connor: 1973). Therefore the developing contemporary mode of state economic intervention that is required is termed by Offe and Ronge - as a conceptual extension of Offe's notion of productive state activities - 'administrative re-commodification' by which the state creates the 'conditions under which values can function as commodities' (Offe and Ronge: 1975; 143), taking measures to enhance the saleability of labour power and capital and to plan for the obsolescence or regeneration of economic units as commodity forms (Ibid.; 142-4).

This makes it necessary to consider the issue of the institutions mediating the relationship between the economy and state intervention, the mechanisms by means of which the latter secures the continuity of the former. This constitutes an important question for analysis since I have attempted to argue that it is not possible to posit an automatic, functional relationship between economic processes and state policies. As Offe puts it, the problem is one of 'charting out the concrete mechanisms mediating between economics and politics' (1976a; 396). The institutions and rules needed to effect forms of state intervention are elaborated at the level of the state for they cannot be developed within the economy. Thus, considerations of this nature direct our attention to analyses of the institutional frameworks devised or utilised by the state to fulfil its role. And it is at this level that the identification of forms and contents of political conflict becomes possible and relevant. It is therefore arguably necessary to hold as problematic, as Poulantzas and trends within Marxist theory do not, the structural relationship between the economy and state policy so as to take account of the 'linking' institutional mechanisms located within this relationship.

ELEMENTS FOR A SOCIOLOGICAL ANALYSIS OF THE STATE

A number of points relevant to providing a framework for analysing the state's role emerge from this discussion, particularly since some of the claims that have been critically examined are by no means mutually exclusive. We can thus begin, for example, to evaluate the respective arguments of Marxist-functionalism and the class conflict theory of the state. The former, despite its deficiencies, tends to concentrate attention upon the systemic or macro-structural, institutional

14

links between the economy and the state. But the social ties between this and the elaboration of class conflict remain unclear save for attempts to reduce the latter to an economic base or for concessionary gestures in the direction of a vaguely defined class struggle, ignoring the specific political and economic conditions which make political and class conflicts possible. The same is true, obversely, of the class conflict theory. Thus here little account is taken of the objective conditions provided by the macro-structural nexus between economy and state for the development of forms of class conflict and political struggle. The constraining impact of class struggles, especially political class struggle, upon the role of the state is often taken to hold irrespective of the objective possibilities established by structural or systemic conditions. This is mainly a consequence of reducing the state's role to its functions in relation to political class struggle.

This is of especial significance for the analysis of the state and the problem of the relative autonomy of the state since, as Laclau indicates, 'the distinction Miliband establishes between class power and state power is entirely appropriate and restores the problem to its true location' (1975; 101). Both levels are appropriate to this question for both class power and state power operate in the course of class and political conflict but under the conditions from which such power derives and which in turn set limits and constraints on the nature of the structure of conflict and the use of power (cf. Thompson: 1965; 322).

Accordingly, with respect to the substantive question of state intervention in industrial relations which I have raised as an issue for study, it is possible to outline some of the factors which need to be taken into consideration in attempting to provide an analysis of the state and to present an explanation of this question. In the first place, it can be suggested that state intervention in industrial relations derives from the logic of capitalist development, from the macro-institutional relationship between the state and the economy within which the state provides certain conditions for the maintenance and continuity of capital production and accumulation, such that just as capitalism entails distinct modes of economic production so it entails distinct modes of state intervention. This means that the processes associated with and between each as definite constraints and limits on action need to be taken into account in dealing with the problem at hand (cf. Block: 1980. J. Hirsch: 1978. Offe: 1975. Strinati: 1980).

But this macro-structural relationship cannot be seen as being determinative or exhaustive of the forms and nature of class and political struggle, particularly since the prevailing institutional structure of capitalism may indeed generate or allow for a number of distinct forms of conflict and a number of strategies to deal with emergent problems and ensure the

reproduction of capitalism as a system. This means that the
structure and influence of class struggles and political
struggles need to be treated as determinants of state intervention in their own right and not as features necessarily
given by the general structure of capitalism. This is especially pertinent since it is precisely as a more or less direct
consequence of these factors that the content of policy formation is determined for they articulate the problems arising
from capital accumulation and connect these to the process of
state intervention (cf. Wirth: 1977; 305 and 309-10. J. Hirsch:
1978).

If we are therefore to take the impact of struggles upon
state action seriously there are a number of points which need
to be established. First, we cannot treat class struggle or
the classes involved in struggle as unitary phenomena, that is
as collectivities which are necessarily homogeneous in terms
of structure and interests in the course of specific, conjunctural struggles (cf. Engels: 1976. Foster: 1976), nor as
being inclusive of all potential class participants in struggle.
Given the discussion and critical comments made above, this is
of strategic relevance, in concentrating upon the relationship
between capital and the state. In an objective sense capital
does not just exist as a class unity, being equally divided
internally, not only in terms of size and the extent of its
international fields of operation, but also in terms of the
kind of economic activity it may be engaged in, be it production, investment or realisation, and it will also be fragmented in terms of the ways these distinct fractions may be
organised politically and be related to the state.[11] Thus,
while capital may have a general interest in the continuity
of capital accumulation, this cannot pre-empt and cannot
inform us about, in any particular, historical conjuncture,
the precise nature of the distinct fractions of capital and
their interests nor the particular political strategies they
will pursue in attempting to ensure the continuity of capital
production and accumulation (cf. Poulantzas: 1973. Idem.:
1975). This therefore needs to be examined empirically in
order to determine its effects in structuring the relationship between capital and the state. The same point can be
made with respect to labour which, again, in the course of
class struggles is not an undifferentiated unity. While there
are many aspects to this, the one we shall stress is the vari-
ation in labour organisation associated with the distinct
levels at which its interests may be represented and at which
industrial conflict may occur.

The structural relationship of and between the economy
and the state provides the context for class formation and
class conflict. In turn, such formations and such conflicts
can influence and alter the structures of the economy and the
state and the relationship between them, but in so far as this
is the case neither classes, nor the economy and the state can

16

be conceptualised as monolithic and undifferentiated totalities
for the purpose of empirical research, even though the determination of their structural nature as totalities is an essential pre-condition for the analysis and the explanation of
state intervention (cf. Przeworski: 1977. Wright: 1978. Hirsch:
1978).

It follows from this that in order to assess the structural relationship between the economy and modes of state
intervention as policy outputs emanating from the state system,
the mediatory and organisational role played by institutions,
mainly state apparatuses, linking and managing this relationship becomes of crucial importance (Offe: 1974; 1976; 1976a.
Wright: 1978. Hirsch: 1978; 98-103 and 107). The state-economy
relation as expressed in modes of state intervention is
necessarily structured and made possible by institutional
forces that integrate and produce such modes of intervention.
The nature and influence of these forces need to be examined
in any explanation of state intervention since they are the
mechanisms which make intervention possible. Thus state action
to manage industrial conflict between capital and labour rather
than being regarded as an expression of economic class conflict
at the level of a relatively autonomous state or conceived of
as the state acting in the interests of capital, can be seen
in terms of the role of the state in relation to maintaining
accumulation, and controlling class conflict. And this calls
for analysis of the operation of already existing institutions
or the construction of new institutions by specific state
apparatuses to attempt to effect regulation and control. In
this case, the problem for analysis becomes one concerned with
the structuring and re-structuring of state apparatuses.

This is of especial relevance to the much discussed notion
of the relative autonomy of the state, for it is in the context
of the institutional linkage between economy and the state and
the state's management of the economy that the autonomy of the
state and its various apparatuses is realised. While accepting
that the state is subject to limitations imposed by the structural constraints of capitalism and class power, I wish to
argue that the state secures autonomy within these limits,
and can even at times undermine such constraints, as a consequence of its mediatory role. This is meant to refer to the
role of the state in exercising a mediating influence between
the interests of dominant classes and those of subordinate
classes in giving effect to policies which sanction the
interests of the former. In doing this, in mediating and
forming class rule, the state possesses a genuine autonomy
by virtue of the properties of this mediatory role. This role,
given the diverse elements and interests of which the dominant
class is composed, consists of the state creating a political
unity from these interests by producing out of them an organised course, or courses, of action designed to secure dominant
class interests and demands, that is those which it chooses to

17

further as policy options to be implemented by state action. Thus, the state's relative autonomy resides in its capacity to select and organise, from diverse interests, an articulation of dominant class interests in an explicit political form. As such, although this does not need to be a conscious process and is subject to the structural constraints of class power, the economy and the state, it is implied that the state autonomously recognises and furthers certain dominant class interests as against others, can introduce interests and aims of its own, and exercises a constitutive role in giving to such interests a politically organised form. And it is this which constitutes the structural character of the relative autonomy of the state and one structural link between class power and state power.

Moreover, the organisation of state apparatuses and the construction of modes of state intervention are not reducible to the influence exercised by the economy and class interests. Rather it is the case that classes and class interests themselves necessitate the construction of representative organisations and they also require their constitution at the level of the political by specifically political organisations and state apparatuses. The formulation and establishment of modes of state intervention is thus a consequence of the role of state apparatuses and political organisations, even if enacted in the face of class struggles and in response to problems confronting capital accumulation. This is bound up with the stress placed upon the need to bear in mind what is termed the specific effectivity and the structural selectivity of state and political forms (Offe: 1974). The claim being proposed here in advancing a framework for study is that the institutional structures of the state and the polity in the process of intervention exercise their own specific and determinative influence and have direct effects upon class struggles, capital accumulation, and state intervention. Even though the state 'responds' to these processes, this response is organised and generated by the state and it is necessarily processed by means of definite procedural norms which are part of the state and which have a constraining impact upon the interests expressed and the form taken by state intervention (cf.Hirsch: 1978).

These are the basic pre-suppositions forming the theoretical framework which will guide the subsequent empirical analysis. But before proceeding to considerations of a more directly concrete character, given the concern of the study with changes in the mode of state intervention, it is necessary to provide a conceptual outline of the changing forms and nature of state intervention.

The Changing Nature of State Intervention

Conceptualising changing modes of state intervention in connection with the changing nature of capitalism and the economy is essential for analyses of the contemporary role of the state since state action like incomes policies and industrial relations reform legislation can be seen as tokens of a more all inclusive change in the role of the state. This transition has been marked in the British social formation by the change from laissez-faire to 'interventionist' forms of state intervention in the economy and industrial relations. Therefore to understand and illustrate the changing nature of state intervention a conception of its phases is set out below in Figure 1. Our immediate concern with these formulations is not so much with the overall long-term process of transition but with its relevance for contemporary capitalism in Britain. However, it is not intended to represent certain phases and structures as totally or completely transcending prior structures and phases (cf. Wirth: 1977; 309. MacPherson: 1977). They may be retained either in the operation of the state though subsumed under subsequent forms, or as the political and ideological objectives regarding the role of the state adopted and supported by certain class and political interests, and as such, they remain highly relevant for our analysis.[12]

We shall now briefly define the conceptualisations employed in the schematic depiction of the development of capitalism and modes of state intervention.[13] I shall not confront explicitly the nature of the changes in the economy, class struggles and the re-structuring of state apparatuses and they will be identified in respect of state intervention in industrial relations in the contemporary British social formation. Let me concentrate here upon the conceptualisations of the state-economy relation, political representation, and forms of state control of industrial relations. The notions of laissez-faire and interventionism as applied to the role of the state are intended to designate the overall complex of factors mentioned. But they are also designed to convey the distinction between forms of state intervention whereby the state provides the limited but essential external conditions for capital accumulation and economic processes but does not directly intervene in such processes, rather orienting its action to preclude such intervention, laissez-faire, and forms of state intervention whereby the state directly intervenes in capital production and reproduction, becomes internally involved in the economy, and orients its action to secure such interventionism. The conceptual distinction is thus intended to denote a qualitative difference in the relation of the state to the economy: between optimising as far as possible the autonomisation of the economy to resolve its own crises and conflicts and secure its reproduction with the minimal but nonetheless indispensable assistance from the state, and, conversely, politicising the economy by the direct intrusion of the state into the economy.

This formulation can be extended if we consider in turn the other conceptions advanced. The distinction between allocation and production, or allocative and productive state

Figure 1: Capitalism and Modes of State Intervention

Economy	State-Economy Relation				Polity and State	
Structure and Problems	General Form of State Intervention	Method of State Intervention	State Strategies (Goals)	Functions of State Re: Economy	Political Representation	Forms of State Control of Industrial Relations
Competitive Capitalism. (Absolute Surplus Value extraction)	Laissez-Faire	Allocation (Politics)	Inaction / Protective - Welfare	Facilitative / Supportive	Liberalism or Paternalism	
Monopoly Capitalism. (Relative Surplus Value extraction)	Interventionist	Production (Policies)	Administrative Re-commodification	Directive	Pluralism or Corporatism	

CAPITAL ACCUMULATION / CLASS STRUGGLES

CLASS STRUGGLES / RE-STRUCTURING STATE APPARATUSES

20

functions, refers to the methods by means of which the state intervenes in the economy (Offe: 1975), and, by extension, in industrial relations. Allocation conceptualises intervention whereby the state allocates resources (e.g. taxes, repressive force) which it already controls, as a consequence of its capacity to authoritatively (e.g. by constitutional norms) allocate such resources in securing the conditions for capital accumulation. Furthermore, decisions over allocation are reached as a result of politics, of direct political struggles between competing interests; and it is also important to note that Keynesian economic policies, the management of aggregate demand through state owned resources like taxation and expenditure, exemplify state allocative functions. However, also occasioned by the changing nature of capital accumulation is the need for productive in-puts which the accumulation process, given its competitive structure of relations between discrete capital units, finds it difficult to provide. Hence allocation is supplemented by and subordinated to productive state functions whereby the state actually produces in-puts for capital accumulation to ensure its continuity. In this case, politics as the struggle of competing interests is no longer adequate for these functions and the state has to 'produce' its own policy decision making rules and organisational forms appropriate to such productive functions. Consequently, 'production' as a state function increases the significance of the need to re-organise and construct state apparatuses for the purpose of intervention in that with productive state functions the means or mechanisms for state intervention also have to be produced.

Turning to the next set of distinctions, those concerning the strategies adopted by the state towards capital accumulation (Offe and Ronge: 1975), first, the state can choose inaction, it can choose to do nothing and orient policy to minimise its intervention. This, however, is undermined by the failure of the putative self-correcting mechanisms of the economy and the market to work to regenerate commodity forms and accumulation. Secondly, the state can be protective, providing subsidies and so allowing de-commodified forms to survive under artificial conditions created by the state until they can be returned to the accumulation process. Since this tends to produce fiscal crises the increasingly dominant strategy adopted by the capitalist state is that of administrative re-commodification by which the state creates the 'conditions under which values can function as commodities' (Ibid.; 143). These contentions are highly relevant to state intervention in industrial relations in that state action to control strikes by one means or another is intervention to prevent labour from renouncing its commodity status and the form and details that may mark this are thus crucial for any concrete analysis.

The types of strategies distinguished above are clearly connected with the functional effects of state intervention

in terms of its relation to the economy, that is, the effects
of the functions performed by the state on the economy (Winkler:
1976). Firstly, state functions in this sense can be facilita-
tive, that is allow economic processes to take place but
strictly delimit the role of the state in these processes.
Secondly, state functions can be supportive by protecting and
buttressing the economy. Thirdly, state functions can be
directive, subjecting the economy to state direction by its
intervention into the economy's decision making processes.

The conceptual distinctions outlined above are connected
in that they collectively define the possible general forms of
the state within the British social formation. These constitute
what may be termed the modes of intervention of the state, i.e.
what is entailed in laissez-faire and interventionism. They
also represent a process of transition although this need not
necessarily imply either teleology or the complete supersession
of one mode by another, for as a process of transition it is
structured by class and political struggles. It is a suggestion
of this study that the role of the state in the contemporary
British social formation is marked by such struggles grouped
around attempts to establish and secure or reverse the institution of the interventionist role of the state. It therefore
becomes necessary to identify as we shall begin to do below
the forces and interests involved in these struggles in order
to move towards a clearer understanding of the role of the
state, taking the area of industrial relations to illustrate
empirically the nature of such struggles and this role and the
extent to which state interventionism has emerged in Britain.
But to do this it is also necessary to consider modes of
political representation and forms of state control of
industrial relations.

State Intervention, Political Representation and State Control of Industrial Relations

Almost inevitably, to raise the issue of the nature of state
intervention in Britain in the latter half of the twentieth
century is to raise the question of whether this will be
marked by the inception of corporatism. A survey of this issue
provides an opportunity for developing our framework further
by clarifying the relationship between state intervention,
political representation and the control of industrial relations in Britain; and a consideration of the dimensions
entailed in the structure of corporatism will allow it to be
distinguished from other modes of political representation
and state control of industrial relations. But much of the
discussion of corporatism is seriously deficient in failing
to locate analysis within the context of a theory of the state
or of the changing nature of its role.[14] The consequence of
this is to leave unexplained one of the central institutional
forces involved in the inception of corporatism; the capacity
of the state to initiate or accommodate corporatism is assumed

and thus unexplicated. Therefore, the conception of corporatism developed here needs to be seen in the light of the formulations established above, since I wish to argue that corporatism is a particular mode of political representation and a particular form of state control of industrial relations. Attempts to institute corporatism are connected with the development of the interventionist state. And, as such, it is not merely a question of the class interests to which corporatism corresponds but also a question of the state's role vis-a-vis capital accumulation and of corporatism as an effective means of securing this role in maintaining accumulation. It is the state's organisation of the conditions for capital accumulation as it is affected and shaped by class and political struggles which constitutes the context for the elaboration of modes of intervention, political representation and control of industrial relations, including corporatism. Corporatism is thus generated by and represents a response to the development of capitalism (cf. Panitch: 1977. Schmitter: 1974. Brenner: 1969). The role of the interventionist state entails, on the one hand, the restructuring of capital, the production of inputs for accumulation, the maintenance of commodity forms, and the control of class conflict, and, on the other hand, the construction of organisational means of intervention and modes of political representation to facilitate such intervention. Corporatism is a potential institutional arrangement organised by the state and class and political interests to provide the political conditions for economic intervention. It thus becomes a potential form of political representation corresponding to the means and purposes of the 'interventionist' state and it is in this sense that we may agree with Panitch that corporatism is a mode of political representation 'within advanced capitalism which integrates organised socio-economic producer groups through a system of representation and co-operative mutual interaction at the leadership level, and mobilisation and social control at the mass level' (Panitch: 1977; 66). A number of points need to be established as a consequence of the use of his definition and its relevance to state control of industrial relations.

In the first place, corporatism as a mode of political representation comes into conflict with parliamentarism, requiring the large-scale hierarchical organisation and political incorporation of socio-economic groups, authoritatively sanctioned by the state, rather than the more fragmented diversity of interest groups and political parties independent of state control (cf. Jessop: 1978 and 1980. Schmitter: 1974; 96). To note this is to address a problem not always confronted in the literature, namely if corporatism is emerging what forms of political representation and state control of industrial relations will it necessarily replace or subsume? We have noted a contrast between corporatism and parliamentary pluralism in terms of political representation, and much of the reality of twentieth century politics in Britain since the war can be viewed as a process of conflicts surrounding the transition to interventionism and corporatism, even though such a process is uneven, reversible and corporatism itself is potentially unstable (Crouch: 1977. Panitch: 1976 and 1977. Schmitter: 1974; 111-112).

However, as it stands this is too simplified a conception, for while pluralism denotes group autonomy from the state it is clearly possible for this to co-exist with the emergence of interventionist forms of state action. The growth of monopoly capitalism and the interventionist state necessarily involve the re-structuring of modes of intervention and political representation. But it is arguable that the limitations thereby imposed do not preclude the adoption of one or another of a confined range of alternatives nor indeed of totally contradictory political structures. For Schmitter, this re-structuring

> can be traced primarily to the imperative necessity for a stable, bourgeois-dominant regime, due to processes of concentration of ownership, competition between national economies, expansion of the role of public policy and rationalisation of decision-making within the state to associate or incorporate subordinate classes and status groups more closely within the political process (1974; 107-108).

In view of the establishment of hierarchically structured and controlled organisations representing 'particular capitals' and 'particular labours', as well as those seeking to represent capital or labour in general, and the political institutionalisation of working class interests and organisations, the state endeavours, for the purposes of intervention, to develop state apparatuses divorced and insulated from popular democratic and working class struggles. Consequently, there develop trends towards the centralisation of power within the state in the hands of the executive (Mandel: 1975; 482. Cf. O'Connor: 1973. Hirsch: 1974) and the corporatisation of political representation in order to incorporate the representative organisations of capital and labour and thus to by-pass and contain class conflict. The political representation of the leadership levels in such organisations and state sanctioning of their formation and/or control structures becomes the mode of political representation structurally connected with the role of the interventionist state.

Thus, bound up with corporatism as a mode of political representation are the following characteristics: the institutional incorporation of the leaderships of capital and labour organisations within state apparatuses and state administration to represent such class interests; the state's sanctioning of the control structures of such organisations, in particular organisations of labour, to buttress their effectiveness as

means of social control over their membership; and the re-
structuring or construction of state apparatuses insulated
from parliamentary and popular-democratic struggles (cf.
Winkler: 1977. O'Donnell: 1977. Hirsch: 1974).[15] Such state
apparatuses are particularly significant in the process of
instituting corporatism, functioning both as a representation
of, and the means to, the secure establishment of corporatism,
and operating in the structural context between political representation on the one hand, and state intervention on the
other.

Still a relatively separate question, however, is that of
the principles which inform such state control. These are given
by the other features, identified with corporatism above,
namely leadership integration and representation in the state
and state sanctioning of the control structures of capital and
labour organisations. Quite apart from opposition to state
apparatuses insulated from parliament, pluralism would thus
also imply opposition to state incorporation and state regulation as intervention in the internal affairs of what are
properly seen as private organisations. Thus, for example,
while countenancing the authoritative allocation of legal
resources legitimately belonging to the state it would reject
the intervention of the state in the internal control structures of such organisations since this would represent, ideologically, a denial of organisational autonomy.

These distinctions between pluralism and corporatism as
modes of political representation can be developed with respect to forms of state control of industrial relations as well
as to other modes of political representation. Pluralism and
corporatism connote a differentiation between autonomy and
regulation which are related to laissez-faire and interventionist forms of the role of the state. If we can combine
these features this will provide us with a social map of the
alternative ways of effecting state control of industrial
relations. Such a map of alternative forms of state control
of industrial relations will allow us to locate the class
interests and political forces associated with and committed
to these varying forms and, thereby, the nature of the
struggles surrounding attempts to institute corporatism.
The foci of analysis centre on, firstly, the external conditions of control of industrial relations provided by the role
of the state - the extent to which this is imbued with the
complex of structural factors defining laissez-faire or interventionism, which involves the incorporation of organisational
leaderships into the state. And, secondly, the internal conditions of control of industrial relations, control by means of
the role of trade unions or labour collectivities, which connects with different modes of political representation in
terms of the distinction between autonomy and heteronomy
(Weber: 1964; 148). This can concern: 1) the extent to which
the state sanctions the internal control structure of trade

unions to ensure leadership control of the rank and file;
2) the extent to which state support is provided for collective
bargaining structures and union incorporation into such structures in industrial enterprises; 3) internally generated,
employer sponsored organisations of labour, contained within
particular enterprises and therefore separated from other
types of labour organisation; 4) the legally coercive denial
of the right of union organisation by the state or the informal
denial of such a right by a particular capital unit. While this
may seem to be a somewhat extensive list, it nonetheless hinges
upon the clear-cut distinction between the regulation of trade
unions by one means or another on the one hand, and their being
allowed to perform, and their taking upon themselves, an autonomous role on the other. Synthesising in this way the elements
that have emerged in our discussion so far provides us with the
means of both differentiating the types of role the state can
play in industrial relations and assessing the relationship
between these types and the articulation of class interests
and political objectives regarding the form to be taken by
state intervention in industrial relations. This is the
rationale of Figure 2 and I shall now briefly define the
respective concepts identified.

Figure 2:   The State and Industrial Relations:
            Competing Strategies

		Internal Control of Industrial Relations: The Role of Labour Collectivities	
		Autonomous	Heteronomous
		Liberalism	Paternalism
External Control of Industrial Relations: The Role of the State	Laissez-Faire		
	Interven-tionism	Pluralism	Corporatism

1. Liberalism. This represents the structural connection of
laissez-faire as the means of intervention and autonomy as
the mode of political representation as the external and
internal conditions for the control of industrial relations.
It thus represents the minimisation of direct state intervention in industrial relations except in exceptional circumstances and by means of the allocation of already existing
authoritative powers, such as the courts or military, relying
thus, in large part, on the initiatives of capital to invoke
the powers of the state against labour, and not involving any

26

means of continuously or systematically regulating the role of trade unions.

2. Paternalism. This form of state control represents the structural connection of laissez-faire as far as external conditions of control are concerned together with the internal regulation of the role of unions deriving from, to varying degrees, corporate forms of political representation allowing for the regulation of unions or labour collectivities by employers without direct, sustained and systematic state intervention of the kind identifiable with interventionism.

3. Pluralism. This represents the structural connection of the external control of state interventionism together with the internally autonomous role of trade unions deriving from, to varying degrees, pluralistic forms of political representation which incorporate and institutionalise rather than suppress working class interests and struggles.

4. Corporatism. This represents the external mode of control of industrial relations associated with state interventionism together with the regulation of the role of unions or labour collectivities as the internal mode of controlling industrial relations consistent with corporatist forms of political representation. It would entail if established in any coherent form (which it can be argued has not yet been the case, certainly not in any stable manner), the direct sanctioning and support of the internal control structure of trade unions and/or their incorporation by recognition procedures into collective bargaining structures together with external control effected by state apparatuses charged with the initiative and responsibility for the control of industrial relations.

These distinct conceptual categories are not intended to refer to empirically clear-cut distinctions but rather to act as the conceptual means of grasping and thereby empirically illustrating forms of state control of industrial relations, the class and political interests associated with and supporting the objectives embodied in each of these forms and thus the structure of conflicts over the role of the state in industrial relations.

The Aims of the Study
The theoretical framework developed above on the basis of a critique of some of the central conceptions of an influential literature will now be used as a basis for conducting an empirical examination of state intervention in industrial relations in Britain. It has in fact been a main assumption of my critique that a major fault in much of the existing literature lies in its failure to construct concepts adequate for such an analysis and I have attempted to fill this gap

accordingly, that is, to provide specifically political concepts appropriate to forms of state intervention which link them to the wider structural constraints within which they emerge and which they can, in turn, influence. Industrial relations and industrial conflict provide highly convenient areas whereby the state as a theoretical and historical problem can be further elucidated, for they are connected directly not only with class relations generally and have been inherent in the organisation and problems associated with capital accumulation and class conflicts in industry, but have taken a central place in the articulation of state intervention. It will be a major aim of this study to show precisely how and why this has occurred. To no small extent this is required because what the recent and extensive discussions have lacked is detailed empirical work on the role of the state, and this study represents one effort to remedy this situation.[16]

It could be contended that my concern with the autonomy of the state is undermined by the fact that I shall not consider fully the state's monopoly of the means of violence or coercive power, since this could be conceived of, quite correctly, as a key determinant of the state's autonomy. The dependence of the state's autonomy upon coercive power is, in fact, an acceptable proposition and it forms a crucial feature of the definition of the state I wish to use which, while focussing on the central institutions of the state, government, parliament, civil service, judiciary, police, military, local government and public sector industries[17] (cf. Miliband: 1973; 30 and 46-51), also attempts to incorporate Weber's emphasis upon the legitimate monopoly of coercive power within a given (national) territorial unit (1970; 77-8. 1964; 156), into Jessop's more general depiction of the state as a system of political domination which embodies both definite means of intervention in the economy and civil society and definite modes of interest representation (1978. cf. Offe: 1975. Hirsch: 1978; 57-8). In this respect, law and money form two strategic links between the state and other sectors of society, even given the state's monopoly or attempted monopoly of the legitimate control and use of the means of violence.[18] Therefore, it will mainly be in terms of the law that I shall attempt to determine the state's autonomy in this book. Although coercive power may be central to the state's autonomy, it is equally possible to analyse such autonomy in terms of the articulation of state power by means of the law.

NOTES

1. This book is an abbreviated version of my Ph.D. thesis, 'The Political Organisation of Capital, the State and Industrial Relations Policy in Britain, 1960-1975', London University, 1981, in which many of the arguments in this book are more fully developed and more extensively documented.

2. For commentaries on Weber's political thought see Beetham: 1974. Giddens: 1972. Spencer: 1977.

3. Plamenatz argues Marx's view of Bonapartism contradicts his overall theory of the state (1954; 135-64). This, as a textual point, is true but it tends to neglect the analytical value of the latter and this is what I wish to establish in this section. For a good, critical over-view of Marx's and Marxist theories of the state, see Jessop: 1977.

4. For discussions of Bonapartism see the Miliband-Poulantzas debate. Miliband: 1973a and 1973b. Poulantzas: 1973a and 1976. For a critique of Marx's analysis of Bonapartism see Spencer: 1979.

5. Cf. Gramsci's analysis of Caesarism. 1971; 219-23.

6. Another variant of this approach, which also fails to avoid economism and functionalism, is the 'capital-logic' school of thought, which I shall not consider in the main text. See Altvater: 1973. Cf.Holloway and Picciotto: 1978. Other examples would be Fine and Harris: 1976. Yaffe: 1973. Murray: 1975. One of the most notable examples of this kind of approach outside of Marxism and drawing on a more orthodox functionalist heritage is the work of Easton which attempts to provide a framework for analysing politics drawn from systems theory. See Idem: 1953, 1957 and 1965. Cf. Parsons: 1967. For a critique of functionalism and of Parsons see Giddens: 1977; Chapters 2 and 10. Still another variant theory within Marxism argues that the state has to be seen as a facet of the value relation of capital, being based upon the generalised alienation to be found in capitalist society (Ollman: 1976. Wolfe: 1974). This has affinities with the attempt to use the concept of commodity fetishism to explain the state's existence as an aspect of the fetishised relations of capital (e.g. Holloway and Picciotto: 1977). It, however, to my mind, still ends up being reductionist - the state and its various institutions and practices cannot exist apart from and independently of the capital relation - while minimising the reality of class conflict and over emphasising the omniscience and reliability of capitalist ideology.

7. Other examples not discussed in the main text are Esping-Anderson et al.: 1976. Bell: 1977. It is interesting to note that an emphasis on conflicts of interest as a major cause of political behaviour is to be found outside of Marxism in the pressure group theory of politics which sees competition between interest groups over legislation as the over-riding force shaping state policy. This assumes a relatively equal distribution of power in society. See, e.g., Dahl: 1965. Dahl et al.: 1959; 36. Polsby: 1963. Dahrendorf: 1959. Kornhauser: 1960. Lipset: 1960. For critiques see, e.g., Miliband: 1973. Lukes: 1974. Offe and Wiesenthal: 1979.

8. For critiques of Poulantzas' use of the notion of relative autonomy which follow many more issues than I wish to take up here, see, e.g. Elster: 1978; 121-2. Cutler: 1971. Block: 1980. Hirst: 1977.

9. Harris (1980) argues that this approach, in its attempt to account for the development of the Welfare State in Britain, fails to take sufficient notice of the importance of the divisions within classes in struggle.

10. For an appreciative view of Offe's work see Frankel: 1979. For critiques see, e.g., Sardei-Biermann et al.: 1973. For a 'tour de force' of 'critical sociology' see Habermas:1976.

11. As a consequence, capital's class consciousness, as we shall see in this study, will be highly problematic as will its political organisation. See, e.g., Block: 1977. Whitt: 1980. Offe: 1975. This may mean that the state will need to legitimate its actions to capital. See MacPherson: 1977.

12. Also, it is by no means viewed as a completed process. In fact, its nature as a process of struggle undermines this view and will form an important consideration in the study.

13. The tentative and exploratory nature of the diagram and the subsequent argument needs to be stressed. However, I think that a move in this direction is necessary, that is, towards specifying the possible relations between the state and economy in a historical and non-reductionist manner. This is so because so many ventures in this area either begin by asking the wrong questions or by pre-supposing answers to more important questions. So, for example, Weberian sociology tends to ask, 'What are the interests specific to politics and the state?', while much Marxist writing tends to come round to the question, 'How are economic interests expressed politically?'. Both of these questions rest upon the assumption that the structural relationship between state and economy is known whereas it is only when this has been assessed that the above questions can be asked.

14. Notable exceptions in this respect are Panitch: 1977. Jessop: 1978 and 1980. Crouch: 1977.

15. Part of the motivation behind this is to prevent the long-term planning and rationalisation that corporatist planning and corporatist economic policies demand from being disrupted by these struggles. As such, it also entails the exclusion and/or control of the interests of certain sections of capital, notably petit-bourgeois capital, at the level of politics. Cf. Offe and Ronge: 1975. O'Connor: 1973.

16. In taking a particular society such as Britain as a case study for the purpose of providing an empirical analysis, I do not wish to deny the importance of either the international dimensions of the state's role, in that it is constructed on the basis of the relationships between distinct nation states, nor the use that can and should be made of comparative evidence on other nation states. Where necessary the international dimensions of the problems I shall analyse will be treated accordingly, but I do, however, wish to make it clear that my object of concern will be the British state. Indeed, case studies of particular societies provide a useful way of establishing a secure basis for the adequacy of com-

parative analyses and for studies of the international role of
any individual nation state. Morecver, far from neglecting the
question, I rather take as a given for the purpose of my own
analysis the fact that the development of the state within and
even prior to the development of capitalist societies has taken
the form of the nation state (and thus has entailed relations
between nation states) and I do not wish to minimise the significance of this issue nor the importance of the need for an
adequate explanation of this fact. For a discussion of this
problem see Giddens: 1981; Chapter 8.

    17. The scope of the state itself, though, can and often
does become an object of struggle and subject to processes of
transformation. See, e.g., Panitch: 1981; 27. It is still
necessary, however, to have a clear conception of what it is
that is being fought over.

    18. For a much fuller treatment of the over all relation
between the state and the means of violence and surveillance
more generally, see Giddens: 1981; 169-81 and Chapters 7 and
9 passim.

Chapter 2

THE STATE AND THE DEVELOPMENT OF TRADE UNION LAW

In this chapter I wish to sketch in some of the historical background to the subsequent study. I shall, accordingly, discuss
changes in the law and legislation relating to the legal status
of trade unions and their activities between 1799 and the mid-
1950s, the latter representing the beginnings of the period on
which I wish to concentrate. The changing nature of the legal
relationship between the state and working class organisation
is important for a number of reasons, not the least of which
is the way its land marks and traditions have informed and
constrained contemporary struggles and interpretations of the
role of the state and the law in industrial relations. But it
is perhaps most important in placing into historical context,
the phase of state intervention in industrial relations that
began to emerge most clearly in the 1960s, emphasising both
historical similarities and continuities, and, more significantly, historical divergences and discontinuities, which together with the analyses set out in Chapters 3 and 4, set the
stage for the study of the conjuncture of the 1960s and 1970s.
Crucial to this is the argument that while the recent episode
of state intervention bears certain similarities to earlier
phases, it has occurred under remarkably different structural
conditions and has involved novel features with respect to the
nature of contemporary capitalism and the role of the state
and class conflict that make redundant the drawing of any
superficial historical analogies. This makes it even more
necessary to clarify this history in order to identify how it
has and how it has not repeated itself, how it has embodied
and how it radically departed from previous conjunctures and
tendencies, tasks central to an understanding of the present
as history.

    With this rationale as its base, this chapter consequently
attempts to identify the following: (1) The transition from
laissez-faire state mediation of industrial relations to the
beginnings of a form of interventionist mediation; (2) The
influence of class conflict and working class militancy in
inducing the state to impose controls on trade unions; (3) The

legal incorporation of trade unions into the state, its controlled and contingent nature, which has been directly determined by the actions of the state; and the way this has been entailed in a social and historical process consisting of judicial coercion of trade unions in the face of increasing class conflict, the politicisation of the response of the organised labour movement in seeking redress through the channels established within rather than outside parliamentary democracy, and the construction of a compromise by government, acting through parliament, revoking judicial constraint, and revealing a split within the state itself over the control of trade unionism and industrial conflict; (4) The way in which it is thus difficult to relate the state and its actions directly to class interests in view of such contradictions in its structure and the way the state is constrained by class conflict; (5) The central importance of the use of the law, in particular the concept of the rule of law, in structuring the state's intervention in industrial relations and its control of industrial conflict and thus in organising not only the coercive but also the hegemonic aspect of class domination.

The Legal Incorporation of Organised Labour

While trade unions and industrial conflict had long been a feature of British society (Dobson: 1980. Pelling: 1971; chapter 2), I shall commence this discussion of the problems I have raised with respect to the combination laws of 1799 and 1800. In the early part of the nineteenth century trade unions, associations of workers for common objectives and for the withdrawal of labour, were illegal organisations, irrespective of the fact that some trade combinations persisted, especially amongst craft workers, sometimes with the tacit acquiescence of employers. At this stage the English working class was 'unincorporated' (Wedderburn: 1971; 304-305). Outright proscription constituted the political method of dealing with the threat that unionism posed for employer prerogatives, and the political threat it posed to the state.

The combination laws exemplify the form that the political and legal exclusion of organised labour took at this phase in the development of state-labour relations. They legally formalised barriers against the collective association of workers to influence their wages and conditions of work and were the first general prohibition of all combinations. The 1799 Act applied only to workers and was designed to prevent 'obstructions to trade' with provision being made for sanctions, including prison and hard labour, for trade union activity. The 'Act of 1800 made all combinations of workmen to regulate their conditions of work illegal' (Citrine: 1967; 5-6) and strike action was a criminal offence (Allen: 1960; 118). Trade unions persisted, either secretly, or where recognised by employers, and a few collective agreements were formed (Thompson: 1968; 546-63). But it was very much the case that

'the Combination Acts of 1799 and 1800 had forced the trade
unions into an illegal world in which secrecy and hostility to
the authorities were intrinsic to their very existence'(Ibid.:
550). It is important to note that the legal prosecution of
trade unions in the early part of the nineteenth century
occurred especially in areas where 'class differences were
becoming more pronounced' (Musson: 1972; 24. Cf. Thompson:
1968; 552). And Musson notes the 'politicizing' influence of
this legislation: 'there were certainly signs that class consciousness was emerging ... in the general opposition to the
combination laws', inducing trade unions to turn to politics
(1972; 37. Cf. Thompson: 1968; 546).

The repeal of the combination laws in 1824,[1] in respect of
the legal incorporation of organised labour, was due to laissez-
faire doctrines and the concomitant hope that repeal would
render trade unions unnecessary (Thompson: 1968; 567). The
Combination Laws Repeal Act of 1824 removed, for one year, all
legal constraints upon the formation of unions, including
liability for conspiracy under common or statute law, while
restrictions were placed upon the use of violence (Citrine:
1967; 6-7). The actual rights afforded by the Act must not be
minimised for, as Engels pointed out, it meant that 'the working men obtained a right previously restricted to the aristo-
cracy and the bourgeoisie, the right of free association'
(1953; 248), even though the intent behind the Act was to
dissipate such association.

With repeal, 'combinations were very soon spread all over
England and obtained great power' (Ibid.; 249. Thompson: 1968;
568). This assertion of militancy posed serious problems for
the control of employers who demanded the repeal of the 1824
Act, a concern shared by the government and by those who had
secured the passing of the Act. Some of this concern was under-
standable in view of the violence that went with increasing
worker militancy, but it must be noted that it also threatened
to erode employer power, even to the extent of some workers
demanding a 'closed shop' (Engels: op. cit. Webbs: 1920; 105).
Employer demands for the re-imposition of the combination laws
were not fully implemented, partly as a result of trade union
protests (Musson: 1972; 27). The Repeal Act Amendment Act of
1825 maintained the rights of combination and collective bargaining over wages and hours of work (Webbs: 1920; 108), and
unions 'were again made subject to the common law of conspiracy
to prevent criminal acts of intimidation and coercion' (Musson:
1972; 27-8). But while the employers did not get all they
wanted, prosecutions of trade unionists continued after the
passing of the Act through the use of other laws (Ibid.; 28),
and prison terms were laid down for coercively infringing the
managerial prerogatives of employers. The legal rights afforded
by the state to organised labour were thus essentially controlled and represented the 'negotiation of a compromise' by
the state with trade unionism. This is illustrated not only by

the fact that the terms 'molestation and obstruction' referring
to union coercion were left undefined, but also by the fact
that associations and strikes concerned with issues other than
wages and hours remained 'criminal conspiracies at common law,
being in unlawful restraint of trade' (Citrine: 1967; 7. Hedges
and Winterbottom: 1930; 36-41).

The next major phase in the development of trade union law
came with the Trade Union Act of 1871, often called the 'Trade
Union Charter' (Citrine: 1967; 10). It signified the inception
of a crucial structural 'contradiction' within the state system,
between the judiciary, on the one hand, which continued to impose controls upon unions, and government and parliament, on
the other, which gradually began to evolve measures to integrate unions into the body politic. This had important repercussions on the legal incorporation of organised labour in two
ways: first, judicial interventionism maintained the controlled
nature of union incorporation; second, it also necessitated,
in the wake of the political responses engendered by such coercion, the adoption by government and parliament of solutions
to accommodate the 'politicised' objectives of the trade union
movement. The process of judicial intervention, political union
reaction, and governmental legislative solution, constituted
a significant structural feature in the development of trade
union law in Britain before the First World War.

The eventual concessionary nature of the 1871 legislation
was set against the increasing organisation of the trade union
movement on a national level with the formation of the TUC
(Musson: 1972; 62) and its opposition to the use of punitive
legal sanctions to control trade union activity, especially
by way of the Master and Servant Act: 'the increase in prosecutions under the master and servant laws in the mid 1860s was
part and parcel of the campaign to curb the rising power of
the unions' (Bagwell: 1974; 36-8).[2] The 1871 Trade Union Act
represents the legislative document of a compromise by the
state with organised labour. It stipulated that trade unions
were not to be regarded as illegal organisations purely because
they were deemed to be 'in restraint of trade' and they were
no longer liable for criminal prosecution for conspiracy in
this respect. This, in turn, afforded protection for trade
union funds. The internal agreements of unions were not to be
legally enforceable, and a system of union registration was
established. To register - and concessions such as exemption
from tax payments and the power to acquire land and property
were laid down as inducements - the objects and purposes of a
trade union and its funds had to be clearly specified in its
rule book and were thereby subject to supervision and amendment by the registrar (Citrine: 1967; 99-336).

This Act is sometimes viewed as the high point of the
securement of legal status by trade unions (e.g. Musson: 1972;
62). But it was accompanied by constraints, in the shape of
the Criminal Law Amendment Act of 1871. This applied specifi-

cally to the use of picketing during a strike and made the use of violence, threats, intimidation, molestation and obstruction criminal offences. Since this, however, included the prohibition against 'watching and besetting' premises or approaches to premises, peaceful picketing was in fact precluded (Webbs: 1920; 284 and 276-7). The legal controls imposed upon trade union activities served to 'politicise' the trade union movement which, led by the Parliamentary Committee of the TUC, agitated for their repeal (Clegg et al.: 1964; 45). The Act 'was bitterly resented by the unions, as a withdrawal of rights already conceded by the Act of 1859', and because 'the terms of the Act made it a potential weapon in the hands of an aggrieved employer and a hostile judge' (MacDonald: 1960; 37), particularly since the judiciary showed it was prepared to give a wide interpretation to these terms (Clegg et al.: 1964; 45).

The result of union agitation was the Conspiracy and Protection of Property Act of 1875 which removed the application of the doctrine of criminal conspiracy to acts in contemplation or furtherance of a trade dispute, and rendered peaceful picketing a lawful activity, leaving violent and seditious activities to be covered by other Acts of Parliament. It also repealed the notorious Master and Servant Act, under which many unionists had been prosecuted and convicted, and replaced it by the Employers and Workmen Act of 1875, whereby employer and employee were formally made legally equal parties to a civil contract. It was thus felt that trade unions, their peaceful practices and collective bargaining had been legally recognised (Webbs: 1920; 290-92. Hedges and Winterbottom: 1930; 115-16).

For the next thirty years the focal point of state-labour relations was largely confined to the role of the courts in controlling trade unionism. This role was crucial in the famous Taff Vale case, set against, as it was, a period of increasing union militancy. In response to the growing unionisation of previously unorganised categories of workers, particularly the unskilled, in the late 1880s and 1890s (Hobsbawm: 1964; chapters 9 and 11), the courts reaffirmed their coercive role in controlling trade unionism and its activities[3] (Saville: 1960; 345-6). For example, in Lyons v Wilkins (1896), the decision of the court of appeal 'declared peaceful picketing unlawful as a common law "nuisance"' (Wedderburn: 1971; 322). In this case, 'certain of the dicta of these appeal judges illustrate the way in which the political arguments for free labour were now finding legal justification' (Saville: 1960; 347 and 346-48).[4] This accorded with the attitude of employers, somewhat typical of which was the insistence of the Chamber of Shipping of the United Kingdom that 'it is desirable ... to render illegal the practice of picketing in force during strikes and labour disputes' (quoted, Clegg et al.: 1964; 307). This situation, structured as it was by working class union organi-

sation, the counter-offensive of employers and judiciary, and
the thereby accentuated political and industrial militancy of
unions, reached its climacteric in the Taff Vale judgement.
The significance of this case is fourfold: it illustrates the
inception of the social structural pattern of judicial constraint, politicised union reaction, and governmental compromise, that has already been outlined; it highlights the
essentially constrained and controlled character of the legal
incorporation of organised labour; it demonstrates the impact
of legal controls on union activities imposed by the state;
and it is indicative of the relative autonomy of the state in
its organisation of an eventual legislative compromise.
    In 1901 the Taff Vale Railway Company sued the Amalgamated
Society of Railway Servants for damages for losses arising from
what were alleged to be the unlawful actions of trade union
officers, namely inducing workers to break their contracts by
striking and using pickets during the strike (Clegg et al.:
1964; 313-16). The court decided that, in spite of what seemed
to be the explicit provision of the Trade Union Acts of 1871
and 1875, a trade union could be made answerable by law for
the actions of its officials, i.e. that a trade union could be
sued for damages in tort, as if it were a corporate body, although previous legislation had refrained from giving trade
unions such a legal status (Milne-Bailey: 1934; 210-15). The
case went eventually to the House of Lords who concurred with
this judgement that trade unions 'could be sued in a corporate
capacity for damages alleged to have been caused by the action
of its officials' (Webbs: 1920; 600 and 526). It was further
decided that unregistered trade unions (allowed for by the
1871 Act) were collectively liable for damages which could be
recovered from its property (Webbs: 1920; 601-603. Wedderburn:
1971; 318-21).
    The rationale lying behind the House of Lords' decision,
the notion of the rule of law, was clearly stated by Lord
McNaghten: 'If trade unions are not above the law, how are
these bodies to be sued?' (Milne-Bailey: 1929; 451-2). The
decision implied, according to the Webbs, that the uncertainty
of the law meant that it could be used as a means of coercion,
especially in view of judicial and employer hostility to trade
unionism (1911; xxvi and xxi). Thus, trade union funds were
open to erosion by employer actions (Webbs: 1920; 526, and
1911; xxxi-xxxiii). The demand was raised that the legal
status of trade unionism thought to be guaranteed by the 1871
Act should be restored (Webbs: 1920; 603-604. Milne-Bailey:
1934; 215-17). Moreover, this pressure took on a directly
political character. Indeed, some authors have attributed the
political organisation of the working class in the shape of
the Labour Representation Committee and then the Labour Party,
in part, to the reaction against legal coercion. As Hobsbawm
suggests, 'Taff Vale made the Labour Party' (1974; 161.
Saville: 1960; 349-50), for Taff Vale was followed by a number

of similar cases in which heavy damages were awarded against trade unions (Clegg et al.: 1964; 316 and 326).

But there was far from complete agreement within the ranks of the trade union movement as to the significance of Taff Vale and the best way of remedying the situation. The decision of the House of Lords to vest trade unions with full corporate legal status to sue and be sued suggested to some trade union leaders a means of buttressing their control, their executive authority and the force of union rules, thereby extending their control over the rank and file (Ibid.; 317-20). However there followed demonstrations, lobbying of Parliament by the TUC's parliamentary committee and attempts to secure remedial legis-lation through the House of Commons. The result was the setting up of a Royal Commission to investigate trade union law (Ibid.; 321-3). The majority report of the Royal Commission supported the Taff Vale decision (Clegg et al.: 1964; 393). The general principle lying behind the Report rested upon the notion of the equality of all institutions under the rule of law (Milne-Bailey: 1929; 455). But the recommendation that the Taff Vale judgement be upheld was not accepted by the Liberal government. The Trade Disputes Act was passed in 1906 which gave trade unions legal immunity, substantially as a result of political trade union pressure (Wedderburn: 1971; 317). The Act removed the applica-tion of the doctrine of civil conspiracy to trade disputes; reaffirmed the legality of peaceful picketing; removed tortious liability for inducing others to break their contracts of employment, and established the general immunity of trade union funds against liability for the tortious acts of its members, servants or agents (Citrine: 1967; 16-17, 551-62).

In terms of the idea of the rule of law the Act of 1906 may ostensibly appear anomalous. Dicey for example, criticised the Act since it 'makes a trade union a privileged body exemp-ted from the ordinary law of the land. No such privileged body has ever before been deliberately created by an English Parli-ament' (1962; xlvi). Empirically, however, it is by no means clear that this interpretation necessarily followed. Lord Haldane in 1913 in fact argued that protection applied only to trade disputes (Henderson: 1927; 74-5). More importantly, as Wedderburn points out, while a trade union was protected by the 1906 Act, this did not apply to its officers and members (1971; 320-21). It was, likewise, still open to judicial inter-ventionism (MacDonald: 1960; 60. Wedderburn: 1971; 360). The state thus represented both repression and redress as reflected in the contradiction between executive, legislature and judi-ciary, which both generated and mitigated the politicising impact of state action upon organised labour (cf. Milne-Bailey: 1934; 186).

The security that the 1906 Act appeared to give to trade unions was to last only three years anyway, when a similar structural process to that already described with respect to the Taff Vale case was again set in motion by the 1909 Osborne

judgement. The 1906 Act had undoubtedly demonstrated to trade
unions the usefulness of independent political action. But it
was this which was now to be subjected to legal inhibitions by
this decision particularly in view of the fact that, 'There can
be no doubt that the privileges given to the trade unions by
the 1906 Act had appeared to virtually the whole legal profession as legally improper' (Clegg et al.: 1964; 415). This
derived, in part, from the class nature of the judiciary and
the legal profession, but it was also due to the anomalous
nature that trade unionism was beginning to acquire within the
definitions and rules of bourgeois law. Furthermore, Taff Vale
did not merely result from judicial hostility but was also
founded upon the legal development of the representative action,
i.e. the legal device whereby ordinary companies could be sued
for the actions of their officers (Pelling: 1979; 72 and 80).

In 1909 trade unions were again regarded as legally incorporated bodies by the Law Lords, and, as such, since corporate bodies could not do anything outside the purposes
detailed in the statute under which they were incorporated,
and as there was no statute explicitly stating that political
activity was a legitimate trade union function, the use of
union funds for political purposes was declared to be illegal
(Milne-Bailey: 1929; 55-6. Citrine: 1967; 17-18). 'As a result
of the Osborne judgement, the courts were flooded with appli-
cations for injunctions against trade unions' (Ibid.; 19).
Hence, 'the result was to threaten with destruction the existing pattern of trade union political activity' (Clegg et al.:
1964; 415).

This attempt by the Courts to de-politicise trade unionism was in fact founded upon a paradox; for deprived of legitimate avenues for political activity, sections of the trade
union movement turned to support the use of the industrial
strike for political ends - the doctrine of 'direct action'
as advocated by syndicalism (Citrine: 1967; 19-20. Pelling:
1971; Chapter 7. Holton: 1976).[5] But more normal ways of obtaining political change, such as lobbying parliament and
introducing remedial Bills in the Commons, continued to be
used, although the use of funds for such purposes could be
construed as unlawful (Clegg et al.: 1964; 417-18). 'The
urgent need to remedy the position established by the judgement once again gave common objective to the trade union movement and the Labour Party' (MacDonald: 1960; 64). The effect
of this on the Liberal government's readiness to 'smooth
Labour's path in politics', Miliband argues, was 'expressed
too in their agreement to remove the inhibitions imposed upon
Labour's participation in politics by the Osborne judgement';
and, noting the influence of increasing industrial militancy,
suggests, 'there is much significance in the fact that this
latter concession should have been made in 1913, at the height
of the industrial unrest' (1972; 373).

The government was constrained by these struggles to

elaborate a compromise. The Trade Union Act of 1913 reversed the Osborne judgement, empowering trade unions to finance parliamentary candidates, hold political meetings, distribute political literature, etc. For trade unions to be able to do such things certain conditions had to be observed: securing the approval of members by a majority vote, and the approval of union rules by the Registrar; union rules had to provide for a special political fund, from which members could claim exemption - i.e. 'contract out'; and payment into the political fund was not to be made a condition of trade union membership. The 1913 Act permitted the expenditure of trade union funds on any lawful object or purpose authorised by a trade union's Constitution (Citrine: 1967; 20 and 377-452). As such, it represents, in statutory terms, the political integration of trade unionism into the British political system by legitimating its 'pressure group' activities. But this incorporation of organised labour was by no means sacrosanct and subsequent events have served to emphasise its constrained and contingent character.

The interruption of this phase by the First World War witnessed an important feature of state-labour relations, namely the legal proscription of strikes by the state, which was also evident during the Second World War. This aspect will be dealt with in the section on 'the role of government'. For the moment I wish to concentrate, in concluding this section, on certain legal changes that preceded the re-emergence of judicial coercion in the 1960s. Though there was some dispute in legal circles at the time as to the legality of the General Strike of 1926, the state ensured the statutory illegality of any future general strikes by means of the Trade Disputes and Trade Union Act of 1927. The provisions of the 1906 Act were to no longer apply to illegal strikes. In the stipulations of the Act strikes were illegal if they had an objective other than or in addition to, the furtherance of a trade dispute within the trade or industry in which the strikers were engaged; and were calculated to coerce the government, either directly or by inflicting hardship on the community (Hedges and Winterbottom: 1930; 75). Since what constituted 'hardship to the community' was left undefined it was possible for the courts to infer that almost any large scale strike was likely to coerce the government (Knowles: 1952; 115). Hence, 'the increasing part played by the government in trade disputes either as an employer or as a conciliator or arbitrator, rendered the expression "calculated to coerce the government" capable of wide interpretation' (Citrine: 1967; 22 and 21).

While the potential of this Act was extensive, its actual impact was fairly minimal in encouraging cases to be brought before the courts (Knowles: 1952; 114-15), though this should not be allowed to obscure its more general significance. In the first place, it signified the constrained character of the legal incorporation of organised labour in the wake of labour's defeat in the General Strike. In obviating strikes against the state, this aspect of the legal structure of state-labour relations denotes the changing role of the state which the Act expresses. The increasingly extensive functional responsibilities of the state for the maintenance of social order and the uninterrupted allocation of economic resources, and hence the need to control organised labour, are clearly conveyed by the terms of the Act. Likewise, the Act illustrates the use of the law as an instrument of this growth in state power and state intervention, with the government, rather than the courts, as the primary agent of legal control. Moreover, the relative autonomy of the state, as structured by its mediatory role, is evident in the legislatively defined function of the state as the representative of the national interest and the upholder of the rule of law and in the state's role as the organiser of the distribution of fundamental resources which the Act sanctioned.

The Role of the State: The Courts

Many authors place great emphasis upon the prejudice and hostility that has historically been expressed by the judiciary against trade unions and trade union activities (Webbs: 1920; 271. Miliband: 1973; 128-9). This type of proposition is related by Engels to the class bias of capitalist law: 'the English bourgeois finds himself reproduced in his law, as he does in his God' (1953; 262 and 316. Cf. Milne-Bailey: 1934; 155 and 163). It is also quite possible to find more general evidence suggestive of the class bias of the courts. Box, for example, argues, on the basis of a number of court decisions, that 'norm enforcement officers proceed more frequently and harshly against members of the lower strata' (1971; 205).

However, I want to argue for the contradictory nature of the law, and for the relative autonomy of the judiciary. Just as the principle of the rule of law, while endeavouring to maintain existing social relationships, through the espousal of the idea of a universal and equitable application of justice also allows for opposition to certain laws to be legitimated precisely in these terms, so the role of the judiciary can likewise be invested with such relative autonomy. The judiciary, like the law, is not the puppet of class power, but attains relative autonomy through its mediatory role in dealing with class relations within the rubric of the rule of law. This resides in the dual components of its role, which Miliband points to, namely, judicial discretion in the interpretation and application of the law, and judicial creativity in the actual making of law (1973; 125). These dimensions of judicial mediation reside in the fact that there 'is no answer to the question whether a given penal statute should be construed narrowly or liberally. It is a policy choice in either case'. This, in turn, means that 'even the sum of legislative and articulated public opinion can be no more than the framework, which judges must seek to fill out' (Friedmann: 1964; 60, and

35-67). The relative autonomy of the judicial arm of the state, within the system of constraints of class and state power, rests upon the dimensions of creativity and discretion inscribed in its role in mediating the relationship between class, politics and the law, which thus forms its basis of power as a law-making agency. This autonomy is similarly indicated by the lack of any necessary or homogeneous connection between employers and the courts in dealing with trade union rights: the courts preserve a class stratified order but do so in a relatively autonomous manner, for there are always sections of capital which will support judicial coercion and others which will turn to other ways of dealing with the working class (cf.Clegg et al.: 1964; 47).

Bearing these propositions in mind, we can now explore the development of the relationship between the courts and organised labour, as revealed by cases and ideology involving the legality of trade unionism. Before 1825, the prohibition of trade union association went hand in hand with a concerted approach by the branches of the state towards trade unionism. But, as we have seen, the 1825 Act gave unions certain limited rights, and this was later followed by an increasing differentiation of the approach of the judiciary from that of Parliament. Hence, during the period 1825 to 1871, the courts developed 'the principles of common law conspiracy and it emerged from their decisions that the existence of a combination might convert an otherwise non-criminal act, into a criminal threat of molestation or obstruction. On this basis, to "threaten" that a lawful strike would take place was a criminal molestation under the statute' (Citrine: 1967; 8). Underlying this approach of the judiciary was an ideology of liberal laissez-faire which stressed the collectivist dangers that unionism posed for Benthamite individual freedom. Dicey, commenting upon the influence Benthamite individualism and liberalism had upon judicial interpretations of the law, commended the general conviction of the judiciary that

> trade unionism was opposed to individual freedom, that picketing, for example, was simply a form of intimidation, and that though a strike might in theory be legal, a strike could in practice, hardly be carried out with effect without the employment of some form of intimidation either towards masters or non-unionists (1962; 199-200).

This formulation of the principle of individual liberty under the rule of law as a means of denying the collective activities of unions was associated with upholding the doctrine that trade union functions were 'in restraint of trade'.

The conflict between judiciary and legislature, expressed in terms of preserving the legal implications of laissez-faire versus the provision of legal recognition of the functions of

trade unionism, was clearly marked by the passing of the Molestation of Workmen Act in 1859. This explicitly removed criminal
liability from peaceful persuasion to induce others to leave
work, albeit not in breach of contract. However, 'many of the
judges' decisions scarcely registered this amendment' (Wedderburn: 1971; 310).

The implications and constraints of the role of the courts
vis a vis the legal incorporation of organised labour became
particularly clear after 1875. The legislation enacted between
1871 and 1875, as already indicated, gave trade unions certain
legal rights. After 1875 the judiciary began to evolve the doctrine of civil conspiracy, leaving unions exposed to actions
for damages in respect of acts committed 'in contemplation or
furtherance of trade disputes'. Inducing breaches of·contract,
and encouraging workers not to enter into contracts, according
to the courts, rendered trade union activity a civil conspiracy
at common law (Milne-Bailey: 1934; 186). It is true that the
most famous legal curtailments of trade unionism occurred at
about the turn of the century, but earlier indications of this
trend are evident. The 1875 Act had made it clear that picketing
a premises purely to communicate and/or obtain information was
not to be regarded as 'watching and besetting', with the intention of making 'peaceful picketing' legal (Webbs: 1911; 855).
But it was held in 1876 in the case of R. v Bauld that the Act
authorised nothing more than the dissemination of information,
and that picketing to persuade others to join a strike was a
crime. This precedent was upheld in Lyons v Wilkins (1896)
(Wedderburn: 1971; 322). Limitations were also placed upon
trade union activities by the judiciary's development of the
use of common law guidelines. It had been decided in Lumley v
Gye (1853) that it was a tort - and therefore liable to civil
action and a claim for damages - to knowingly induce a breach
of contract without justification (Wedderburn: 1971; 349).
This made the calling of a strike unlawful if it was in breach
of contract to the express or implied knowledge of those
calling the strike: 'on this ground numerous successful actions
were brought against trade union officers and members'(Citrine:
1967; 44). The 1875 Act was designed to prevent the law of
criminal conspiracy being applied to trade disputes but its
influence was vitiated by the judiciary's elaboration of common
law and 'the extension of the doctrine of conspiracy into the
realm of·civil law as a separate species of tort' (Ibid.: 15.
Cf. Wedderburn: 1971; 314-15).

While such a legal doctrine had gradually been evolved
the assertion of its use against organised labour became most
pronounced from the late 1880s onwards as one response of the
state to the 'New Unionism'. The arousal of judicial creativity
that this entailed went hand in hand with the employers' demands
for 'free labour': the law had to be re-interpreted and·organ-
ised·into a new form for controlling trade unionism (cf.Saville:
1960; 340-41). This was made evident in a number of cases, such

as Temperton v Russell (1893) which served as a precedent for
a number of similar cases (Jencks: 1934; 334. Saville: 1960;
345). This orientation of the courts was not without some
notable exceptions. It was occasionally possible for a worker
to bring a successful action against an employer (Jencks: 1934;
334n). Differences in legal opinion as to the validity of the
above judgements were aired and criticisms were put forward
(Hedges and Winterbottom: 1930; 138-41. Clegg et al.: 1964;
307 and 316). But these serve to qualify rather than undermine
the characteristics of the posture adopted by the judiciary
towards organised labour as described above and the general
thrust of legal interpretations construing trade unionism as
a civil conspiracy at common law in fact received further con-
firmation in Quinn v Leatham (1901) (Citrine: 1967; 15).

After this manifestation of judicial coercion which lasted
until the First World War, the orientation of the judiciary towards trade unionism, with the exception of the General Strike,
exhibited a more tolerant, liberal and accepting character up
till the 1960s. Trade unions were increasingly recognised as
legitimate social institutions by employers in the form of
collective bargaining and by the state in the form of union
incorporation within its administrative structures. The contours of this process were exemplified by the Government's
establishment of conciliation and arbitration procedures by
the Conciliation Act of 1896 and the Industrial Courts Act of
1919, and by the inclusion of trade union representatives on
governmental advisory committees, and the formalisation of
contact between government and the trade union movement. That
organised labour was involved in an uneasy alliance with the
state was clearly demonstrated whenever trade unionism called
into question this evolving consensus, as in the General Strike
of 1926. Nevertheless, the state was, at this juncture, developing a more accommodative approach to trade union demands and
activities (Middlemas: 1979. Phelps-Brown: 1959; 114-293).

Before the 1960s the courts were largely inclined to
accept as given and secure certain fundamental political and
legal rights of trade unions, including, most significantly,
the right to strike. This principle was clearly expressed by
Lord Wright in the Crofter case of 1942: 'The right of workmen
to strike is an essential element in the principle of collective
bargaining .... A perfectly lawful strike may aim at dislocating
the employer's business for the moment but its real object is
to secure better wages or conditions for the workers' (Quoted,
Wedderburn: 1971; 340 and 346). This judicial development reflected judicial acceptance of trade union activities in cases
such as Reynolds v Shipping Federation in 1924, and the Crofter
case, 1942 (Ibid.: 340-45). In the first case, Justice Sargent
held that it was a legitimate right of trade unions to insist
upon a closed shop and stressed the advantages for employers
in freely adopting this policy. The decision also emphasised
the benefits that could be derived from collective bargaining

(Wedderburn: 1971; 28-29). Even the tendency to construe union action as 'unlawful coercion' or as amounting to the issuing of threats was negated by the courts themselves (Ibid.; 359). This period may therefore be considered, especially since the 1927 Act was rarely invoked, as one in which it was believed that the law had laid down (in the 1906 Act and the common law rules) a set of rules within which the autonomous bargaining and conflict of capital and labour could be conducted (Ibid.; 360-61). Correspondingly, it witnessed 'the development towards a more liberal view' such that 'judges now placed workers' collective interests on a level as valid as those of employers' (Ibid.; 301 and 29). As we shall see later, this was to change again in the 1960s, away from liberalism and towards paternalism.

The State: The Role of Government and Parliament

The transition in the role of the state from that in the nine-teenth century based on laissez-faire principles to state interventionism is quite commonly regarded as the characteris-tic form of state development in British society (Taylor: 1972. Supple: 1973). What is actually conveyed by these types of state and, hence, the nature of the transition, are important problems not only in so far as the relative autonomy of the role of the state is concerned, but also in so far as such problems refer to changes that have profound links with and repercussions for state-labour relations.

It is usually taken as an axiomatic and unproblematic fact that the state, including the government, played a rela-tively minor part in the social and economic life of nineteenth century Britain. Intervention to regulate and maintain economy and society was kept at a minimum, only being activated as an instrument of social control when order was threatened or thought to be threatened. The logical corollary of this was the idea that institutions could act 'in restraint of trade' (cf. Citrine: 1967; 34). This ideology, in part, was used as a means by which the courts legitimated their coercive atti-tude towards organised labour. It also served as a platform from which attacks on state intervention could be mounted.

But, as Roberts has cogently affirmed, despite much ideo-logical opposition to the bureaucratisation and centralisation of government in the early Victorian period, especially amongst upper and middle class groups, there emerged between 1833 and 1854, however inchoately, a welfare bureaucracy concerned with alleviating the worst social abuses concomitant upon the growth and extension of industrialisation (Roberts: 1969; 100). It would be unwise to overstate this case for even 'early Victor-ian Collectivism was ... social and not economic in emphasis', in that the powers of the state were not designed to interfere with 'economic freedom', except 'to correct scandalous social evils, such as child labour or distressing living conditions' (Ibid.; 95). And state legislation making trade unions illegal, like the Combination Laws, should warn us against accepting an ideological picture of the distinction sometimes maintained between laissez-faire and state intervention.

This is clearly shown by the fact that the socio-economic conditions underpinning the realisation of laissez-faire forms were created by state legislation. Nowhere is this more clear than in the proscription by the state of trade unions because they were thought to be associations 'in restraint of trade'. State intervention was required in order to ensure that 'liberalism' prevailed in economic and industrial affairs. This is not meant to suggest that the state has always been interventionist in the same way nor to obscure the qualitative change that characterised state development in Britain leading to the explicitly interventionist role assumed by the state in the twentieth century. The intention is rather to clarify further the concept of laissez-faire and what it entailed, empirically, for the role of the state.

In this context, it is as well to note the high degree of legislative regulation that occurred in the nineteenth century. Brebner, for example, argues, 'British laissez-faire was a political and economic myth ... a slogan or war cry employed by new forms of enterprise in their politico-economic war against the landed oligarchy' (1962; 252). This myth was undermined by the facts on state intervention.[6] We can thus indicate the transition from the form of intervention characteristic of laissez-faire to that in which the state assumes a role in managing sections of the economy and in ensuring the re-structuring of capital and the maintenance of the distribution of social and economic resources that has come to be more characteristic of state intervention in the late twentieth century. For it is crucial to recognise that the relative autonomy of the laissez-faire state resided in state legislation designed to preclude more than a minimum level of state intervention: the state intervened in order to provide against the necessity for its continual intervention, save as a 'law and order' state entrusted with the task of preserving social integration. As Polanyi makes this point,

> laissez-faire itself was enforced by the state ... the 1830s and 1840s saw not only an outburst of legislation repealing restrictive regulations, but also an enormous increase in the administrative functions of the state, which was now being endowed with a central bureaucracy able to fulfil the tasks set by the adherents of liberalism (1957; 139).

Polanyi argues that the formally free labour market, the gold standard and free trade, leading characteristics of nineteenth century economic structures, were directly established by state legislation, by, respectively, the Poor Law Amendment Act of 1834, the Bank Act of 1844 and the Anti-Corn Law Act of 1846. These Acts created and ensured 'free' markets in labour, money

and land (1957; 138 and 136-49).[7] The social and economic conditions underpinning the laissez-faire ideology of liberalism
were created by the state.

If it is granted that the state in British society for
most of the nineteenth century can be typified in this manner
then the combination laws, their repeal, the limited nature of
this repeal, and the generally coercive posture adopted by the
state towards organised labour, in particular, by the courts,
can be interpreted in this light. As Milne-Bailey comments on
this phase of state-labour relations: 'What had hitherto been
forbidden on the ground of non-interference with the functions
of the state was now forbidden on the principle of non-interference with the rights of the individual to dispose of his
capital or his labour as he chose' (1934; 176-7). The provision
of formal economic freedom, which also provided the rationale
for judicial control of trade unionism, was effected by state
intervention that had this as its objective, whereas with the
interventionist state, legislation, rooted in the law-making
capacity of government and parliament, began to provide for
state regulation, supervision and support and thus for a different approach to the problem of legally controlling trade
unionism. The role of the liberal state centred upon its repressive, or social control function to maintain law and order.
It took on little responsibility for the economy apart from
ensuring the 'legality' of the labour contract, and enacting
legislation to implement the principle of laissez-faire in
economic matters, to mitigate the worst forms of social abuse
associated with the industrial revolution, and to impose strict
legal controls upon organised labour in the name of economic
liberalism.

That the whole tenor of state legislation culminating in
the establishment of laissez-faire principles in economic life
had repercussions upon the general condition of labour is un-
deniable. In this vein, Hobsbawm remarks:

> The first half of the nineteenth century is anything but
> laissez-faire in its labour relations. In Britain it saw
> the codification of the Master and Servant law which
> penalised breaches of contract more harshly for men than
> for masters, the systematic, if not always effective,
> outlawing of trade unions and strikes - the repeal of
> the Combination Acts made relatively little difference
> to this - a marked taste for long-term and inelastic
> labour contracts like the miner's annual or monthly bond,
> and that ruthless piece of legal-economic coercion, the
> New Poor Law (1968; 352).

The Conspiracy and Protection of Property Act of 1875, so far
as trade union law was concerned, signified an incipient transition in the role of the state that was to affect the structure
of its relationship with organised labour. Section 4 of this

47

Act stated that a criminal breach of a contract of employment
would occur if it were committed by a person employed in the
public supply of gas or water and if the loss of such supply
were likely to lead to serious injury to people or property
(Citrine: 1967; 13). What is significant is that this stipulation represents a change, albeit nascent, in the role of the
state in the direction of taking on the responsibility for
maintaining continuity in the supply of certain key and strategic economic and social resources by legislatively preventing
the potential disruption that strike action posed to such distribution (Allen: 1964; 119).

Conciliation and Arbitration
One respect in which the extent of this change was noticeable
was in the field of conciliation and arbitration, for as governments became more directly 'interventionist' in the late nineteenth century, and in view of the escalation of class conflict
in this period, the need to establish statutory guidelines for
conciliation and arbitration as a means of controlling industrial conflict and to provide for government intervention in
disputes, became more pressing. Thus, in 1896 a Conciliation
Act was passed, based on the recommendations of the Royal
Commission of 1894. It conferred on the Board of Trade statutory authority to intervene in industrial disputes to:
(1) inquire into the causes and circumstances of disputes;
(2) facilitate meetings between contending parties under a
mutually agreed upon, and Board of Trade nominated, chairman;
(3) appoint a conciliator on the application of either party;
and (4) appoint an arbitrator on the application of both
parties. The Act was used increasingly despite some employer
opposition. Also, as Phelps-Brown argues, the result of the
1896 Act was that 'it was decided that British industrial
relations were to consist of voluntary negotiations between
employers and employed. Government would not regulate them,
save in so far as it had already provided a special legal
status for the trade unions' (1959; 187). Prior to the 1896
Act, the coal strike of 1893 which threatened both industrial
and domestic supplies, represented a new stage in industrial
conflict, for it was the first time that the government intervened in a dispute (Ibid.: 160-61). This trend continued after
1896 with government intervention in disputes, especially
national strikes which disrupted, or possessed the potential
to disrupt, industrial production on a large scale (Ibid.:
320-25 and 286-343. Milne-Bailey: 1934; Part 1).
    What the government, in effect, had begun to do through
the agency of the Board of Trade, was to use conciliation to
enable parties to a dispute to reach a settlement and then aid
the setting-up, or improvement of, machinery allowing for more
regular future transactions. Such joint boards of conciliation
imposed collective bargaining on employers from the outside.
Thus, 'in the disputes on the railways in 1907 and 1911 and in

the mines in 1912 what it [the government] in fact did was to
coerce the employers by legislation or the threat of it'
(Phelps-Brown: 1959; 342). Needless to say, workers were also
coerced in this fashion, as in the Miners' strike of 1912.

This intervention was still, however, quite limited in its
extent. Most of the more powerful trade unions were against
compulsory arbitration and they 'shared the employers' dislike
of bringing government into their private business' (Ibid.: 285
and 187). However, the government did enhance its conciliation
and arbitration powers to a degree with the Industrial Courts
Act of 1919. This established a permanent tribunal composed of
independent personnel and representatives of employers and
workers. Any dispute could be referred to the Minister of Labour
but he could refer it to the Industrial Court only, (1) if it
was a trade dispute as defined by the Act; (2) with the consent
of both parties; and (3) only if the negotiating machinery in
the industry had been fully used beforehand. Under Part 2 of
the Act the Minister had the power to appoint a Court of Inquiry
into a dispute, whether or not it had been reported to him, and
without the consent of the parties. This court could make recommendations but had no powers of enforcement.

This Act, together 'with the Conciliation Act, 1896, which
still remained on the statute book, was the authority for most
of the Minister of Labour's interventions in industrial disputes until 1940' (Allen: 1960; 62). Between 1940 and 1951 the
Conditions of Employment and National Arbitration Order (1305)
set up a National Arbitration Tribunal to which disputes were
referred by the Minister of Labour at the request of either
side, and strikes and lockouts were only legal if the Minister
had failed to take action within 21 days. This system of compulsory arbitration was repealed by the Industrial Disputes
Order of 1951 which nonetheless maintained compulsory arbitration in a modified form, in the sense that either side could
take a dispute to the Minister who could refer it, in turn, to
the Tribunal without the consent of the other party and any
award the Tribunal made was legally binding upon both parties
(Ibid.; 95 and 104-105). This ended in 1958 and the government
reverted to the 1919 Act (Ibid.; 67).

The State, Law and Strikes
From the point of view of the political sociology of the legal
regulation of industrial conflict some of the most significant
empirical examples have involved direct attempts by government
to legally prohibit strikes, in the context of the growth of
the interventionist state. By the First World War, governments
had begun to assume responsibility, not only for maintaining
national security and law and order, but also for the distribution of resources, the preservation of general welfare and
the protection of economic interests, and in more deliberately
and purposively upholding the social order, 'was becoming involved in the organisation of society' (Allen: 1960; 299).

Hence, government was increasingly constrained to regard most major strikes as direct challenges to its authority and functions. In order to maintain such authority and to ensure that such functions as it was taking on could be fulfilled, government armed itself with legislation, distinct from that passed previously, to enable it to legally control strikes which threatened its organisational and cohesive functions. Undoubtedly, the two world wars combined with industrial conflict played a crucial part in the development of the state. The constraints that war imposed on government in the shape of the need to plan the national economy led to a re-assessment of its relationships with organised labour and to the co-optation of union leaders (Miliband: 1972; 47-8) as well as the legal proscription of strikes. For wars gave labour a more strategic position in the economy and in considerations of national interest (MacDonald: 1960; Chapter 7). This situation enhanced the process whereby the state became more and more self-consciously the political custodian of the national interest (Allen: 1966; 32). This was also generated by the fact that the economy was becoming more inter-dependent and industries had grown up which encompassed and integrated the national society, such as the railways and the mines. The rationale of government intervention and regulation rested upon its claim to protect the interests of the community and therefore the maintenance of essential services and supplies became more and more the province of the state. Thus the government's guarantee of the supply of necessary and strategic economic resources meant that strikes which interfered with this function challenged the 'national interest' and posed a threat to the authority of the state (Allen: 1960; 121-3. Knowles: 1952; 291).

This was made manifest by a series of legislative enactments central to this phase of state development. The Munitions of War Act, passed in 1915, made arbitration in the munitions industry compulsory and thereby made strikes illegal unless the dispute was reported to the Minister of Labour and he failed to refer it to arbitration within 21 days (Allen: 1960; 131-3). This was buttressed by the more extensive Defence of the Realm Act, 1916, which dealt with workers inciting others to strike (Ibid.). The 1919 Electricity Supply Act extended the stipulation of Section 4 of the Conspiracy and Protection of Property Act of 1875 to prevent workers engaged in the supply of electricity from calling a strike legally (Citrine: 1967; 638). The Police Act, 1919, passed in the wake of a police strike and the attendant disorder, was designed to prevent policemen from striking and from belonging to a trade union (Knowles: 1952; 104-105). Most decisive was the Emergency Powers Act of 1920 (Milne-Bailey: 1929; 350-1. Bunyan: 1977). It provides that if action is taken or immediately threatened which is on such an extensive scale as to be calculated to deprive the community or any substantial portion of the community, of 'the essentials of life', a state of emergency will be declared. It confers upon the government powers and duties designed to secure 'the preservation of the peace, for securing and regulating the supply and distribution of food, water, fuel, light, and other necessities. for maintaining the means of transport or locomotion, and for any other purposes essential to the public safety and the life of the community'. It further provides that 'no such regulation shall make it an offence for any person to take part in a strike, or peacefully persuade any other person or persons to take part in a strike'. The emergency powers of the government could, however, have such an effect, de facto, and the Act did mean that 'the government may, moreover, assume powers of search and arrest without warrant' (Bunyan: 1977. Citrine: 1967; 638-40).

However, while it may be insisted that statute and case law provide a means of identifying the controlled nature of the legal incorporation of organised labour and the changing role of the state, it is essential to assess the empirical application of legal devices by the state to control strikes. The war-time strikes that governments have had to deal with have mainly been illegal and unofficial. A strike by South Wales miners over wages in 1915 came within the purview of the Munitions of War Act. The government was thus confronted with maintaining the authority of the Act by imposing penal sanctions on 200,000 miners. Instead the Minister of Munitions obtained a settlement on the miners' terms (Allen: 1960; 137-9). As Allen notes, 'this was the first indication of the fact that if a large enough number of workers in a vital industry ignored anti-strike legislation there was nothing the government could do about it except behave as if no such legislation existed' (Ibid.; 138). However, on a number of occasions, the state was prepared to proceed with legal action against strikers rather than accede to their demands. Clydeside workers were dealt with under the Defence of the Realm Act and arrests were also made during an engineering strike (Ibid.; 133, 139-43). In this period, a notable feature of internal structural change within trade unionism, to re-emerge in the processes leading up to the I.R. Act, came to be highly significant in that a shop steward movement developed (MacDonald: 1960; 87-9. Hinton: 1973).

The government equipped itself with similar but new measures to deal with strikes during the Second World War. The Emergency Powers (Defence) Act, 1940, gave the government the power to authorise orders for the execution of government control. For our purposes here the major part of this Act concerned Order 1305, the Conditions of Employment and National Arbitration Order, 1940, Part 2 on 'lockouts and strikes'. As already indicated, under this Order a dispute had to be reported to the Minister of Labour and 21 days had to elapse from the time of this report and it had also not to be referred by the Minister for settlement during that time, before strikes and lockouts were deemed to be legal. This was buttressed by a new Defence Regulation, passed by an Order in Council in 1944, which made those persons who incited or instigated strikes liable to imprisonment or fines; peaceful picketing was also declared to be an illegal act (Allen: 1960; 134-6). This legal machinery was used by the government in the Kent miners' strike in 1941-1942 but the fines imposed were not paid and the miners returned to work after management had granted them a satisfactory wage offer (Allen: 1960; 140. Donovan Report: 1968; 340-1). This evidence clearly illustrates the point that 'it was administratively difficult to make so many arrests and if they were made they were likely to have repercussions in the form of another strike covering a wider area' (Allen: 1960; 140. Cf. Knowles: 1952; 119).

Legal sanctions against strikes have been similarly used in peace-time: Order 1305 was retained until 1951 when its use as a normative system of social control had been seriously undermined by working class opposition. The Order was brought to bear in two cases. A strike of gas maintenance workers in September 1950 led to 10 strikers being summonsed under the Conspiracy and Protection of Property Act, 1875, for depriving the public of gas supplies, and under Section 4 of Order 1305, for not giving 21 days' notice of their intention to strike to the Minister of Labour. Each striker was sentenced to one month's imprisonment, but on the same day the men went back to work, and on appeal, the sentences were reduced to fines of £50 each (MacDonald: 1960; 156-9).

The government's action may appear to have been effective but powerful trade union pressure against the Order was mounted and the government exacerbated the situation by again using the Order in February 1951. On this occasion seven dock workers, members of the T.G.W.U., were arrested for conspiracy to incite other dock workers to strike contrary to article 4 of Order 1305 relating to unofficial strikes. The dockers staged one day strikes during the court hearings (Wedderburn: 1971; 393). The decisions reached by the jury on different counts were inconsistent and it was therefore announced that, for this reason, the prosecutions were to be withdrawn. In August 1951, Order 1305 was withdrawn and a new Order, without provisions making strikes and lockouts illegal, was introduced (Allen: 1960; 268-70. MacDonald: 1960; 160-2 and 166). Thus, as Clegg concludes on the effectiveness of this measure of legally controlling strikes: 'Virtually every strike between 1940 and 1951 was a criminal offence ... but the order was rarely invoked, and proved difficult to enforce even when it was invoked. It appeared to have very little effect on the number of unofficial strikes' (1972; 479-80).

These examples clearly demonstrate the ineffective and politically precarious nature of legal sanctions. Such measures were only readily enforceable when a relatively small number of strikers were involved or where the strikers were not prepared to resist; in other words, where social consensus could be maintained or already prevailed. That this consensus was not attainable very often, even under war-time conditions when the overwhelming ideological stress was placed upon national unity and upholding the national interest, is a telling enough indication of the constraints that the legal control of strikes held for the state. In both World Wars governments were not particularly willing to make use of the legislation and regulations they had devised to prevent strikes. Nor were workers, for the most part, put off by these measures from using their strike weapon, nor by the fact that they were striking against the state (cf. Allen: 1960; 141. Knowles: 1952; 118-19). It is equally true, however, that for its part, organised labour has refrained from taking potentially explosive conflicts between itself and the state to their logical conclusions by directly threatening the constitutional legitimacy of state rule. While this may suggest the strength of state legitimacy, it has also occurred when the power of the coercive force of the state has been made apparent to strikers and potential strikers.[8] Thus, the state, in pursuing its expanding interventionist role and its ideological custodianship of the national interest, has been prepared to mobilise its military-coercive powers, to uphold the rule of law and to meet the challenges posed by strikes to the authority of its role as was the case with the General Strike of 1926[9] (Knowles: 1952; 107-109).

The State and the Institutions of Collective Bargaining

Concomitant with the above developments and a somewhat different response to the same periods of intense industrial conflict, was the move towards more co-operative and institutionalised forms of collective bargaining. For contrasting with and growing out of the processes so far discussed was the growth of the principle of voluntarism, which rested upon union-employer co-operation as the means of resolving industrial relations problems, with only the minimal degree of state assistance.

This concerned, firstly, the industrial council of 1911-1913.[10] This was an attempt to establish at national level co-operation between unions and employers in improving investigation, conciliation and arbitration in industrial disputes, under government direction, its board consisting of union and employer representatives. It was largely ineffective in its immediate cases not merely because of its inability to handle class conflict, but also because where it intervened, the norms of collective bargaining, which its role pre-supposed, had not been prevalent. But it did represent a move away from laissez-faire since it 'emphasised that government could no longer simply hold the ring but had to have a positive and forceful policy for industrial relations in support of voluntarism' (Charles: 1973; 72 and Part 1, passim).

The next stage in this process was the Whitley Committee scheme, the evolution of Joint Industrial Councils. In preparing for post-war reconstruction the government, in 1916, set up a Committee of employers and unions to make recommendations

on how to secure permanent improvements in industrial relations.
This, the Whitley Committee, amongst its reports, proposed the
setting up of permanent joint bodies of employer and union representatives, namely joint industrial councils. This allowed
the government to provide for industrial order (which was also
sought by capital and some union leaders) without becoming over-
committed to interventionism at this stage. But this had relatively little substantive effect: it was more or less irrelevant
to industries in which collective bargaining was already developing and it had most impact in the public sector and certain
other industries where trade unionism was weak (Charles: 1973;
Part 2. Goodrich: 1975; 113-14 and passim. Garside: 1977; 247-9).

Deriving out of the Whitley proposals, the government con-
vened a National Industrial Conference, in 1919, comprising a
large number of union and employer representatives, to consider
and recommend ways of improving industrial relations. This was
something approaching the notion of an 'Industrial Parliament',
a national advisory and representative forum for tri-partite
collaboration on resolving difficulties in industrial relations
and restoring industrial peace. A number of meetings were held
during 1919 and 1920 but due to the then relative abatement of
industrial disruption and class conflict and the absence of
constraints impelling the government (and capital) to cross the
divide between laissez-faire and interventionism, the Conference
fell into disuse in 1921 (Charles: 1973; Part 3. Garside: 1977;
249-50).

In the aftermath of the General Strike an attempt was made
by certain sections of capital to develop class collaboration
through the Mond-Turner talks of 1928 to 1929. These represented, in the main, an attempt by large-scale capital in the
newer, technologically 'advanced', and 'science-based' industries like chemicals, rubber and oil, and other domestic based,
capital-intensive industries, to take advantage of the opportunity opened for national collaboration with the trade union
movement in order to more effectively control the economy by
securing labour co-operation in policy, and to devise permanent
institutions for such co-operation. This capital, with its
large-scale operations and complex division of labour and
organisational structure, sought more sophisticated and consensual or hegemonic forms for industrial relations, rather
than direct coercion and legal repression, and received the
support and co-operation in the venture of some union leaders
within the TUC. But the Conference on Industrial Re-Organisation
and Industrial Relations, as it was called, despite some 'con-
versions' amongst unionists and employers, failed to have any
great impact, mainly because of the opposition of employers in
the more basic and traditional industries within the FBI, NCEO
and EEF (Charles: 1973; Part 4, Chapters 18-20. Garside: 1977;
258-62).

Thus, as Garside notes, 'despite the efforts made since
the formation of a National Industrial Council in 1911 no

54

permanent relationship had been successfully forged at national level between the two sides of industry'; this is attributed to employer opposition (1977; 261). Though interest in such schemes persisted throughout the 1930s and 1940s amongst sections of capital, both industrial and financial, and also within the state (Carpenter: 1976), the establishment of tri-partite, corporatist style institutions for industrial relations, involving a more extensive role for the state, failed to materialise very strongly either as a structural fact or a serious political strategy until the 1960s. This observation must lead us to ask what has changed in the structure of British capitalism to make corporatism a more appealing and practical option for certain fractions of capital and state apparatuses in the present conjuncture?

Conclusion

I have attempted to establish in this chapter the points I set down at the outset. I have therefore covered some of the history of the relationship between the state, capital, organised labour and industrial relations before the contemporary period on which I wish to concentrate. History, however, is not merely more of the same. It is therefore necessary to consider if the contemporary phase of state intervention is similar to those we have just considered. And it also needs to be determined if it occurred under similar conditions to previous phases. In order to answer this question I shall analyse the social character of modern British capitalism. As we shall see, clarifying this structure goes some way towards explaining the present juncture of state intervention in industrial relations.

NOTES

1. For two examples of the 'relative autonomy' of the state in this period see Pelling: 1971; 27-8.
2. For discussions of this Act and its extensive use by employers see Clegg et al.: 1964; 44, and Simon: 1954. The Act was opposed by the unions precisely because of its unequal legal treatment of breaches of contract by employers and workers; the former were only liable to a fine and the latter to imprisonment for the same offence. It represented a significant aspect of the legal repression of union activity, continually resorted to by employers,
3. In fact, a group of members of the Royal Commission on Labour in 1894 'recommended an alteration in the law to make union funds liable for damages' foreshadowing the Taff Vale decision. See Bealey and Pelling: 1958; 14.
4. Picketing was condemned by employers because it infringed upon their capacity to introduce strike breakers into their factories when faced with a strike: this is what was meant by free labour. Also 'the process of strike-breaking had become systematized by the establishment in 1893 of the National

Free Labour Association, which was designed to provide employers with alternative sources of labour in the event of difficulty with unionised employees' (Bealey and Pelling: 1958; 14. See also Saville: 1960; passim).

5. Of course, the Osborne judgement was only one amongst a number of factors contributing to mounting industrial discontent (see Clegg et al.: 1964; 423-65).

6. On this, see the comprehensive list of legislative intervention by the state during the nineteenth century provided by Brebner: 1962; 260-62.

7. The perspective adopted by Polanyi is similar to that used by Gramsci in his critique of the theoretical foundations of economic liberalism. Gramsci argues, 'laissez-faire too is a form of state "regulation", introduced and maintained by legislative and coercive means. It is a deliberate policy, conscious of its own ends, and not the spontaneous automatic expression of economic facts' (1971; 160).

8. For a discussion of the use of the armed forces to prevent strikes see, for example, Knowles: 1952; 133-8. Bunyan: 1977; Chapter 7. Cf. Phelps-Brown: 1959; 323-5.

9. On the General Strike see, for example, Farman: 1974. Foster: 1976. Symons: 1957. Mason: 1969. Pelling: 1971; Chapter 8. It is also discussed at greater length in Strinati: 1981.

10. This and the other aspects discussed in this section are covered in much greater detail by Charles: 1973. Cf.Garside: 1977. The latter provides interesting details of the objectives of employers in the inter-war period.

Chapter 3

STATE INTERVENTION AND THE POLITICAL ECONOMY OF BRITISH
CAPITALISM

This chapter attempts to analyse certain trends in the development of British capitalism in order to begin to provide a sociological account of changes in the structure of industrial relations in Britain from the late 1950s onwards, especially the
state's mediation of these relations. In the next chapter I
will examine the specific, conjunctural characteristics of the
crisis of British capitalism in the period mentioned, to comp-
lement the analysis of more long-term changes in class and
political structure with which this chapter is concerned,
namely the relationship between the structure of industrial
relations and the overall socio-economic development of British
capitalism. But it is not only because they inform particular
interests in the re-structuring of industrial relations that
the themes of this chapter may be considered important, for it
is also necessary to establish the extent to which British
capitalism has changed so as to identify the influence of such
changes in the formation of often conflicting strategies for
the reform of industrial relations and the institution of state
control of industrial conflict. What I wish to do is to extract
a limited set of contentions from the protracted and extensive
debate on the nature of modern capitalism which are germane to
the considerations raised by this study (cf. Giddens: 1973;
Chapter 9, especially p. 164. Habermas: 1976; 33).[1]
    The relevance of this requirement to the issue of the con-
trol of industrial relations, as well as being implied in the
historical survey in the last chapter, has been stressed by a
number of authors. For example, Goldthorpe remarks: 'increases
in the scale of production, advancing technology and more integrated and competitive markets place increasing pressure on
industrial enterprises to engage in the long-term planning of
their activities.... In this attempt, however, the factor of
labour represents, at least potentially, a source of major
difficulty' (1977; 204. Cf. Jessop: 1978; 42. Kidron: 1970; 129).
The changing social structure of capitalism constrains monopoly
capital units and the state to become engaged in some kind of
planning of labour control. This makes it necessary to consider

in some empirical detail the nature of contemporary British
capitalism which can be conveyed by the growth of economic
concentration, both financial and technical, increasing structural interdependence, bureaucracy and specialisation in the
political economy, the rise and separation of monopoly capital
from petit-bourgeois capital within competitive markets, the
separation of money and industrial capital, the socialisation
of labour and union centralisation, and the development of the
interventionist state and economic planning. I shall now consider these trends by empirically indicating the extent of
their presence in British capitalism, because for an adequate
sociological explanation of the class and political interests
and conflicts over, and the actual processing of, the state's
mediation of industrial relations, such changes in the structure of capitalism provide the context in which these interests
and conflicts have their effects; and since, at the same time,
they are bound up with changes in the state's structuring of
work relations, they thereby exert a determining influence
upon both of these processes.

Economic Concentration and Forms of Capital
A number of detailed studies have exhibited a high degree of
agreement on the predominance of oligopolistic capital in the
industrial and financial sectors of the British economy. One
study[2] has defined this trend as follows:

> In the course of the present century British industry
> has witnessed a transformation from a disaggregated
> structure of predominantly small, competing firms to
> a concentrated structure dominated by large, and often
> monopolistic corporations. The top 100 corporations
> which now occupy the dominant position account for
> something approaching one half of total manufacturing
> output, whilst at the turn of the century the largest
> 100 firms accounted for barely 15% of output (Hannah:
> 1976; 1).

It similarly needs to be noted that this trend accelerated
between the middle 1950s and early 1970s (Ibid.; 166) and that
'over the period as a whole, mergers were the major cause of
increasing concentration as they were in the 1920's' (Ibid.).
What this has entailed in Britain has been the rise of monopoly capital centred more upon financial centralisation rather
than, though by no means excluding, technical, industrial concentration. The very fact that merger and take-over activities
are tied in with the growth of financial and banking institutions (Aaronovitch and Sawyer: 1975; 240 and Chapter 12)
suggests that monopolisation in sectors other than that of
industrial manufacturing needs to be considered. Aaronovitch
and Sawyer question whether 'non-manufacturing sectors are
predominantly of low concentration. Rather there is a mixture

of levels of concentration, and several sectors show high and/
or rising concentration' (Ibid.; 113). They also indicate the
heavy involvement of manufacturing giants in some service industries (Ibid.; 108-10) and infer that 'concentration in these
financial sectors is very high' (Ibid.; 112-13).

The empirical persistence of small-scale capital provides
another means by which the monopolisation of capital, the
changing organisation of the economic dominance of capital,
can be identified. This is expressed in an accentuated division
between oligopolistic industrial and money capitals on the one
hand and petit-bourgeois capital on the other. The dimensions
of this can be described as follows. Between 1935 and 1963 the
number of small firms, that is those employing a work force of
200 or less,[3] fell from 136,000 to 60,000 and over the same
period their share in manufacturing output was reduced from 35
per cent to 16 per cent. More specifically, between 1958 and
1965 the share of such firms in manufacturing output declined
from 20 per cent to 16 per cent, and the demise of more than
half of these small companies was due to their acquisition by
larger units (Hannah: 1976; 1 and 166). This is not to suggest
that petit-bourgeois capital is no longer of any economic or
political importance. It still employs about 6 million people
or 25 per cent of the employed population and is responsible
for 20 per cent of GNP, facts indicative of the preservation
of a competitive, private enterprise, small firm sector within
the economy (Bolton Report: 1971; XIX and 33-35). Nonetheless,
the position of petit-bourgeois capital has been subject to a
marked degree of erosion over time, manifest in the fall in the
number of establishments in this sector from 93,000 in 1930 to
35,000 in 1968 (Prais: 1976; 10-11), and the employment provided by these establishments which has fallen from 44 per cent
of the total employed in 1924 to 29 per cent in 1968, while
their share in net output fell from 42 per cent in 1924 to 25
per cent in 1968 (Bolton Report: 1971; 58-9 and 67).

This changing structure of the economy has been connected
with a change in the structure of its industrial control. Large
scale, oligopolistic capitals have been characterised by
increasingly differentiated industrial structures in terms of
production chains, products, plants and management structure.
As Channon has shown, in a study of 92 of the top 100 British
manufacturing companies between 1950 and 1970, more than half
by 1970 were multi-national, multi-product concerns possessing
multi-divisional management structures, although this had been
true of only a quarter of the companies in 1950 (1973; 66-8,
73 and 78). Central to this diversification of industrial
structure has been corporate growth through mergers and takeovers. Thus the problem for management administration concerns
not merely the production structure but a number of different
and discrete production structures. Moreover, many modern
products, their production relations and their requisite tech-
nologies are based in large scale plants: 'typical plant sizes

59

measured in terms of the number of employees have doubled in a
general way in the past forty years', acccmpanied by a reduction in the number of small plants (Prais: 1976; 58 and 52).
However, 'plant sizes seem to be largely irrelevant to the rise
in the concentration of firms' (Ibid.; 48). The relative importance of the large plant has not increased: 'In the 1930's the
hundred largest plants accounted for 11% of manufacturing net
output, and in 1968 - surprisingly enough - the proportion was
still at that same level' (Ibid.; 59). Also there has been a
'threefold increase from an average of 27 plants per each individual enterprise comprising the hundred larger enterprises in
1958 to an average of 72 in 1972' (Ibid.; 62). There has thus
been a somewhat phenomenal acceleration in this process of the
rise of the large, multi-plant firm since 1958 (Ibid.; 64-5
and 85). However, the largest firms do not necessarily own
most or all of the larger plants, for, 'one should rather
think of the typical giant enterprise as owning a host of
plants, most of which are only of medium or small size, though
in some cases there may be a "nucleus" of a few very large
plants' (Ibid.; 61-2). Hence, it is not merely a question of
planning control within plants but also co-ordinating control
between plants and groups of workers for the administrative
organisation of monopoly capital, especially if it is realised
that such capitals employ a large and increasing proportion of
the labour force (Bullock Report: 1977; 5-8).

If this is the case, it would tend to accentuate the
problem of managerial administration for monopoly capitals in
so far as such a problem becomes very much a question of admin-
istering production on the basis of the effective integration
of distinct, technically and structurally fragmented industrial
plants. For the overall administration of capital, integrated
production in one or a few large plants would not form as great
a constraint but rather assist the logic of planning. However,
the fact that this would not appear to be the case only com-
pounds the problem of control engendered by multi-divisional
management structures. Moreover, in so far as plant size
increases it in and of itself increases the managerial need
to socially control industrial conflict in that there is a
positive relationship between plant size and industrial conflict, i.e. the larger the plant the greater the likelihood
of conflict (Prais: 1978. Ingham: 1970). This constraint
applies both to internal managerial control and to the external conditions of control provided by the state for with
greater socialisation, larger plants and the multiplicity of
plants and plant sizes characterising the structure of particular monopoly capitals, a qualitatively distinct, more co-
ordinated, systematic and planned form of control becomes
necessary. It may be noted in this context that the often mentioned practical difficulty of using penal and financial sanctions against large numbers of strikers may be a consequence
of the growth of large plants and denotes a specific structural

60

condition limiting legal coercion by the state and favouring
the adoption of incorporative methods of labour control.

The Structure of Organised Labour
The mere existence of large-scale production plants has been
found to be conducive to shop steward organisation (Brown et
al.: 1978; 154). This has been particularly apparent in the
conjunctural re-emergence of work place based rather than
national, union based industrial conflict in Britain from the
mid 1950s onwards. The nature and influence of work place union
organisation and the assertion of shop floor power in collective
bargaining and the securing of delimited job control has long
been a feature of work relations in Britain, declining in extent
and influence after the defeat suffered by labour in the General
Strike of 1926. But the expression of shop floor power in post-
war Britain has had very different conditions and consequences,
especially for the mode of state intervention, than that
experienced in previous phases of ostensibly similar conflicts.
The re-assertion of shop floor power at the point of production
has different conditions and consequences depending upon (but
also, in turn, conditioning) the extent of monopoly capital's
growth, whether planning is becoming such capital's logic of
action and whether state economic intervention is laissez-faire
or interventionist and is therefore taking a more direct role
in the re-structuring of capital. It is also dependent upon the
extent to which the institutions of organised labour have become
bureaucratised and centralised.

Even if we concentrate on the period 1948 to 1974, certain
notable characteristics in the unionisation of the labour force
in Britain become apparent. In this period the density of
union membership within the labour force increased from 45.2
per cent to 50.4 per cent. The growth in union density has
occurred at a time when industries noted for their traditions
of unionism, such as mining and railways, have seen a decline
in the numbers employed, while the opposite has been the case
in areas such as white collar work in the financial sector
where unionism has been traditionally weak (Price and Bain:
1976). It is also the case that union density is generally
much higher in large-scale enterprises and establishments in
the industrial manufacturing and public sectors of the economy
(Ibid.). Of particular significance is the concentration of
union membership into fewer and larger trade unions. For
example, in 1900 there were 1,323 trade unions officially
recorded in existence; by 1960 they had been reduced to 664,
and by 1974 to 488. This has gone hand in hand with increasing
membership density. Also, in 1960, unions with 100,000 members
or more totalled 17 in number, organised 6,590,000 members
which represented 67 per cent of the total union membership;
by 1974 such unions totalled 25 in number, organised 9,259,000
members, which represented 77.5 per cent of the total union
membership. The fact that in 1974 the 88 unions with 10,000

members or more accounted for over 95 per cent of total union membership, makes the concentration of members in the top twenty or so unions strikingly evident (D of E: November 1976; 1250-1).

The consistency of this with corporatist forms of political representation has tended to be over-exaggerated in accounts which either emphasise the manipulable accommodation of political structures to interest bargaining or which tend to ignore the extent to which such consistency is structurally undermined by shop floor opposition and by the ideological perpetuation of an attenuated liberalism amongst the ranks of organised labour;[4] for such trends in union centralisation occur not only in the context of the monopolisation of capital and growing and changing state intervention but also in the context of the re-emergence of shop floor based, workgroup power often inimical to official union organisation. In post-war Britain organised labour has been subject to more or less simultaneous centrifugal and centripetal forces: it has been marked by the centralisation and bureaucratisation of its organisations but at the same time it has also been marked by the re-assertion of unofficial union power at the workplace (cf.Clegg: 1976; 17-18).

This contradiction within trade unionism in Britain (Hyman: 1971) constitutes a crucial structural feature vis-a-vis state intervention in industrial relations and state control of industrial conflict. On the one hand, the trend towards union centralisation facilitates and indeed provides an institutional channel for organised interest group bargaining with government in the context of the changing and growing economic role of the state. Therefore the development of strong unionism to contain industrial conflict entails both the state encouraging union organisation and the maintenance and extension of the institutionalisation of interest group bargaining with organised labour at the level of the state. However, bound up with and in part engendered by this trend is the accentuation of industrial conflict as a result of the power exercised by organised but unofficial rank and file work groups in the context of an increasingly socialised political economy. This serves, among other things, to undermine union control of industrial conflict, especially insofar as they are constrained to represent their members' interests and yet at the same time may appear to be incapable of containing their members' aspirations and actions. Thus, the centralisation of union organisations and the formalisation of their relationship with the state comes to be undermined by conjunctural changes in the intensity of class conflict consequent upon the devolution of power to the work group at the point of production. Unions as forms of social control for employers and as channels for political attempts to maintain order in industrial relations thereby involve the control of shop floor power.

In general terms this can be related to the fact that as

the labour process itself becomes more collective, socialised
and co-operative this has gone hand in hand with the fragmentation and specialisation of tasks in more precisely differentiated occupational categories. It may therefore be suggested
that these processes will tend to be reflected, to some extent,
in labour's presence in class conflict, the former in the shape
of large-scale, 'official', bureaucratic trade union organisation, the latter in the shape of discrete, localised work
groups confined to more narrow arenas of conflict which nonetheless can still affect the rest of society due to the socialisation of the political economy. Such centrifugal and centripetal forces within the ranks of labour have obvious implications not merely for the structuring of conflict between such
'fractions of labour'[5] but also for that between labour and
capital and the state in the context of the state's mediation
of economic and industrial relations, forming a constraint
shaping the interests and strategies of capitals and the state
in developing mechanisms of control for industrial relations.

State Intervention, State Planning and British Capitalism
The growth of and changes in the role of the state are intimately connected with the other trends which, it has been
suggested, characterise the development of the political
economy of British Capitalism. Details of this with respect
to its relationship with changes in trade union law have been
provided in the previous chapter. The task now is to examine,
empirically, changes in the overall complex of state mediations
of the economy in order to determine the nature of the growth
of the interventionist state so that it is possible to clarify
and assess its impact upon the structuring of industrial relations in contemporary British capitalism.

The transition of the state from laissez-faire to interventionist forms of mediation of the economy can be conveyed
by employment in state administration (which is associated
with the increasing structural complexity of the political
economy), as well as by the extension of the control the state
possesses over economic resources. As far as employment is
concerned, the percentage of the total labour force employed
by the state (including the armed forces, central, civil and
local government and, after 1945, the nationalised industries
and government services) increased from 2.4 per cent to 24.3
per cent between 1851 and 1950 with the greatest increase
being in the second half of this period. By the 1970s this
trend has tended to stabilise, especially with the running
down of the armed forces, with about 25 per cent of the total
working population in state employment (Abramovitz and Eliasberg: 1957; 19 and 23-4. Barratt-Brown: 1971; 222-3). If
nothing else this provides the minimal basis for the state's
implication in economic production and industrial relations
control since the state becomes a major employer of labour-
power.

Increases in public expenditure (which includes the national debt, military, civil and local government expenditures), as a percentage of gross national product can be delineated as follows: 'From 1841 until 1890 the share of government changes little, declining very slowly from 11 per cent of GNP in 1841 to 9% in 1890. This compares with a share of 12% in 1905, 24% in 1923 and 37% in 1955' (Peacock and Wiseman: 1967; 38). It has been estimated that subsequently public expenditure rose to 43 per cent in 1964, 52 per cent in 1968, and 56 per cent in 1975.[6] Concomitantly, government revenue has risen in percentage terms from 11 per cent in 1910 to 44.6 per cent in 1973 (Gough: 1975; 60). The relationship of this with the functional composition of public expenditure has also to be stressed. Gough notes a number of changes in this respect: the expansion of expenditure on social services in total, save for the 1930s, rose from 4.2 per cent of GNP in 1910 to 24.9 per cent in 1973; the declining share taken by armaments and military expenditure which fell from 10.8 per cent in 1951 to 6.4 per cent in 1973; and, lastly, 'two further notable increases have also occurred in the 1960's: a growth in state economic aid to the private sector and a growth in state expenditure on its legal and coercive apparatus' (Ibid.; 62).

This has been bound up with a general growth in the overall extent and complexity of state institutions. This is highlighted not only by public expenditure and the functions towards which it is directed, but also by such features as the increasing number of government departments, the continued creation and amalgamation of departments, the transfer of functions between departments, the setting up of larger departments with wider responsibilities, the integration of departments, the extension of their structures functionally and geographically, and the attendant need for inter-departmental co-ordination. This is not to be seen as a functionally smooth process since it only aggravates the need for centralised co-ordination within the state (Chester and Willson: 1968; 391 and passim). Moreover, the very re-structuring of state apparatuses derives from, shapes and affects conflicts both within and outside the state.

Connected with the changes so far described has been the growth of what have been termed 'fringe bodies' or 'quangos'. These are governmentally constituted state apparatuses which are ideologically construed to be independent from government, representing a form of government at 'arms length', while, at the same time, being government funded, relatively permanently established and subject to government appointment of a number of their officials. They are generally conceived of as bodies outside the 'core institutional order' of the state which consists of Parliament, armed services and police, the judiciary, government departments, nationalised industries, the National Health Service and local authorities (Bowen: 1978; 5-7). Operating in the social zone between the legally defined and

64

differentiated public and private spheres but still forming
part of the state, they have arisen out of a context in which
the role of the state has been widened as its structure has
been extended and re-organised. In 1900 such bodies totalled
10 in number, by 1949 they had increased to 84, by 1959 to 103,
by 1965 to 150, by 1971 to 196, and by 1975 to 235 (Ibid.; 1).
Although they are accountable to Parliament this has to be
weighed against the fact that the majority are in fact 'executive' agencies, i.e. implementing a policy or carrying out a
prescribed function of government (Ibid.; 31-4).

The often-remarked upon growth of state functions after
1945 in some ways obscures developments in the inter-war period
and the contribution of the Second World War itself to this
process (Chester and Willson: 1968; 39-47 and 104-105. Addison:
1975). What is evident is that the state came increasingly to
administer the economy. As Dobb has pointed out, with reference
to the emergence of political means of assisting economic
recovery: 'The recovery phase of 1933 to 1937 stood in contrast to previous periods of this kind in the extent to which
the expansion of production depended on government policy'
(1963; 333). The use of the power of the state to open up markets abroad had already been leading to a growing integration
between the state and private capital (Feis: 1961). Also
equally indicative of this trend was the fact that 'one of the
original impulses towards the foundation of I.C.I. came from
the direction of public policy' (Reader: 1977; 227). In such
ways it was beginning to become evident that the state had
begun to engage in economic intervention of a kind distinct
from that to be found in liberal capitalism.

State intervention in a more directive and productive
form became apparent during the Second World War with its combined imperatives of optimising economic efficiency by means
of state planning and of building a national consensus transcending class lines. As a result it had a major influence
since 'Social security for all, family allowances, major reform in education, a National Health Service, Keynesian budget-
ary technique, full employment policies, town and country
planning, closer relations between the state and industry' had
begun to emerge by 1943 (Addison: 1975; 14). This entailed the
integration, control and direction of labour and hence 'the
installation of the TUC virtually as a department of government
in Whitehall ... [and] ... the dissemination of social democratic ideas' (Ibid.; vi). Such TUC control of labour as was
possible was a quid pro quo for the development of state planning (Ibid.; 234), and forms of 'tripartite consultation among
industry, labour and the government', such as the joint production committees emerged (Rogow: 1955; 102). Needless to say,
the more direct, physical controls like the direction of labour
were gradually removed after 1945 and highly centralised and
directive planning gave way to Keynesian techniques of state
intervention such as the use of the financial budget to manage

the economy, to control the business cycle, maintain full employment and further incorporate labour on the basis of consensus politics, re-orienting state policy towards intervention,
though, despite some important measures of nationalisation, it
still rested primarily upon influencing market forces (Dobb:
1963; 387-8).

However, the basis for more direct intervention had been
developed before 1960. During and after the Second World War
governments had endeavoured to channel their intervention in
industry via representative, often quasi-executive, tripartite
institutions: a 'main characteristic of the war economy was the
gradual introduction of corporate forms of organisation (Leruez:
1975; 35-6). This involved closer relations between the state
and large firms combined with the state's acceptance of the
autonomous self-government of private industrial organisations.
Representatives of employers' associations and trade unions
were increasingly to be found on state boards and committees
(Rogow: 1955). In this context, a notable institutional innovation of the post-war Labour Government was the Development
Council system established in 1947, similar to the sectoral
economic development committees set up in the 1960s and designed
to provide additional manpower research and other services so
as to improve industrial efficiency (Shonfield: 1965; 88).
Although ineffective due to employer opposition (despite some
initial enthusiasm) amid fears of the 'corporate state' and
much concern over the future of private capital's trade associations, they still provided a structural prototype for state
planning, even though state direction and control were fore-
saken for the voluntarism residing in the autonomous regulation
of economic relations by privately constituted and organised
interests.

Thus, before 1960 the Conservative government tended to
utilise demand management techniques of economic intervention
like monetary and fiscal policy, relying upon the primacy of
market forces, with the stop-go character of this policy being
the major consequence (Dow: 1970; Chapter 3 and Part 2). But
since 'the fatal flaw in stop-go was that it crippled both
long-term and short-term expansion' (Leruez: 1975; 84), the
lack of accumulation, the desire of some sections of industrial
capital for long-term economic stability and planning and a way
of countering the influence of money capital (Blank: 1973.
Longstreth: 1979), the need for economic consensus, planning
as a quid pro quo for an incomes policy acceptable to the trade
unions, and the state's re-assessment of intervention led to
attempts to institute state planning in Britain in the 1960s
(Leruez: 1975. Longstreth: 1979. Shonfield: 1965). To illustrate this, the cases of the NEDC and IRC can serve as suitable examples.

The NEDC was established in order to study 'the plans and
prospects of our main industries, to correlate them with each
other and with the Government's plans for the public sector,

66

and to see how in aggregate they contribute to, and fit in with, the prospect for the economy as a whole including the vital balance of payments'.[7] In order to effect such intervention, it was thought necessary for 'both sides of industry to share with the Government the task of relating plans to the resources that are likely to be available'.[8] It was also accordingly designed 'as a forum for the establishment of a new consensus among the main economic interest groups ... a second parliament with a corporatist character - and because of that character, expected to be able to conclude binding agreements between major interest groups of a type which a traditional British parliament could not compass' (Shonfield: 1965; 151-3). Supporting this, a system of economic development committees (EDC's), separate planning bodies for each industry under the aegis of the NEDC, operating on tripartite lines and with similar objectives was also set up (Denton et al.: 1968; 112-17). This was 'welcomed by both employers and unions. This represented a major change in employers' attitudes from 1947' (Leruez: 1975; 110). Indeed, the initiative taken by domestic, industrial, and large-scale private capital within the FBI played an influential part in the inception of planning in Britain in the early 1960s (Longstreth: 1979. Blank: 1973).

Despite the importance of this system in promising to mobilise consensus on the priorities to be realised regarding the reproduction of capitalist relations in the process of economic intervention by integrating corporatist political representation with interventionist state policies, the essentially voluntaristic normative definitions which have marked such intervention must be emphasised for they indicate the ideological limitations which confront state planning in Britain, and which tend to 'under-determine' corporatist representation and state intervention. Private control and initiative has rested with and derived from autonomously constituted organisations, like employers' and trade associations and trade unions, and since these are regarded, normatively, as being independent of government interference and control by government departments, they tend not to embody the statism opposed by their members but required by corporatist state intervention (Leruez: 1975; 153). As Shonfield has argued, a major difficulty in establishing planning in Britain has centred on the appropriate co-ordination of state and private economic power and the institutional responsibility for planning. And this, in part, rests upon prevailing ideological conceptions of 'the proper role of government in a system of guided capitalism' (Shonfield: 1965; 161). This episode shows how certain institutional developments attendant upon the growth of interventionist state power have not attracted the corollary of strongly hierarchical, even politically sanctioned, structures for interest representation, although, as will subsequently be shown, some moves in this direction have been attempted. The support of capital and labour interest representatives for planning institutions,

though at times considerable (Leruez: 1975; 153), has been
denominated in an ideological coinage not easily exchangeable
for the corporatist alternative.[9] This has limited their
effectiveness as forums for consensus building for what consensus has already been available has been either inimical to
or inconsistent with the entrenchment of corporatist representation.[10]

Equally instructive in this context is the example of the
IRC,[11] especially in terms of the productive re-structuring of
capital by means of state interventionism, for, unlike the
NEDC, which remained wedded to Keynesianism, it represented a
response to the lack of capital accumulation by means of state
sponsored rationalisation aimed at production and not just at
market forces. For the Labour government which introduced it,
the IRC represented an alternative to the National Plan as a
way of directly moulding the structure of industry so as to
make British capital more competitive internationally (Young
and Lowe: 1974; 133-76). This entailed varying shades of state
inducement to ensure industrial and technical re-structuring,
such as the adoption of new product lines, the use of the most
up-to-date technology, reducing over-manning, rationalising
assets to lower unit costs, and changing marketing practices,
all of which have been aimed at increasing industrial efficiency, productivity and competitiveness (Ibid.; 175). The IRC
was to assist industrial re-organisation and profitability,
in particular by encouraging industrial concentration, mergers
and rationalisation, for the government argued that market
forces were not a sufficiently compelling force in restoring
productive efficiency (Ibid.; 40. Cf. Leruez: 1975; 140-41,
210, 212-13). Armed with wide and unspecified powers, a board
consisting mainly of businessmen and normative independence
from government (Young and Lowe: 1974; 40. Leruez: 1975; 212-13)
major amalgamations resulted from its operations like General
Electric, British Leyland and International Computers, as well
as the re-organisation of the nuclear and mechanical engineering industries (Young and Lowe: 1974; Chapters 4 and 6).

The IRC was heavily criticised from the perspectives of
distinct class interests and political objectives. Sections of
trade union and left-wing opinion considered it to be too independent of government and an instrument for furthering the
interests of monopoly capital (Leruez: 1975; 214). Some
businessmen thought it brought Britain to the verge of Commu-
nism (Smith: 1974; 101 and 94). The Institute of Directors
called it 'trapdoor nationalisation', while the CBI promised
to ensure that the government did not 'envisage nationalisation
by the back door!' (Smith: 1974; 94. Young and Lowe: 1974;
80-81). And yet it was equally true that 'larger companies
with a tendency towards monopoly or oligopoly benefitted most'
(Leruez: 1975; 215). In fact, the work of the IRC depended
very much on the consensual co-operation of private capital,
especially in view of its reliance upon voluntary rather than

68

statutory powers; and due to the wide co-optation of industrialists, the funds made available for investment and the progressively clearer nature of its aims, the IRC eventually
managed to secure the co-operation of business, particularly
large-scale capital, with an increasing number of projects
being born out of approaches by firms and trade associations
to the IRC (Young and Lowe: 1974; 30-83). There were, however,
important constraints upon the operations of the IRC for it
'was quite unable to force companies to act against their will'
(Ibid.; 83-4). Consequently, the economic re-structuring
associated with state intervention was still constrained by
the political and ideological components of voluntarism more
characteristic of state laissez-faire. Moreover, it was mainly
opposition from petit-bourgeois capital and its political
supporters which led the Conservative government to abolish
the IRC in 1971 (Leruez: 1975; 215, 242, and 269).

What I have attempted to do in this section has been to
identify empirically the nature and extent of the changes
associated with the transition from the laissez-faire to interventionist state in the British political economy. Accordingly,
I have also been concerned to begin to demonstrate concretely
the relevance of the typology developed in Chapter 1 insofar
as it can be argued that state mediation of the economy can
be seen to be marked by certain characteristic paradigms, such
that with the interventionist state it is possible to identify
an emergent and contradictory tension between corporatism and
other forms of political representation. State intervention
depends upon the co-operation of organised producer groups and
the state has attempted to secure this by constituting such
groups as organised interest groups and by accentuating the
mobilisation of consent in order to more effectively manage
the economy, which has led to what Beer has called the 'new
groups politics' (1965; 395 and passim).

This analysis is germane to the study of the role of the
state in industrial relations in two important ways. Firstly,
it is indispensable in illustrating key features of the developing structural context in terms of which the subsequent discussion can be placed and understood. It therefore provides an
explanatory identification of some of the conditions within
which class, intra-class and political conflicts over the
structuring of state control of industrial relations have
taken place, for the rise of the interventionist state imposes
constraints upon the forms of such control and the interests
associated with them. The change in state economic mediation
from laissez-faire to intervention is a central structural
factor in determining the role that the state began to play
in British industrial relations in the 1960s and 1970s,
informing the class and political interests and conflicts
grouped around such changes. Secondly, the empirical identification of the changing mode of state economic intervention
from laissez-faire to interventionism, will allow us to discern

and understand the parallels between this and the state's mediation of industrial relations.

The Changing Structures of Class and Political Power
The above analysis has attempted to detail some structural
constraints engendered by the changing structure of economic
and state power in British capitalism for the articulation of
class and political interests and conflicts associated with
state intervention in industrial relations and the state's
control of industrial conflict. It is now necessary to consider the state's control of class conflict for what is equally
required is an examination of the economic and political
crises to which British society has been subject and to which
it is still elaborating a response.

NOTES

    1. By this debate I mean the voluminous literature that
has been written on the issue of whether contemporary societies
in Western and Eastern Europe and North America are best considered capitalist or industrialist, whether they are best designated monopoly capitalism, state capitalism, or advanced industrial societies. For a discussion of this see Giddens: 1973
and Scott: 1979; Chapter 1.
    2. See also, e.g. Aaronovitch and Sawyer: 1975; Part 2,
chapters 4-6. Perhaps the most useful work mainly because it
provides a comprehensive summary of most of the evidence is
A Review of Monopolies and Mergers Policy: A Consultative
Document, Cmnd. 7198, London, HMSO, 1978 (hereafter referred
to as A Review of Monopolies).
    3. This may not appear to be the best criterion since an
arbitrary quantitative measure would not appear to give the
precise social referent required. However, such a measure is
empirically consistent with other more meaningful measures,
such as combined owner-managership, small plant size, the inability to re-shape markets, etc. See Report of the Committee
of Inquiry on Small Firms (Chairman, J.G. Bolton), Cmnd. 4811,
London, HMSO, 1971 (hereafter referred to as Bolton Report),
paragraph 3, pp. XV-XVI and Part 1, chapter 1.
    4. Or, indeed, ignore the effects of political structures
altogether. Particularly noteworthy in both regards is Winkler:
1976.
    5. It has become quite orthodox to talk about 'fractions
of capital' and the consequences of this for the role of the
state. See, e.g. Poulantzas: 1973. Idem: 1975. And this study
carries on this emerging orthodoxy. But the suggested fractions
are an attempt to conceive of the fractionalisation of labour
with respect to the problem I am analysing. Other obvious form-
ulae come readily to mind like the division between productive
and unproductive labour, skilled and unskilled labour, etc.
These, however, are less relevant for an understanding of the

problem to which this work is addressed.

6. On this and public expenditure in general see Peacock and Wiseman: 1967 (2nd ed.); especially Tables 1 and 2, pp.37 and 42, and Table A6, p. 166. Gough: 1975; Table 2, p. 60. Warren Nutter: 1978; Figure 2, p. 11 and Table 4, p. 12.

7. Quoted in Chester and Willson: 1968; 351. On the related development of the National plan and the setting up of the Department of Economic Affairs by the 1964-1970 Labour Government, see Longstreth: 1977. Leruez: 1975; chapters 6, 11 and 12. Budd: 1978; chapter 6.

8. Quoted in Denton et al.: 1968; 112. Cf. Leruez: 1975; 100.

9. This applies both to ideological practices and to the political and industrial dimensions of interest organisation. The structural sources of this support for and opposition to the development of corporatism are discussed more fully below.

10. This is particularly true of the relationship between planning and the securement of trade union support for incomes policy. See Corina: 1975; 181. Longstreth: 1977. Shonfield: 1965; 154-7.

11. My discussion of this relies heavily on Young and Lowe: 1974; especially Part II and pp. 231-6. It also provides general coverage of state intervention in the period 1964-1974. Cf. Leruez: 1975; 140-41, 210, 212-15 and 242.

Chapter 4

CLASS CONFLICT AND THE ECONOMIC AND POLITICAL CRISES OF
BRITISH CAPITALISM

The argument of this chapter suggests that it is not merely
the macro-structural developments detailed in the previous
chapter which provide the conditions for changes in the nature
of state intervention for these are equally derived from the
extent and nature of the way in which such developments and
their consequences are dependent upon the particularity of
their combination within the institutional structure of different capitalist societies, in terms of the extent to which they
are implicated in the generation of crisis. It is to a consideration of this, the conjunctural crises of capitalism within
the British social formation, that I now wish to turn. Moreover, these features are of significance in so far as they
allow us to begin to determine clear and direct links between
such crises, class conflict, class interests, and modes of
state intervention.
     In order to conduct this empirical examination I shall
make an analytical distinction between forms of class conflict,
namely between struggles in the spheres of production and distribution. The former refers to class conflict inhering in
relations of production as evinced by struggles over such
issues as productivity rates, the rationalisation of capital,
work organisation, accumulation, restrictive practices and
technical changes, and so on - in effect, struggles grouped
around the production and appropriation of surplus value from
the industrial production of commodities within the labour
process. This is analytically if not substantively distinct
from conflict inhering in relations of distribution as evinced
by struggles over such issues as wage demands, labour costs,
profitability, the structure of the wage form, e.g., time or
piece rates, wage drift, and so on - in effect, struggles
grouped around the realisation and circulation of profits and
wages arising from the exchange of commodities within the distributive labour process. This distinction not only provides
a convenient organisation for the subsequent discussion but
also, as we shall see in later chapters, can inform the consciousness of the classes and state agencies engaged in

conflict (cf. Esping-Anderson et al.: 1976; 199. Stedman-Jones: 1975; 49, 55 and 60). Objectively constituting the structural link between the two sets of conflicts is class struggle, the struggle between capital and labour in both the spheres of production and distribution. From the point of view of the analysis being presented in this chapter such a link is marked by the conjunctural nature of the class struggle which characterises production and distribution relations. In this case this centres upon the growth in the power of shop floor based groups of unionised workers estranged from the control and authority of official union leaderships and often militant in the pursuit of economic rewards and job control by means of various strategies of industrial action. The different indices of industrial conflict, once the precise nature of such rank and file power has been identified, thus prove to be crucial as indicators of class struggle. Conflict arising from the use of unofficial work place union power is, in effect, the specific, concrete form that the class struggle in industry has generally taken in Britain, re-emerging at least from the mid-1950s onwards.

This needs to be detailed since, in the first place, we need to be clear as to the dimensions of the crisis before we examine how its features began to inform the consciousness, interests and objectives of classes, class fractions and political groups as well as the state. It will be seen that it is at this level that an increasingly greater commensurability can be discerned between socio-economic conditions and subjective and ideological evaluations of those conditions. Moreover, and secondly, it allows for the discernment of the manner in which the structural determinants upon the role of the state are actually revealed to the state as compulsions to action. One of the major problems which has confronted theoretical discussions of the state has centred on the question of defining the mechanisms by which the state responds to the features of its socio-economic environment to which it is supposed, conceptually, to respond. How do the state and its agencies know that intervention in economic and industrial relations is required? (cf. Wirth: 1977; 305-307). Although it is not predicated upon a view of the state as a functionally omniscient agent, the answer suggested to this question here is that the features of capital accumulation requiring state intervention are revealed, in general, by means of crises in the reproduction of economic and political relations and, in particular, by the ostensible generation and accentuation of class conflict in production and distribution relations (cf. Ibid.). Thus, the empirical detail in this chapter possesses a theoretical importance in both affording part of an explanation of the specific features of the state's role in industrial relations in Britain which will subsequently be described and in identifying the impact of economic and political crises in the shape of class conflicts upon the role of the state.

Class Conflict and Production Relations

The first factor to be noted in this context is the overall
rate of economic growth characterising the British economy.
This can be indicated as a first approximation by the annual
percentage growth in the Gross Domestic Product, which averaged
2.8 per cent for the period 1955 to 1968 (Gamble and Walton:
1976; Table 1, p. 6. Bacon and Eltis: 1978; Chart 1, p. 2).
On a more long-term basis this can be placed in perspective:
between 1900-1913 the annual percentage increase in GDP averaged 1.09 per cent; between 1922-1938, 2.3 per cent; between
1950-1960, 2.6 per cent; between 1960-1970, 2.8 per cent; and
between 1970-1976, 1.6 per cent (Prest and Coppack: 1978; 48).
It is also necessary to consider the more refined measure of
GDP per capita which for the periods mentioned, excluding the
first, varied from 1.1, 2.2, 2.5 and 1.4 per cent (Ibid.). It
can be conceded that, historically, the productive growth of
the economy has been greater since 1945 than it had ever been
previously[1] although the figures cited do not suggest a dramatic increase, and they indicate a decline from 1970 onwards.
As far as the significant variable of labour productivity is
concerned it can be concluded that 'output per man hour in
manufacturing industry increased at an annual rate of only 3.0
per cent from 1955-65, but at an increased 4.0 per annum from
1965 to 1974' (Bacon and Eltis: 1978; 9. Cf. Sargent: 1979).
Although this represents an improvement and by UK standards
high productivity, even the latter compares unfavourably with
an average of 6 per cent for W. Germany, France and Italy
(Ibid.; 9). Hence, the relative ability of workers in Britain
to resist by a number of means the compulsion of capital to
increase productivity constituted a central barrier to capital
accumulation.

Investment as an aspect of the appropriation of surplus
value provides a similarly striking index of the crisis that
confronted capital accumulation in the period under scrutiny.
It would be fair to say that the aggregate rate of investment
would not at first glance appear to be unduly low or problematic for accumulation since its pattern is typically cyclical
rather than declining tendentially though certain significant
low points have been reached as in 1962 and 1963 and again in
1969 (Glyn and Sutcliffe: 1972; 120-26. Prest and Coppack:
1972; 34). It is however possible to discern some kind of
trend in that the proportion of industrial production between
1961 and 1975 which was 'invested in industry itself, net of
capital consumption, fell by one-fifth from 8.2 per cent to
6.8 per cent of sales of industrial production' (Bacon and
Eltis: 1978; 18). Furthermore, the quality and the underlying
objectives of investment in Britain may be less than favourable for accumulation in view of the fact that it is often
less than productive, being dominated by the 'consolidationist'
ideology of money capital, which is one of 'maintaining the
value of money wealth ... its monetary holdings but at the same

time to earn a return on these', rather than the 'accumulation-
ist' ideology of industrial capital which emphasises 'rationali-
zation' in the productive process;'a technocratic outlook concerned with efficiency; a preparedness to take risks in the
search for additional surplus, etc.' (Thompson: 1977; 270-71).
In the UK the former tends to dominate 'the practices of the
financial and the industrial sector itself' (Ibid.; 271).
    The actual constraints entailed in the labour process
which hinder productivity growth are neither as clear nor as
susceptible to statistical demonstration as production, productivity rates and investment per se. These concern the organisation of production and work practices, the managerial impetus to ensure control of this process and the opposing impact
of the organisations and practices of workers at the point of
production (Friedman: 1978. Benyon: 1975). They thus can be
represented by conflicts over managerial efforts to restructure
work to increase productivity, in a way the most notable in
Britain being the attempt to remove work group opposition to
technical change because of its effects on employment and job
control, thereby generating struggles over such 'restrictive
practices' as the maintenance of existing labour units to run
labour-saving technology. The significance of such struggles
and of employer responses, for example, productivity bargaining,
can be seen in this light as will be shown as the subsequent
analysis unfolds. Equally crucial is work group organisation
for the purposes of conflict over the production process. This
can reasonably be conveyed by a consideration of the nature of
industrial conflict and this will be attempted in the third
section of this chapter.

Class Conflict and Distribution Relations
Closely connected with the workplace organisation of labour are
changes in wage and earning rates and labour costs, and, more
generally, conflicts over the wage-form which also includes
struggles over such issues as overtime, piece as opposed to
day or time rates, and the character of bonus payments. Much
of the substance of these issues emerges below but it is possible to indicate here the magnitude of overall changes in
wage and earning rates. The general point to be noted in this
connection is the way in which such rates at least in money
terms have risen, leading, albeit by no means automatically,
to an increase in labour costs. From 1953 to 1956 the annual
percentage weekly wage rate increased from 3.0 per cent to
7.9 per cent from which it fell to 4.1 in 1960, with a low
point in 1959 of 1.1 per cent. However, for most of the early
and mid 1960s it ranged at this level of between 3.4 to 4.6
per cent until 1967 when it reached 5.9 per cent. From this
it rose to between 11 and 13 per cent for the early 1970s
until escalating to over 25 per cent in 1974 and 1975 (Prest
and Coppack: 1978; 43. Cf. Glyn and Sutcliffe: 1972; 108-10).
This tended to have its effect not only in potentially

increasing labour costs and thereby costs of production so inducing employer strategies to control such costs. But also, due to the collective bargaining tactics adopted by certain work groups with a basis of power on the shop floor, it led to the phenomenon of 'wage drift', that is the securement of actual earnings significantly in excess of negotiated, agreed and nationally ratified wage rates (cf. Dow: 1964; 343-50).[2] The nature of this trend from the 1950s onwards and before the 1969 'wage explosion' has been adequately conveyed by Crouch:

> Much of this pressure for increased pay stemmed from local increases in excess of nationally negotiated rates.... The association between shop-floor militancy and [wage] drift is seen in those sectors where workers have been able to take conscious advantage of their strong market situation in order to turn certain payment systems to their own advantage. The most striking cases of this occur with piece-work systems (1978; 208).

It can also be noted that the incidence of taxation on the rising net real income of manual workers effectively reduced the latter so that it more or less stagnated after a notable increase from 1958 (Jackson et al.: 1975; 103). The consequence was an acceleration in industrial militancy. This response by workers to stagnating real income contributed to the wage explosion from 1968 onwards (Ibid.: 86-7 and 101-103). However, this sudden rise has to be seen as a consequence of an already rising level of pay demands, and to a certain, albeit correspondingly lower, extent, in increasing real incomes (DOE: May 1978; 521-3),[3] and it is interesting to note that when this consistent though modest rise in pay was halted, industrial conflict over this very issue began to escalate, again an accentuation of an already growing process.

Centrally bound up with such trends has been the power derived by sections of the working class from the low levels of unemployment that have tended to characterise the British economy since the war. The percentage rate of unemployment in the UK between 1953 and 1966 stayed below 2 per cent, ranging around the 1.5 per cent mark, only going over 2 per cent in 1959 and 1963. However from 1967 up to 1970 the rate consistently averaged over 2 per cent, going up to 3.5 per cent for 1971 and 1972, before dropping again to 2.5 per cent for 1973 and 1974 and then climbing for subsequent years to around 5 per cent (Prest and Coppack: 1978; 43). No doubt this was due in part to employer hoarding of labour (Ulman: 1968; 329-31) arising out of the competitive nature of capital. But it was undeniably also due in part to the state's commitment to full employment as part of the post-war social democratic consensus with organised labour (Panitch: 1977. Gough: 1975. Warren: 1972; 3-4). The maintenance of such a low level of unemployment has important consequences for class relations in industry, for,

76

as Kalecki recognised: 'Under a regime of full employment "the sack" would cease to play its role as a disciplinary measure' (1971; 140-41. Dobb: 1963; 23-4). This illustrates how certain changes in the conditions and structuring of distribution relations, namely state expenditure to control aggregate demand and employment levels, can influence production relations by enhancing the power of workers through mitigating the control and authority of the employer over the hiring, deployment, and discipline of labour in the production process, and by giving labour the leverage to increase the price that capital has to pay for its labour-power.

Connected with this in making manifest by means of the crisis mechanism the need for state intervention and seen by many as an inevitable corollary of full employment has been the problem of inflation. Inflation is in many ways one of the most visible expressions of the effects of class conflict (Goldthorpe: 1978). Needless to say, price rises must, in some part, be conceived of as circulatory ramifications of the power of monopoly capitals to exert some influence over the prices of their products as well as a response by capital to declining profits (Holland: 1975. Kidron: 1970; 69. Rowthorn: 1977; 21). The shape and effect of the inflation rate is clear for governments have long been concerned with inflation and what they have generally seen as its root cause, excessive and unproductive wage claims (Panitch: 1976). The rate of price changes in the British economy has tended to be subjected to substantial, and at times almost meteoric, increases. As far as the annual percentage change in retail prices is concerned this can be demonstrated as the following tabulation for selected years shows: 1953 - 3.1; 1959- 0.6; 1961 - 3.4; 1965 - 4.8; 1968 - 4.7; 1969 - 5.4; 1971 - 9.4; 1973 - 9.2; 1974- 16.1; 1975 - 24.2; 1976 - 16.5 (Prest and Coppack: 1978; 43). This, although of course hotly contested, has its proximate sources in wages increases and import prices (Crouch: 1978; 193) as well as monetary expansion, for there is some evidence to support the view that inflation derives most immediately from the link between worker demands for money wage increases to maintain real wages in the face of price increases as engendered by increased pay expectations (Jackson et al.: 1975). The notable effects of inflation in terms of an attempt to identify the conditions for state intervention in industrial relations concern international competitiveness, the element of unpredictability and uncertainty it introduces into the price level and economic environment in which capital has to operate (Gamble and Walton: 1976; 13), eating into profit margins and increasing the prices that companies have to pay as well as receive.

Obviously linked with the investment aspect of capitalist production discussed above has been perhaps the crux of the issue, the profitability crisis of British capitalism. The link between stagnating investment and declining profitability

in the UK economy has been made clear since a low or zero
profit rate 'means that ... companies' gross incomes were
insufficient to meet all the claims on that income quite apart
from providing further funds for expansion. This must imply
both an erosion of capital and an increasing inability to
secure external finance' (NEDO: 1975; 6 and 16). The trend
towards industrial concentration and the increased merger
activity apparent in the 1960s have been directly associated
with the declining profitability of British industry: 'The
merger movement has been partly a defensive response to falls
in the rate of return on capital' (Sinclair: 1978; 71). It is
clear that the rate of profit has been in decline from at
least the mid-1950s onwards (Bank of England Quarterly Bulletin:
December 1978; 513-20). Inflation has tended to obscure this
but a NEDO study aimed precisely at taking this into consideration, computed that the rate of return on capital assets in
manufacturing industry fell between 1965 and 1973 from 10.2
per cent to 6 per cent (1975; 1-6 and 15). The Director of
NEDO saw these conclusions as a dramatic indication of the
nature of the crisis: 'If this process were to continue it
would jeopardise the chances of improving performance and
could lead to the erosion of our industrial base' (Ibid.; iv).
Or as the seminal study carried out by Glyn and Sutcliffe
(1972) notes, 'British capitalism has suffered such a dramatic
decline in profitability that it is now literally fighting for
survival. This crisis has developed because mounting demands
from the working class for a faster growth in living standards
has coincided with growing competition between capitalist
countries ... [which] has prevented British capitalism from
simply accommodating successful wage demands by pushing up
prices correspondingly' (1972; 10). And this is so even though
the discernible decline in the gross trading profits (after
deductions for stock appreciation) of UK industrial and commercial companies between 1965 and 1976 has been to some extent
offset by the maintenance or growth of other sources of income,
like rent, non-trading incomes such as interest on investments,
and income from abroad (Thompson: 1978; 424-5).

This crisis has served as a mechanism to trigger state
intervention in the economy and industrial relations. The NEDO
study and its conclusions already cited, as well as much of
the evidence which follows, affords credence to such an infer-
ence although our analysis attempts to avoid the mechanistic
instrumentalism colouring Glyn and Sutcliffe's analysis of the
role of the state which conceives of it as a more or less automatic consequence of the recognition of the profits crisis
(Glyn and Sutcliffe: 1972; Chapter 8). The declining rate of
profit constitutes and makes manifest, as do the other features
of distributional struggle considered here, the crisis of
capital accumulation; but they do not automatically determine
and guarantee, although they motivate, state intervention;
they are conditions within which modern state power in Britain

has had to act and move but its actions have not merely been
reflective of these conditions. Furthermore, the crisis of
contemporary British capitalism is not just the result of autonomous, insulated, and 'pure' economic forces working themselves out over time; they have been determined and 'over-
determined' by the state. This has been apparent, for example,
not only in the way in which inflation has been exacerbated -
or has even emanated from - state induced increases in money
supply to finance its intervention in capital accumulation
(Gamble and Walton: 1976). It has also emerged in the way in
which governments have produced rather than reduced fluctua-
tions in demand through fiscal and monetary policies (Dow:
1964; 211, 369-73 and 391-2), and through deflationary policies
designed to deal with balance of payments deficits, which have
tended to lead to or aggravate low investment and low productivity (Pollard: 1969; 442-7). But perhaps the most illustrative
example is the politicising, educational and even inflationary,
effects of incomes policies (Tarling and Wilkinson: 1977; 408).
A point somewhat specific to the profits crisis but which can
stand as a comment on all of the features of crisis considered
here and to be followed up subsequently is that the objective
fact of declining profitability began to constrain, structure
and inform the interests of capital. Hence, the CBI submission
to the Wilson Committee of Inquiry into financial institutions
stressed that British industry has been characterised by low
investment mainly because of low profitability, resting its
case on an estimated fall in the profit rate from 10 per cent
in the 1960s to $3\frac{1}{2}$ per cent in 1975 and 1976 (The Times,
12.8.77, p. 16). It can thus be seen to constitute a key
structural constraint on the motivation to action of classes,
class fractions and political groupings involved or implicated
in class conflicts in production and distribution relations.
The other factors so far analysed may therefore be seen in a
somewhat similar light. But of equal and compelling force in
articulating the economic crisis and notably in the very obvious way in which it has informed and constrained class and
group objectives and actions has been the manifestation from
the late 1950s onwards of the various indices of industrial
conflict in British industrial relations. It is essential that
we now turn to analyse the connections between the production
and distribution dimensions of class conflict in as much as
these are affected by the nature of the organisation of
industrial conflict.

Class Conflict and Industrial Conflict
I shall in this section consider the incidence of industrial
conflict as expressed mainly in strike activity before proceeding to assess its bases and nature. A rigorous attempt to
decipher strike trends in Britain has concluded that 'the frequency [number] of strikes ... remained remarkably stable
throughout the 1950s, since which time it has risen almost

continuously to the highest levels ever recorded' (Shalev:
1973; 95. Cf. DOE: November 1978; 1256-8). This increase in
the rate of stoppages has been notable for the evenness of its
distribution between industries, such that other industries
began to join and even outpace the traditionally more militant
workers like those in transport and engineering, with car
workers increasingly becoming protagonists predominant in
industrial conflict from the 1950s onwards (Shalev: 1973; 73-6.
Crouch: 1978; 220-5). The point here is that there has been a
general increase in strikes in virtually every industry outside
coal-mining since the mid-1950s (McCarthy: 1970; 231-3). Similar conclusions can also be drawn regarding the other major
indices of strike activity, the size and duration of strikes,
that is the numbers of workers involved and the number of working days lost: 'in recent years not only the frequency of
strikes [outside of coal mining] but also the numbers of workers involved in strikes and, most of all, the amount of working
time foregone, have shown strong upward tendencies' (Shalev:
1973; 95 and 79-85). This overall growth in strike activity
is thought to be the case particularly from 1968 onwards but
it is also part of a more long-term increase which escalated
rather than emerged in the late 1960s (Shalev: 1973; 80.
Crouch: 1978).

In order to exemplify the relevance of such trends for
the articulation of state intervention in industrial relations
the structural nature of strike activity needs to be clarified.
This can be achieved by considering the forms taken by indust-
trial conflict, which can be approached in the first instance
by indicating changes in the reasons given for striking: 'by
far the lion's share of the rise in strike frequency since the
early 1960's is attributable to disputes over wage claims....
Strikes over working conditions and employment issues form a
smaller proportion of the total today than they did at the
beginning of the period, although ... the frequency of strikes
in both categories has more than doubled' (Shalev: 1973; 85 -
my emphasis).

Conducive to such struggles is the actual structure of
industrial conflict which informs much of what has so far been
claimed, namely the growth of unofficial and unconstitutional
strike activity, often shop steward led, and undertaken by
workplace based union groups rather than by official union
organisations: the rise of shop floor power. As Clegg has
commented,

> Britain is now widely known as a country of two-level
> bargaining because of the post-war development of sup-
> plementary plant bargaining, mainly by shop stewards....
> the distribution of workplace bargaining is uneven.
> It has grown up with little help from national union
> headquarters and none from the law, so that it exists
> where shop stewards have been able to establish it and

managers have been willing to recognize it, either formally or informally (1976; 17, 51, 56-7. Cf. Donovan Report: 1968).

The connection between the extension of workplace bargaining and shop floor power and the gradual accentuation of industrial conflict has likewise been noted:

> The rise in unofficial shop-floor militancy, [is] indicated by: an increasing number and proportion of 'unofficial' or 'unconstitutional' strikes; an increase in the extent to which wages are settled at plant level (associated with the wider phenomenon of wage-drift); and a rise in the importance of shop stewards as opposed to full-time union officials. Although much has been made of the novelty of these developments, it is important to bear in mind that they mark a return to much earlier patterns of industrial relations; the pattern of trade or industry level bargaining through union hierarchies and employers' associations which has become known as the traditional pattern dates back only to the late 1930s. It should also be noted that the rise in unofficial disputes began in the 1950s, and was not a sudden phenomenon starting in the late 1960s (Crouch: 1978; 204 - my emphasis).

This extension of the shop floor power of workers is not only rooted in features generic to industrial relations per se but also in the wider framework of the socialisation of production and the labour process, the rise of monopoly capitalism and the interventionist state that has come to characterise the contemporary capitalist political economy.

The Donovan Commission estimated that 95 per cent of all strikes in Britain have been unofficial,[4] as well as being also both relatively small and short-lived (1968; Pa. 368). However, since about 1970 it has again become more common for officially sanctioned strikes to take place, and they started to increase in number, size and duration, often in response to incomes policies, and more stringent state control of industrial relations (Hyman: 1973; 102-103 and 107-110). This reflected 'a gradual recognition by union officialdom that attempts to suppress rank-and-file militancy may prove unsuccessful and merely discredit their own position in the eyes of members and employers alike' (Hyman: 1973; 108). But by 1974 the previous pattern of small, short, unofficial strikes began to be re-established, albeit now larger in size and longer in duration than before (Shalev: 1973; 89 and 92). Unconstitutionalism is similarly engendered by shop floor power and has clearly figured in, if not at times almost consuming, complaints and conflicts over its use. But reliable evidence by no means matches the intensity of the arguments and it is superficial to equate unofficial with unconstitutional strikes. Nonetheless on the basis

of what evidence there is, Shalev indicates that there is a
generally high cyclical rate of unconstitutional strike activity in the engineering industry (Shalev: 1973; 92-4 and 96).

Closely connected with the foregoing have been the effects
of shop floor power and strike action within the context of an
increasingly socialised political economy. One crucial index
of this is the number of workers involuntarily thrown out of
work by strike action elsewhere which they have neither initiated nor supported. This has been an important condition in
the articulation of employer and state control of work group
power because of its very effects in undermining the socialised
and co-operative nature of what still remains capitalist production. Shalev concludes, 'the implication would seem to be
that lately an increasing number of workers have been laid
idle because of industrial conflict through no wish of their
own' (1973; 81 & 99). As Phelps-Brown has noted, 'Increased
complexity and integration of processes has given some quite
small groups the power to halt wide sectors of production.
Increased capital per employee has raised the cost of a stop-
page relatively to the cost of the settlement that will avoid
it' (1973; 333).

The variant indices of conflict analysed express the
growth of shop floor based, union power (cf. McCarthy: 1970;
233 and 234). The short, sharp, unofficial strike pattern that
has arisen concatenates with fragmented pay bargaining, and
serves as a token of the militancy and combativity of work
group power at the point of production (cf. Clegg: 1976; 78).
And local shop floor bargaining plays a key role in strike
action over wage determination (Daniel: 1976). Socialised production, shop floor power and work place bargaining thus have
their effects in a form of unpredictable, unofficial industrial
conflict that is particularly intractable to planning and
control.

A central role has been played in this growth of workplace
bargaining and unofficial industrial action by shop stewards
and shop stewards committees in the organisation of industrial
relations (Goodman and Whittingham: 1969). A number of studies
have attested to the growth and extension of the role and
functions of the shop steward in collective bargaining in association with the development of workplace bargaining, within
the context of the overall rise of shop floor power (McCarthy:
1966. McCarthy and Parker: 1968. McCarthy and Ellis: 1973.
Donovan Report: 1968). As Fox notes, 'shop stewards have leapt
in numbers from around 90,000 in 1961 to an estimated 300,000
today. The number of full-time shop stewards alone has risen
in private manufacturing industry from around 1,000 in 1966
to about 5,000 in 1976' (1978; 2). This has been closely linked
with the attentuation of the influence of collective bargaining
and negotiated agreements at national and/or industry level
between employers and/or employers' associations and trade
unions and its gradual replacement by discrete, autonomous,

82

fragmented and localised bargaining between shop stewards and
shop steward led work groups, on the one hand, and managements
on the other, at plant and company level (cf. Hyman: 1973; 110).
It has accordingly been discovered that there has been a clear
trend towards workplace bargaining in British industry, that
shop stewards have taken a more central and influential role
in such collective bargaining as a consequence and that a large
number of shop stewards have it as their aim to subject wider
areas of work organisation and a larger range of issues to
joint regulation with management (McCarthy: 1966; Sections B
and D. McCarthy and Parker: 1968; chapters 2 and 5). The focus
of industrial relations and industrial conflict has thus tended
to shift once again to the work place and the initiative has
tended to return to shop floor, working class organisations
(cf. Goodman and Whittingham: 1969).

The structural sources giving rise to shop floor power
have in the main resided in factors already analysed, most
especially the socialisation of labour processes in the political economy and the development of full employment and labour
scarcity. But there are also more proximate causes rooted in
the internal structure of industrial relations which incorporate the effects of these macro-structural processes. Fox points
to the fact that increasing technical complexity favours bargaining with work groups involved directly in sophisticated
industrial and technological production rather than with remote
'outsiders' without this detailed work knowledge, like union
officials and employer association representatives (Fox: 1978;
3. McCarthy: 1966; Section G). Concomitantly, centralised collective bargaining institutions and collective agreements laying down minimum standards are by their very nature incapable
of being meaningfully applicable to local concerns and their
inherently general provisions allow scope for work place bargaining in any case (Goodman and Whittingham: 1969; 11-12 and
146. McCarthy: 1966; Section G). Trade union structure itself
by virtue of the phenomenon of multi-unionism within and between particular plants, the relative weakness of branch organisation, the fall in the number of trade union officials in
relation to members, and the lack of provisions in union rule
books for the shop stewards' role and duties all facilitate
workplace bargaining (Goodman and Whittingham: 1969; 9-13, 38
and 184). Furthermore, the appearance of wage forms such as
payment by results schemes and piecework rates are directly
conducive to shop steward bargaining over the ever-changing
quotas and time measurements that are generic to such forms
(Goodman and Whittingham: 1969; 147. McCarthy: 1966; Sections
F and G. McCarthy and Parker: 1968; chapter 4). The diversified
industrial and technical structure of monopoly capital is also
germane here in that the very increase in size of manufacturing
establishments has led to an increase in steward representation;
and the need for co-ordination between plants, as well as between unions, leads to the establishment of shop steward

combines and committees, especially since the interdependence of the social and technological organisation of industries is such that work groups are affected by changes in managerial practice, collective bargaining or industrial action elsewhere and thus require work group co-ordination to control and influence such changes and their consequences (Brown et al.: 1978. Brown and Terry: 1978).

Shop steward led workplace bargaining has by means of industrial conflict in its various guises - unconstitutional and unofficial strikes, overtime bans, work to rule, go-slows, withdrawal of co-operation, insistence on formal rights and customs, and, where possible, the subtle diminution of output targets - extended the field on which industrial class conflict has been fought (Benyon: 1975). But it has to be remembered that the shop steward is more of a representative than a dema-gogue vis a vis his work group constituency and plays as great a part in controlling as in articulating conflict (Hyman: 1972; 45-7 and 56-8). It is therefore the work group which is the real social reference point. And it is this, coupled with its characteristic shop steward leadership structure, which has since the 1950s endeavoured to extend the struggle within work relations to 'subjects such as the reinstatement of workers; promotion or re-employment after redundancy; attempts by manage-ment to change conditions of employment, i.e. alterations in the systems of working, and attempts by management to impose discipline ... previously been considered by managements as being within the scope of their managerial prerogative' (Coker: 1969; 136). There is little doubt that many managements have been constrained to accept and negotiate with shop stewards in workplace bargaining and some have even fostered or welcomed it for a number of reasons, usually ones of convenience, speci-alised knowledge of the particular industry, its technical pro-cesses and local workforce, and the potential afforded for expeditious and informal settlement of disputes (Clegg et al.: 1961. Boraston et al.: 1975; 187). It is therefore suggested certain managements may have a need for shop steward organisa-tion in terms of securing industrial efficiency and industrial order (Turner et al.: 1977; 34 and 33).

But equally crucial has been the threatened and realised erosion of managerial prerogatives and employer control over the labour process; and this in itself should warn us of poten-tial differences in the administration of their work relations by distinct capitals. It accordingly needs to be maintained that effective workplace based shop steward organisation has managed to encroach upon practices previously regarded as inte-gral to the managerial function of capital. Managements and employers engaged in the administration, deployment and organi-sation of capital have quite clearly been confronted with direct challenges to the control and authority they exercise over work processes by the development of shop steward organisation, work-place bargaining, and industrial conflict. The rise of shop

84

floor power in structurally connecting production and distribution conflicts has thus constituted a major barrier to the continuity of capital accumulation. And it is to an analysis of the role of capital in industrial relations and its responses to the changing structure of class forces that we shall therefore turn in the next chapter.

Although it has been implicit in much of what has been said in this chapter, I have not directly addressed the nature and consequences of the political crisis of industrial relations. In essence this refers to the construction of an appropriate mode of state control for industrial relations, the lack of which interacts with and exacerbates the economic and industrial relations crises. This has been present throughout the processes analysed above in so far as the absence of effective political control of industrial relations has been one condition for the articulation and accentuation of industrial conflict. Little has so far been made of this factor because the rest of the study is in a way concerned with this very political crisis of industrial relations. The complex of factors and the consequent crisis discussed above, have thereby formed a condition for state intervention to organise the control of industrial relations. Moreover, the fractionalisation of capital, the wage competition between capitals for labour and the acceptance by particular capitals of shop floor bargaining has meant that capital in Britain has not itself been capable of organising, nor would particular capitals necessarily agree to, political policies to deal with the problems which have been hindering the process of capital accumulation as a whole. But while the potential for state intervention as such has been generated, it has not been pre-determined but has rather been the outcome of class and political interests and conflicts.

NOTES

1. 'The rate of growth of output achieved between 1963 and 1973 was exceptionally high compared with previous British experience, and probably higher than in any period this century' (Wragg and Robertson: 1978; 513).
2. Influential in this has been the fact that overtime working and overtime rates have formed an increasing part of the 'working' day and real earnings. See Whybrew: 1968. DOE: May 1978; 520-22.
3. The gradual and almost steady rise in earning rates is clearly demonstrated by the DOE survey cited. The rise in real incomes depends of course on price levels as well as taxation; this means that the rise in price levels, which is considered more fully below, has generally attenuated and frustrated the maintenance of increases in real income and this has served to exacerbate industrial militancy and wage conflict (Jackson et al.: 1975. DOE: May 1978; 523).

4. For a consideration of the extent to which the distinction between official and unofficial industrial action can realistically be maintained see Crouch: 1978; 225-8. Hyman: 1972; chapters 1 and 2. Turner et al.: 1967; 56-7 and 117.

Chapter 5

FRACTIONS OF CAPITAL AND THE ROLE OF THE STATE IN INDUSTRIAL
RELATIONS

1. Industrial Monopoly Capital and the Corporatist Control of Industrial Relations

Despite the power and control exercised by capital the sociological study of its role in the structuring of work relations
and its impact upon the policies of the state towards such
relations has been neglected. It is one aim of this study to
attempt to redress this balance a little by discussing the
national role of capital in industrial relations. So far we
have considered the social conditions which provided the pressure and potential for certain developments in industrial relations in Britain, and for changes in the state's role in these
relations. It now becòmes necessary to see how these worked
themselves out historically in definite social forms. This
entails analysing the patterns that the programmes, objectives
and influence of the major groups involved in these events
took so that the preceding arguments can be adequately comple-
mented.

    We begin this task therefore with an examination of the
role of capital in industrial relations, by considering the
consciousness, aims and actions of employers in the British
social formation. In this section I shall, firstly, try to
outline the decisive structural features of the nature of the
capital which the CBI represents. I shall then present the
CBI's stated rationale for, and objectives towards, plans for
the reform of industrial relations structure, attempting at
the same time to bring to light, clarify and systematise the
assumptions and interests in state control of industrial relations that articulate and animate the espoused and explicit
programmes for change.

Big Business, British Capitalism and the CBI

It is, of course, the case that the monopolisation of capital,
in terms of the concentration of power and the conditioning of
labour's capacity to engage in conflict, as well as the rise
of the state, has had a considerable impact upon the CBI; and
it is indeed a by now familiar claim to trace the formation of

the CBI to the need for a single organisation to represent business which arose from the state's formalisation of tripartite economic planning in the National Economic Development Council. What is of more immediate interest here is the nature of the capital implicated in such processes which have come to be represented by the CBI. What I wish to argue and establish is that the CBI from its inception has in the main served as a forum, both industrially and politically, for the representation of large-scale, mainly monopoly capital, usually operating from a domestic base in the industrial or manufacturing sector of the UK economy.

This more precise identification of distinct sets of capital and interests can clarify the nuances in the conflicts of interest over the re-structuring of industrial relations by connecting types of group support and class objectives with both the actual expression of interests and struggle and with whatever ensues in the form of accomplished policy outputs. This kind of analysis allows us to understand the _class_ and _intra-class_ links between distinct structural locations and sets of class interests, their ideological expressions in conflict and their outcomes in the degree to which they are imbricated in the products of state policy. State policy is a formative and constructed process and class interests and political conflicts provide the key to its explanation.

As will be seen when we come to consider them, multinationals, particularly those with foreign bases, for a large part of the period under consideration, pursued the organisation and manipulation of their internal industrial relations practices outside the ambit of existing employer organisations. This reliance on capital autonomy formed an important ingredient in the highly liberalistic orientations that marked the practices of such companies during the 1960s and the period of the Industrial Relations Act. Moreover, as a Commission of Inquiry into business representation noted, the large company 'stands in greater need than the small of the services which only a national body can give ... direct contact between the CBI and the big company is likely to be beneficial to both, enabling the company to play a part in the formation of national policy commensurate with its resources' (Devlin Report: 1972; 10-11). It has likewise been found to be the opinion of a majority of officials of National Employers' Associations that large firms wielded more influence in employers' organisations than other firms (Munns and McCarthy: 1967; 97). Perhaps the most illuminating conflict surrounding the development of the CBI has been the continuous dissatisfaction of small firms with the general tenor of CBI policies and practices. And this is so despite the fact that the CBI has managed to maintain in membership a high proportion of small firms (Devlin Report: 1972; 10). As the Devlin Report indicates, the CBI has tended to be less responsive to the needs and interests of petit-bourgeois businesses which by reason of structural

88

differences tend to be local rather than national or international in character and possess a distinct order of priorities in terms of economic change and political action.

It is equally possible to find direct and dramatic indices
of the tensions within the CBI between large and small capital:
the most notable and extreme is defection, as was the case with
the SIM which was formed in 1965 substantially out of the
membership of the NABM which was united (formally at least)
with the BEC and the FBI to form the CBI in the same year
(Blank: 1973. SIM, ME, 32, 1966, WE, 129, p. 1372). The SIM
represented only manufacturing companies and its average member
employed between 80 and 200 employees (SIM, RC, WE, 129, p.1372
RC, ME, 32, pp. 1375-6). Although it stated that it was not
opposed to the CBI the society was formed because the need was
felt for a separate association 'for those of a smaller size
to represent their views where they might be at variance with
the bigger boys' (Ibid.).

More direct evidence on the capital interests predominantly
represented by the CBI can be derived from the available data
on trends in its membership rates. Between 1965 and 1969 commercial companies, that is banks, insurance companies, as well
as retailers and also nationalised industries had only been
accorded associate membership. From 1969 onwards, however,
they have enjoyed full CBI membership and this is reflected in
the rise of commercial membership (CBI, Annual Report, 1969,
pp. 79-80). Now as a consequence 'all the clearing banks as
well as twenty merchant banks and ten major insurance companies are members' (Grant and Marsh: 1977; 33, cf. 68-71. CBI,
Annual Report, 1977, pp. 15-16). However, CBI attempts to
secure the integrated representation of manufacturing and
financial interests have tended to flounder; 'although the
CBI has made some headway in the City, its initiatives have
been largely unsuccessful', for 'many City Bodies ... are
anxious not to sacrifice the channels of access to the government which they developed for themselves over the decades',
namely the Bank of England and the Treasury (Grant and Marsh:
1977; 34, 40 and 68-71. Longstreth: 1979). Furthermore, the
majority of the large companies in membership of the CBI tend
to be engaged almost exclusively in industrial manufacturing,
despite the rise in commercial members. The majority of large
companies which are not members of the CBI are, generally
speaking, commercial or financial rather than industrial in
character. Hence, Grant and Marsh argue that the efforts of
the CBI to increase membership amongst companies listed in
The Times top 1,000 companies are thereby severely limited
(Grant and Marsh: 1977; 34, 39-41). Thus, 'in the case of the
CBI it is particularly significant that the great majority of
large manufacturing companies are in membership' (Ibid.; 34).
Although there are a number of significant and outstanding
exceptions, the CBI includes 75 per cent of the companies in
The Times list of the 200 leading companies and approximately

50 per cent from the list of the top 2,000 companies (Ibid.).

The validity that can be accorded this contention is further enhanced by the information on the CBI's sources of finance: '50 percent of the whole income of the CBI comes from member companies listed in the top 500 in The Times list of a thousand leading companies. Once again this illustrates the dominant importance of manufacturing industry within the CBI and the strong position of large companies' (Ibid.; 37). In effect, this percentage of income comes from 13 per cent of the CBI's company membership (Ibid.; 34). This is compounded by the fact that it is usually large companies which can spare executive and managerial manpower to undertake what are often full-time duties for the CBI (Ibid.; 85-7). Also the committed presence of large firms within the CBI is thought by such companies to accentuate the influence of the CBI with government and to help in enabling it to counteract the power of the unions and the TUC (Ibid.; 49-50).

The CBI, the State and the Reform of Industrial Relations: the inception of corporatism

Having identified this particular section or 'fraction' of capital we can now consider its characteristic strategies towards the re-structuring of industrial relations, the motivation for the adoption of such strategies, their impact upon the state and changes in their form and substance over time. We can thus analyse the CBI's objectives towards the reform of work relations, in order to discern its dominant orientation and the changing emphases that have emerged within this orientation. The main argument that I wish to advance in this section is that the CBI and industrial monopoly capital in Britain, has, despite an avowed ideological commitment to voluntarism, moved to an identifiable corporatist position on the organisational shape to be assumed by industrial relations. The central dilemmas or contradictions in this position, which has had considerable influence upon the state and political agencies, concern the extent to which the state, as opposed to 'private' capital, has to take the responsibility for the establishment and maintenance of corporatist structures in industry. Associated with this has been the tension over whether corporatism should be institutionalised in a formal and legal manner, as evinced, for example, by the I.R. Act of 1971, or an informal and 'administrative' manner, as evinced for example by CBI and Conservative Party proposals for a national forum on economic policy, involving capital, labour and government. This latter point highlights another central and attendant dilemma which concerns the level at which corporatist regulation of trade unions is most effectively and practically implemented, that is, whether it is realised at the level of state, or at the level of the industrial enterprise.

In terms of the social-structural factors conditioning the CBI's motivation towards the reform of industrial relations

significant amongst them has been the concern over declining
profitability. There is little doubt that the problem and its
growing intensity have been recognised by the CBI: 'before tax,
both profit shares and rates of return have been in decline
since the early 1950's' (CBI Economic Directorate, 1974, p.3).
The reasons for the decline in the profitability of British
industry are seen to arise from price controls combined with
rapid increases in wages and other production costs. The inevitable consequence has been to reduce the rate of investment in
manufacturing industry in Britain for it is primarily profits
which either provide finance or attract capital from external
sources (CBI, Economic Directorate, 1974, p. 6). Given also
the fact that high inflation erodes profit levels (CBI, Annual
Report, 1974, p. 5) it is clear that it is in these senses
that wage inflation is conceived to be a major factor in inducing a decline in capital accumulation.

The stress placed on wage inflation indicates that for
the CBI a crucial cause was to be found directly in the actions
of organised labour and thus in the structure of the industrial
relations system. This is indicative of the recognition of the
working class challenge posed to accumulation in the form of
increasing industrial conflict and of the need to mobilise in
order to meet this threat. In turn, this threat at the same
time constituted a political crisis for capital in emphasising
the lack of an effective institutionalisation of conflict in
industry. The CBI judged the British industrial relations system to be lacking in not producing the following effects:
'(1) in preserving industrial peace and good relations between
management and workers; (2) in producing earnings levels which
are not inflationary in effect; (3) in promoting the efficient
use of labour' (CBI, Written Evidence to Donovan 1968; p.260).

The CBI pointed to the generally damaging consequences of
strikes for the control of production, especially given the
prevailing interdependent and integrated organisation of modern
industry (Ibid., p. 261). This was compounded by the fact that
the character of industrial conflict had come to be marked
increasingly by the unpredictable and unofficial strike. The
increase in such a form of industrial conflict, when associated
with the availability of alternative methods of conducting conflict like, over-time bans, working-to-rule, go-slows, etc.,
has been viewed by the CBI as extremely damaging and disruptive,
particularly in breaking collective agreements and union rules
and in undermining production and efficiency (Ibid., pp.262-3).

This development is traced in the first instance to full
employment in strengthening the bargaining power of workers.
However, given that this is also true of other societies,
greater emphasis is placed upon shop floor power per se: the
rise in local, shop steward organised bargaining and 'the
failure to integrate shop stewards into union organisation
and the inability of many unions to exercise control over
union officials, stewards and members' (Ibid., p.262). This

decentralised patterning of union bargaining has been regarded as the fundamental source of the disruption posed to accumulation not only by conflict as such but by inflationary wage earnings, low productivity, and the general lack of efficiency and profitability.

It follows for the CBI that such an organisation of collective bargaining has been conducive to the inflationary gap between the growth in earnings and the growth in national productivity. This means that the former grows more rapidly than the latter and contributes to inflation because money earnings rise much faster than productivity and this leads to declining international competitiveness because of the inflated prices of export commodities (Ibid.; pp.263-4). This entails not only the power of unions to obtain higher wages through strike threats and strike action which inflates workers' earnings but also 'the temptation to employers to grant wage increases when they can pass these on to consumers through higher prices' (Ibid.; p.263). The point in many ways therefore is for the CBI to endeavour to mobilise employer solidarity to prevent such occurrences, though this comes up against the constraint of competition between capitals which provides a social space through which the state can intervene.

The need for some such remedy similarly derived from what the CBI saw as the failure of the industrial relations system to ensure the efficient use of labour. In particular, this entailed the problem of restrictive labour practices (Ibid.; pp.265-6). This refers to the extent to which workplace union organisation and bargaining involves practices like the maintenance of manning levels on machinery ('over-manning'), demarcation rules, go-slows, informal 'ceilings' on earnings, opposition to technical innovations leading to redundancies, and opposition to work study and to merit as the criteria for promotion, restrictions on recruitment, over-time or shift work, and the reduction of normal working and increases in over-time working to boost earnings (Ibid.; pp.266-8). These practices have therefore become obstacles in the way of the technological changes and rationalisations required by capital for the furtherance of the production and accumulation processes (see Ibid.; p.266).

At the root of all this for the CBI has been the development and extension of shop floor bargaining. The fact that such bargaining, because it builds upon the rates set in industry-wide agreements and can be buttressed by workplace job controls, leads to wage drift (Ibid.; pp.273-4) underlined for the CBI its centrality in the structuring of industrial conflict (Ibid.; p.274). Plant bargaining, as the CBI saw it, meant that unofficial strikes could have their main 'effect on earnings and work practices; they create inflationary wage drift and perpetuate restrictive practices and inefficient manning scales. How, therefore, can we prevent this?... we cannot continue with exactly the same sort of system we have got today' (CBI, ME,

9, 1965, 1574). The effect of the economic crisis of declining
profitability coupled with the escalation of industrial conflict
and the changing nature of working class power in production
was producing a crisis for capital in the institutions of the
existing, industrial relations system. It was therefore necessary for changes to be made to this system to provide the basis
for the re-assertion of employer control and the retrenchment
if not re-invigoration of more effective and more profitable
capitalist relations in industry.

We thus now need to consider the reforms the CBI thought
from its vantage point in the mid-1960s were required in order
to make the industrial relations system more consistent and
more symmetrical with the requirements of the capital accumulation process. These can be considered in terms of their implications regarding respectively the role of trade unions, employers and the state.[1]

(a) Trade Unions. The most notable general feature of the CBI's
objectives apropos trade unions has been the implied effort to
move their organisational principle from autonomy to heteronomy,
and more specifically, to evolve an externally guaranteed and
supervised heteronomy. But it has to be remarked that a great
deal of ambiguity can be noted in the CBI's ideas regarding the
role to be played by the state. This has been compounded by the
fact that the CBI's aims with respect to trade unions have been
directly connected with the prevention of breaches of procedure
agreements by strikes and other types of industrial action, the
attainment of greater complementarity between national and
industry bargaining on the one hand and local and plant bargaining on the other, the possibilities for industrial unionism,
the integration of rank and file and shop stewards into official
union structures with the aim of increasing the control and
authority of the leadership over union members, and the scrutiny
and surveillance of union rules in order to more effectively
constitute them as agencies of social control (CBI, WE, 1968,
passim). In a sense, the CBI's most insistent, albeit submerged,
aim has been strong, centralised authoritative trade unionism
for this has not been seen as the real source of industrial
conflict.

The problem posed by the specific nature of trade union
structure for employer control rested on the fact that 'there
is insufficient control by union leaders over their local officials and their representatives on the shop floor, i.e. the
shop stewards' (Ibid.; p.286), which 'can lead to e.g. non-
observance of collective agreements; unofficial strikes [often
a direct result of the usurpation of power by shop stewards];
challenges to management authority; and general embitterment
of plant relations' (Ibid.; p.287). This led to CBI support for
the idea of industrial unionism. This it was thought would allow
for the more effective resolution of demarcation disputes and
hence inter-union rivalries; the reconciliation of industry and

plant bargaining; and 'Industrial unions would make easier the integration of shop stewards into union organisation and the improvement of communications between union officials and wor-, kers on the shop floor' (Ibid.; p.288), particularly as it seemed suited to conditions of complex socialised production and the power this gave to local work groups (CBI, ME, 6,p.220).

(b) The role of employers and management. The CBI saw its own formation as a crucial ingredient in the more effective class formation of capital. It provided greater co-ordination, cover-age and centralisation of employer activities and interests than prior organisations and worked to ensure that employers took account of the national interest (CBI, WE, 1968, pp.282-3). This objective is especially important for state policy as well as centralised employer policy in view of the types of competi-tion which inevitably arise between employers and which promote the pursuit of the short-term gains of particular capitals as opposed to the general and long-term interests of the class as a whole.

     With a view to fostering what it conceived of as this general interest the CBI urged employers at industry level to pay more attention to linking local and national bargaining. This concerned controlling increases in earnings and ensuring the more efficient use of labour power with organisational changes at industry level being canvassed as one way to effect this, including the amalgamation and rationalisation of emp-loyers' organisations in relation to the changing structure of industry, i.e. moves towards centralisation, sound finance, improved CBI support and increased membership (Ibid.; pp.284-5). The CBI's injunctions serve to re-emphasise the nature of the divisions within capital in general and even within particular fractions of it in the face of the need for an organised and practicable response to the effects of shop floor power upon accumulation and upon the role of the state. This does not mean, of course, that attempts were made to deny this; it was argued for example that the competitive bidding up of wages to attract labour between employers would be curtailed and pre-vented by employers themselves (CBI, ME, 6, 1965, p.239). Relatedly the CBI has been noticeably reticent about buttress-ing its authority and control over its members by sanctions or by other means. This may go a long way towards explaining its commitment to the ideology of voluntarism, but it may also represent a recognition of the realities of the competitive nature of capitalism (CBI, ME, 6, 1965, pp.225-66). But this voluntarism was still seen as being conducive to the CBI's efforts to secure the long-term interests of employers as against the precarious benefits that could be derived in the short term from employer autonomy (Ibid.; 226), even though it conceded: 'in the present time of extreme shortages of labour employers do take part in bidding against one another for existing labour' (Ibid.; p.227). But this has not been seen

94

as a reason for strengthening the control exercised by employer organisations. The imperatives of economic accumulation and market competition have been deemed to demand priority over the imperatives of organisational co-ordination which therefore implies a problematic relationship for capital between economic constraints and political organisation.

(c) The state and the law. The relationship of the state to the control of industrial conflict, as with its relationship to private capital accumulation as a whole, assumes for capital a deeply contradictory nature. On the one hand capital accumulation persists on the basis of economic production and commodity exchange and its separation from the state; on the other hand capital accumulation and thus the containment of class conflict come to rest upon the support of the state. This is expressed in an ideological aversion on the part of capital to an interventionist role for the state which is associated with a factual acceptance of such intervention. This obviously varies as we shall see between different capitals and sectors, and the very fact of increasing state interventionism can by no means be represented as an inevitable process although political attempts to transform and reverse it will have their own contradictory effects. But the articulation of the dilemma over the role to be played by the state in industrial relations can be clearly seen in the aims and objectives of employers and capital.

What, then, did this consist of? In its evidence to the Donovan Commission the CBI stated that while employers usually had little recourse to the law even when they could traditionally use it - for example, to sue an individual worker for breach of contract of employment for going on strike - it was still willing to 'consider' changes in the law (CBI, WE, 1968, pp.290-1). This included the legal enforcement of procedure agreements (Ibid.; p.291) but also and most importantly the legal immunities enjoyed by trade unions in tort since with this, unlike the legal enforceability of agreements, the responsibility for enforcement was to be given to the state and was not to rest on the shoulders of individual employers. Legal action taken by individual employers has rarely been countenanced because the main interest of the employer is in the resumption of production and the maintenance of good relations with the work force, neither of which are achieved by employers themselves taking strikers to court (Ibid.; p.289). In general terms the CBI argued that the immunities given to the trade unions by the 1906 Trade Disputes Act were no longer relevant since the unions were no longer the weaker parties in industrial relations. It therefore wanted the immunity of trade unions in tort restricted to: (1) acts in furtherance of trade disputes between members of a union and their employers, thereby excluding sympathetic strikes, secondary boycotts and picketing and inter-union disputes from immunity; (2) strikes and other forms of industrial action taken in accordance with agreed procedure or where notice to terminate employment had been given, thereby excluding strikes and industrial action in breach of such constraints; and (3) registered trade unions 'and conditions of registration would be introduced which would help unions in the proper performance of their functions, strengthen their position against unofficial elements and provide protection for individual members' (Ibid.; pp.292-3).

The CBI's proposals on trade union registration are important not only because they identify the functions carved out by this fraction of capital for trade unions to perform in the future arrangement of industrial relations but also because they identify its recognition of the need for outside intervention in industrial relations in the shape of the state sanctioning trade union structure. The registration of a union was to be <u>voluntary</u> but acceptance of a union for registration was to be dependent upon the Registrar's scrutiny and approval of the Union's rules. These had to provide for: the control of the union by its members and the use of proper disciplinary actions; the appointment of union officials and shop stewards; the payment of benefits (i.e. benefits had to be paid for actions taken in accordance with union rules); the imposition of penalties (e.g. 'certain penalties might be provided for action in connection with unofficial strikes'); no penalty provisions for inadequately defined offences 'or for failure to apply a restrictive practice'; and the publicising of rules and accounts (Ibid.; p.293. ME, 9, 1965, pp.283-5).

The powers of the Registrar, which covered the right to withdraw registration, were thought to be effective if they included the power to: inquire into cases where the rules may not have been followed; 'to instruct the union to take action, e.g. to encourage observance of agreements, discontinuance of unofficial strikes, withdrawal of overtime bans'; and to impose penalties on unions (Ibid.). It has to be noted that this intention was associated with the vesting of the authority and responsibility for controlling and strengthening the structure and actions of trade unions vis a vis their members not with individual employers but with the Registrar of trade unions, an external 'public' body. However, the paradox of voluntarism and its contradictory connection with state interventionism is graphically captured in the following passage: 'if you could have a legal system of enforcing collective bargaining which would still leave the voluntary system, and the main virtues of the voluntary system, intact, then we would support it' (ME, 6, 1965, p.245). Thus while such ideological and normative preoccupations were retained, the CBI's political practice and objectives were moving in the direction of corporatist state intervention and a definite conception of the role of trade unions: 'We are trying to alter the surrounding circumstances by isolating the unofficial strikers from the help of the unions - by encouraging the unions to take certain action against them' (ME, 9, 1965, p.286). As a central part of this attempt to alter the 'surrounding circumstances' of industrial conflict, embodying as it did both the heteronomy of trade unions and state interventionism, has been the tactic of the legal use of sanctions against strikers.

The use of legal sanctions against strikers
A year later when the CBI returned to the Commission to give further oral evidence its attitude had hardened even further in favour of legal sanctions, most notably because the then Labour government was intending to include such sanctions against strikes in its Prices and Incomes legislation (ME, 22, 1966, pp.806-807). But the CBI still prevaricated about the use of sanctions,[2] still rejected the possibility of legislation, and still placed greatest reliance upon the Registrar's powers over the breach of union rules by unofficial and unconstitutional strikes (Ibid.; pp.808-10).

The institutional responsibility for the activation of this machinery was still left very unclear by the CBI at this stage. But the importance of the role of the Registrar was confirmed as a means to activate the legal machinery to control shop-floor power so as to minimise the involvement of employers and because it would provide, unlike the ad hoc, specific and isolated interventions of the law courts, a systematic, generalised and comprehensive mode of regulating industrial conflict (Ibid.; pp. 811-13). The consequence of this for the role of trade unions, notwithstanding the maintenance of the CBI's commitment to voluntarism (Ibid.; p.818) remains clear: 'the whole of our purpose is to strengthen the hands of the trade union against certain of its members ... the penalty ... is a penalty imposed by the union itself on its members according to its rules. It is the Registrar's business to see the union observes its rules' (Ibid.).[3] Only if such a strategy were to fail because the unions could not be encouraged to perform such a function would the CBI 'then have to look again at more radical proposals for a much greater intervention of the law' (Ibid.; p.814). We can thus see that by 1966 the CBI had already begun to adopt a directly corporatist plan of action, combining the heteronomy of trade unions and the intervention of the state, as its articulated response to the constraints that it saw class conflict imposing upon capital accumulation.

Conclusions
I have spelt out at some length the social consciousness, class interests and objectives with respect to the reform of industrial relations represented by the CBI on behalf of large-scale, monopoly capital, generally operating from bases in Britain,[4] in the mid-1960s, in response to the accentuation of class conflict in industry and the problems posed for capital accumulation. In particular I emphasised the emergent corporatist strategy advanced by the CBI as a response to the industrial

relations crisis. I have done this for a number of reasons.
Not only does the economic power represented by the CBI have
an influential impact upon the conditions and content of state
policy, but it also forms part of a more general constellation
of capitalist class interests in the retrenchment of bourgeois
domination, and it thus provides a particularly good example
of what is entailed in bourgeois class mobilisation, as this
is organised by a particular fraction of capital and by one of
its specific political organisations. But it is also important
to recognise some of the crucial divisions and differences
that can and do arise within the capitalist class, both structurally and as regards strategies of class domination in industry which are central to an analysis of the state's role.

2. Petit-Bourgeois Capital, Paternalism and the Control of Industrial Relations

The concerns and objectives of monopoly capital differ very
much from petit-bourgeois capital,[5] while still sharing the
same universe of employer rights and prerogatives over labour,
the black and red arithmetic of the profit and loss accounts
and the legal and effective ownership of property. The quantitative empirical measure generally used, including this study,
to distinguish small business is the criterion of the employment by a company of 200 or less employees. This is not merely
an arbitrary and purely quantitative measure since it tends to
be associated with other central structural features associated
with small business, namely, single plant, small scale manufacturing, restricted and precarious market shares, independence from external, financial control via ownership, however
nebulous and camouflaged, and the economic control of an owner-
manager, not excluding of course the possibility of self-
employment (cf. Bolton Committee: 1971; pp.XV-XVI and Chapter
1). As Bechhofer and Elliott have pointed out, it is of the
essence of petit-bourgeois capital that it employs a
low level of capital, and material and social technology, such
that 'the social organisation of work is simple, the span of
authority small, the petit-bourgeois concern cannot be given
a bureaucratic structure' (1976; 76-7). These features combined
with a paternalistic ideology towards industrial relations are
what it is my intention to convey by the concept of petit-
bourgeois capital.

There exists a quite popular conception of the quality of
industrial relations in small-scale establishments which regards them as essentially harmonious, co-operative, consensual,
free from strife and conflict, embodying undistorted communication and the agreed-to betterment of the fortunes of the enterprise to the total exclusion of the irreconcilable and unwarranted claims of the class war and the amphitheatre of politics.
The survey of the industrial relations of small firms conducted

by the Bolton Committee tended to endorse this view (1971; pp. 19-22). It found that only 8 per cent of small firms were completely unionised and these tended to be the larger firms in each industry, some two-thirds of small firms employing no trade union members whatsoever. The firms which responded to the survey registered the general absence of industrial conflict in the sector: under 8 per cent had experienced any strikes between 1967 and 1969[6] and only 1½ per cent of these experienced strikes in their own establishment, the other 6 per cent being accounted for by strikes in other firms (Ibid.; p.19). It can also be noted here that about 40 per cent of the small firms studied were members of an employers' organisation, this again increasing with size and with the increasing level of unionisation faced by a small-scale employer (Ibid.). Freedom from unions was seen as one main advantage of owning a small business (Golby and Johns: 1971; 44).

However, Curran and Stanworth have argued that the Bolton Committee's research 'relied on owner-managers' views of their relations with employees, and on the data for strike rates ... the Arbitration, Conciliation and Advisory Service spends a disproportionate amount of its time in small firms ... around 50 per cent of registered unfair dismissal claims involve firms which employ less than 100 people' (1978; 627. Cf. Idem: 1979). They found that small firms had 'markedly high levels of labour turnover', which more than questioned 'the stereo-type of close, warm relations, free from conflict' and 'the idea that workers in small firms identify more strongly with their employers' (Ibid.; p.628). A majority of workers in small firms felt out of touch with management and there was a genuine lack of adequate communication. This research was conducted on the basis of a comparison between small and large firms, and little difference was found between workers in each type with respect to the question of whether they saw industry resting on 'teamwork' as opposed to 'conflict' (Ibid.; 629). The authors also argue that unionism is very weak in small firms not so much because of the prior orientations of the workers but rather because of the inordinate amount of effort required by a union to gain membership, the virulent and sustained anti-unionism of small-scale employers, and the 'hegemonic' inculcation of this into the ideology of their employees (Ibid.; 628).

Clearly the sociological realism provided by this evidence must determine the extent to which the paternalistic ideology of petit-bourgeois industrial relations can be held to represent their factual nature, particularly as this has been expressed in the interests of petit-bourgeois capitalists themselves. The Bolton Committee's research evidently tapped the mainsprings of this ideology as well as some survey data. But it would be as well not to be too dismissive of the hold or the effects of this ideology. It is central to the structuring of the political objectives of petit-bourgeois capital, forming a link between its material conditions and its demands upon the role of the state. And in so far as it comes to be shared by the labour employed by this capital then there will exist determinants ensuring that, to some degree, it becomes a reality, limited while being conditioned by the effects of the material class inequalities in industry (cf. Batstone: 1975; 129). It is towards containing these effects of class conflict that the paternalistic ideology of petit-bourgeois capital (like all ideologies of capital) is directed and with which it comes into conflict.

In so far as the reality of petit-bourgeois work relations has tended to coincide with its ideological pretensions, then this paternalism must have become subjected to severe strains in the 1960s as a result of the direct, and more importantly, indirect impact, of the increasing scale of class conflict. A survey of the attitudes and motivation of small businessmen, conducted for the Bolton Committee, found that it was generally felt that 'labour was increasingly becoming irresponsible as well as inefficient' (Golby and Johns: 1971; 43, cf.pp.41-4). And it consequently follows on from this that if our depiction of the nature of industrial relations in small-scale enterprises may be judged to be reasonably accurate then petit-bourgeois capital will have continued to seek ways and means of retaining or regaining a structure of control consistent with the ideology of paternalism.

With the foregoing analysis in mind we now need to examine these latter points by way of a political sociology of petit-bourgeois capital's objectives towards industrial relations in order to determine the impact of economic and political crises on its operations and objectives, its structure of interests and consciousness of the dimensions of the crisis, and its own impact upon the course of events, especially upon the role played by the state. The retrenchment and consolidation of paternalism in the small business sector will involve, as we have seen, encouraging a corporate team identity amongst its workforce and the familial acceptance of inequality in tasks and rewards within a closely knit and integrated system that implies the exclusion or the heteronomy of trade unions. In many ways, corporatism is paternalism writ large. But if this is so a very different role is envisaged for the state. As we shall now attempt to illustrate in detail, it is more usual for petit-bourgeois capital in British society to favour the laissez-faire as opposed to the interventionist form of the state's mediation of work and class relations (Bechhofer and Elliott: 1976; 81-9 and 92-6. Idem: 1978; 63-6, 73-8 and 82).

The State, Industrial Relations and Petit-Bourgeois Capital
The two major bodies representing small business which gave evidence to the Donovan Commission, the NABM and the SIM, were very much involved with and affected by the formation of the CBI in 1965. In fact, the SIM was formed as a response to the demise of the NABM within the newly formed CBI. There existed

a great deal of opposition within the NABM to its merger with the BEC and FBI in 1965 to form the CBI precisely because of the effects this would have in reducing petit-bourgeois representation and in linking the CBI more closely with the state (The Times: 3.3.65, p.18).

There is very little doubt that petit-bourgeois capital combines with its paternalistic view of work relations a very profound antagonism towards the state in general and government and bureaucracy in particular. The Bolton Committee, for example, found that 'small firms and their representative organisations complained of generalised hostility or indifference on the part of Government, calling in evidence what they see as the total effect of Government policies in many fields' (1971; pp.92-3). As far as the overall role of the state is concerned, the general tenor of petit-bourgeois ideology, aspirations and politics tends, usually, to gravitate towards the laissez-faire rather than the interventionist form of state mediation (cf. Ibid.; Chapter 9).

This, in more precise terms, entails principled opposition to such things as tri-partite economic planning, political collaboration between government departments and large companies, the excessive paper work demanded by government intervention and the bureaucratic proliferation of rules, state encouragement of mergers and rationalisation, government imposed credit restrictions, high taxation, high interest rates, and the state's accentuation of the cyclical economic vicissitudes to which the small business sector is subject in any case without the aid of government policies of deflation and expansion (cf. Ibid.; and Golby and Johns: 1971; 23-32, 47 and 51-2). But what does this orientation entail for small businesses' political objectives and actions with respect to the role to be played by the state in industrial relations, when seen in the light of its accompanying practice of seeking to secure the paternalistic regulation of its own work relations? We can begin to attempt to answer this question by looking at the evidence provided by the policy programmes of petit-bourgeois capital.

The NABM, expressing concern at the power of unions and the growth of unofficial strikes (WE, 1, 1964, p.1) confined its policy aims to changes in the law regulating industrial relations. The legal immunity of unions for actions in tort was to be confined to registered trade unions and to acts undertaken in a trade dispute, involving the respective union and employer, and concerning terms and conditions of employment (Ibid.; p.1). This meant that unofficial strikes would receive no legal protection, strikers being open to legal proceedings because they would no longer be protected from breaches of contract since they would not be giving adequate notice to terminate their contracts of service – an inevitable feature of unofficial strikes. The unofficial strike was to constitute a breach of an employee's contract of service

101

thereby negating any rights under the Contract of Employment Act as did the other suggested reform of the Act requiring seven days' notice of the desire to suspend such a contract (Ibid.; p.1). This would also allow a seven day 'cooling off' period before an official strike could be called. Arbitration could then be used but this had to be at the discretion of the parties concerned though provision for a secret ballot of union members at this stage was to be laid down in order to determine whether they wanted to strike or continue to negotiate (Ibid.; p.2). However, the right to strike was to be prohibited in services and industries 'essential to life or to the national economy', compulsory arbitration being suggested as one suitable, alternative means of handling disputes (Ibid.; p.2). Trade unions were thus to draw up rules providing safeguards for members, 'establishing disciplinary procedures, with the necessary fines and penalties for their enforcement'. Union rules were to be registered with the Registrar of Friendly Societies who was to have the power to check, revise, rescind or approve the rules: 'This would restrict the exercise of arbitrary powers over individual union members and would at the same time enable the union to control its own members' (Ibid.; p.2).

There is much in this that is indicative of the common concern of employers at the changing nature of industrial conflict, notably the way in which unofficial strikes are seen as a major problem and the stress placed upon ensuring that unions accept their fair share of responsibility in a modern society for the success of industry (Ibid.; p.3). However, a reasonably clear implication of the NABM's suggested changes in the law concerns how its proposals rested upon making relatively minimal changes in existing laws and institutions - re-formulating the 1906 Act or the Contract of Employment Act, adding certain functions to the role of the Registrar of Friendly Societies - rather than pursuing the construction of new institutions and the systematic and detailed intrusion of the state such as have marked the CBI's policies. Greatest reliance is placed on existing legal forms and procedures. Trade unions are still to become responsible for their own internal order and thus for unofficial strikes but little of an elaborate external structure to ensure this is envisaged. This intention is coupled with the liberalism and individualism associated with opposition to union coercion of individual employees who do not wish to become union members, to the closed shop and any other attempt to legislate for its enforcement (Ibid.; p.2). In ideological terms, it is very much the rights of the individual under the rule of law rather than the obligation of corporations under administrative law which emerge as the guidelines governing the state's response to the industrial relations crisis.

The successor to the NABM, the SIM (ME, 32, pp.1372-5), laid much greater stress on the co-operative and more personal

102

work relations possible in small rather than larger companies.
It argued that it was much easier to achieve 'better' industrial relations in small companies because the owner or manager maintained direct contact with the employees. Small businesses tended on the whole not to engage in collective bargaining with unions, were party to few national agreements, relying on work place negotiations (if indeed they needed to do, or agreed to, even this) and felt constrained to <u>follow</u> the wage rates paid by larger companies as well as those set by supply and demand. It argued that small firms experienced relatively few industrial disputes, those that did occur most usually being over trade union recognition. But it did make the important point that small business was indirectly affected by the rise in industrial conflict since disputes in larger companies tended to rebound on firms in this sector by, for example, interrupting the supplies of raw materials from, or the delivery of finished orders to, the monopoly corporate sector (Ibid.; pp. 1375-6 and 1388-91).

One of the most graphic illustrations of the ideology and reality of paternalism was provided in the evidence of Sir Halford Reddish, then Chairman of Rugby Portland Cement.[7] This policy was embodied in the practices of the company. It entailed the use of works committees internal to company plants rather than trade unions as the channel for dealing with employees for this was considered to be capable of handling most issues and maintaining close and co-operative relations with staff.[8] The trade union is therefore seen as an outside influence which is capable of damaging this and thereby the overall teamwork and company identity established. It was claimed that the company had thus had little experience of disputes and those that did arise were settled immediately and on the spot by the works committee. However, it is clear that the works committee while aimed at ensuring the heteronomy of worker representation also helped to buttress the employers' control for not only did they not normally deal with cases of dismissal - the prerogative solely of the employer - but pay rates were set unilaterally by executive directors, though the committee could decide on the loss of bonus under the profit-sharing scheme. In this structure, industrial relations is viewed as a partnership in which, while the employer maintains the role of leadership, all members of the team are working towards the common aim of the profitability and well-being of the company, and trade unions as outsiders can only wreck this order of things (ME, 68, passim).

Coupled with this full-blooded paternalism has been the emphatic espousal of free market principles as far as the role of wage labour within the wider economy is concerned. As such, the worker is regarded as being free to accept or reject on the labour market the conditions of employment and rates of pay provided by any company. There is no external coercive force leading the worker to work for any particular capital according to the beliefs of this type of laissez-faire capitalism; while bound by the economic requirements, conditions, aims and leaderships of a specific company no such compulsions are thought to apply to the role of the worker within the economy and the labour market as a whole. In effect it is the individual worker who bargains over conditions and pay by deciding where to work and where not to work and management which ultimately decides what these conditions and rates of pay should be. From this point of view, the free sale of wage labour rather than the right to strike is the major defence of the workers' interests (Ibid.; pp.2937-44). For these reasons the collective organisations of trade unionism as much as the state and even monopoly corporations, are held to interfere with the optimum functioning of the liberal and competitive capitalist economy. The interests of petit-bourgeois capital entail individualism in the economy, paternalism in the enterprise.

It is thus to uphold the sanctity of the contract which this type of economic structure has handed down that the role of state is required: 'if you do not in all walks of life uphold the sanctity of contract, the whole fabric of civilization falls apart' (Ibid.; p.2940). This includes the need for trade unions to honour agreements and contracts and to ensure that their members do so (Ibid.; p.2942). The company itself did not tolerate the right to strike for strikes were seen as a breach of the sanctity of the contract. Since the sanctity of contract has been seen to be breaking down under the escalation of industrial conflict, the need is for the state to re-establish the conditions under which the labour contract becomes sacrosanct, while allowing for the paternalistic structuring of work relations. The law and the state and legislation are not capable of intervening and altering industrial relations in order to ensure that they are more orderly, co-operative and consensual in character, and fostering as a consequence the profitability of capital units (Ibid.; pp.2937-40). Nor is this possible by compromise rather than employers' principled stands in the face of unions' and workers' demands (Ibid.; pp.2935-6 and 2944-5). Paternalism thus comes to rely on employer initiative and the use of existing legal and state institutions to uphold the sanctity of the labour contract, to oppose the power of collective forces within society and the individual enterprise and to support the rights of the individual under the rule of law, as the mechanisms by which employer control of industrial relations can be guaranteed. And in following this practice its proponents base themselves upon the exclusion of the law and the state from the internal regulation of industrial relations save as and when demanded by the need to uphold the rule of law and the liberal principles of the freedom and sanctity of the contract and when called for by private individuals and groups rather than by agencies of the state.

Conclusions

The connection between opposition to the extensive and detailed intervention of the state and the paternalistic regulation of its work relations on the part of small business finds its factual basis not only in its political programmes and objectives outlined above - its response to the 'industrial relations crisis' which is also a political crisis - but also in its more micro-level class mobilisation of its social relations and ideological resources. Nichols (1969: Chapter 14) has found that non-owner managers in large firms have tended to support a business ideology that favoured 'long-term-company interest'. This means that profit is the underlying condition of the economic enterprise but in order to achieve this it is necessary to be able to actively nurture the co-operation of others on whom the enterprise is dependent, including and especially labour. On the other hand, owner-managers, who are archetypically small businessmen, have been shown to be more likely to hold to a laissez-faire ideology (cf. Stanworth and Curran: 1973; 115-20). This centres on the pursuit of profit not just to the exclusion of all else but with reliance on little else save the market: workers are merely accepted as individuals towards whom the responsibility of the employer is accepted as an employer of wage-labour but both of whom must accept the realities of the market (Nichols: op.cit. Stanworth and Curran: op.cit.; p.116).

It would be hazardous to deny that certain consequences did not follow from these sets of relations and their ideological forms for prescriptions upon the role to be adopted by the state. If the long-term-company-interest is generated by the managerial milieux of the large bureaucratic corporation this imposes some pressure to recognise unions and the part that the state has come to assume in the regulation and administration of the economy and industry. While this is by no means a pre-determined process it does tend to encourage support if not struggle for the extension of the state's role in industrial relations by more direct, systematic and administratively organised and sustained means. Conversely, and again albeit tendentially, the unmitigated laissez-faire ideology given rise to by the competitive capitalism of the small firm economy imposes recognition of the market and opposition to monopolies, organised unions, and the state, while the small-scale and non-bureaucratic authority of work-relations tends to impose recognition of the individual worker. The effect of all this for the petit-bourgeoisie is to encourage opposition to the collectivism of workers and to any role for the state (outside the preferential treatment that may be but is not usually that possible for small business by way of pressure-group politics) other than one of guaranteeing the minimal legal and coercive conditions for the functioning of the economy and of the individual company.

3. Foreign Multi-National Capital and the Liberal Autonomy of Corporate Bargaining

In many ways the requirement to plan and account for the control of labour, rationally and systematically, on the basis of a corporate strategy geared to the structure of the capital unit concerned, rather than placing too great a reliance upon the state, has been noticeably characteristic of multi-national companies. Exceptions can be and will be cited but this approach has usually gone along with the toleration if not recognition of the de facto collectivism and organisation of labour. I shall argue that this overall strategy of 'corporate bargaining' with some notable exceptions, during and in response to the overall breakdown in industrial relations institutions in the 1960s, has been much more normally followed and much more available and feasible as an option suited to the capacity and requirements of multi-national companies; and it has been particularly characteristic of foreign based, mainly American, multi-nationals. In other words, a significant attempt has been made to retrench the control of monopoly capital which proceeded upon the foundation and strategy provided by the structure of the multi-national enterprise, consolidating control at this level as opposed to seeking control through the power of the state. In contrast, those American based corporations operating in the British car industry not only adopted corporatism as a response to class conflict but played a leading and constructive role in paving the way for the acceptance of certain of the changes that this entailed.

North American Capital in the UK Economy

First let me consider briefly the quantitative economic dimensions of this capital in the UK economy. This has three notable aspects: 1) American owned firms tend to be found in the fastest growing, most technologically advanced, science and research based, export oriented and capital intensive industries; 2) some three-fifths of the sales and more than one half the employment of these firms is to be found in seven sectors, viz. food, tobacco, mineral oil refining, metal manufacture, instrument engineering, office machinery and computers, and vehicle manufacturing. These same sectors account for 38 per cent of the sales and 28 per cent of the employment of all UK companies (Dunning: 1972; 4); 3) most US companies are to be found in industries which are already highly concentrated (Ibid.; 23). These features gave US capital in manufacturing industry a capacity and flexibility in handling (as well as constraining and shaping) its industrial relations policies which set it off from other capitals in the 1960s. A more rapid rate of accumulation, international, integrated production systems, commitment of investment to science, research and exports, capital intensity plus the power of monopoly and multinationalism all facilitate while at the same time making more imperative, the containment and control of the demands of labour.

The ccnsequential higher profitability and productiveness of US as compared with British capital (Dunning: 1972; Part 2) should not be allowed to obscure the accumulation problems that the former faced. While from the 1950s, onwards, capital in general began to experience a profitability crisis and US companies normally and consistently earned higher rates of return, they did not escape the downward slide in profits (Ibid.; 75). Thus, US capital was not immune to the economic crisis that began to affect British capitalism. Neither was it free from the obstacles deriving from working class militancy and industrial ccnflict.

Foreign multi-nationals have been affected by industrial conflict in much the same way as other capitals,[9] although some qualifications regarding its form and volume should be stressed. Steuer and Gennard argue their comparison for the years 1963 and 1968 'suggests very strongly that the foreign-owned firm is less strike-prone than its domestic counterpart' (1971; 123). Furthermore, they argue that the patterns of conflict tend to differ for 'very big and very small strikes are mcre important in the domestic total. The foreign-owned firms are given to nice, medium-sized disputes' (Ibid.; 125). This pattern is related to bargaining structures in that domestic firms tend more to engage in national bargaining while foreign-owned firms tend more to engage in plant and company bargaining, though the latter has not been immune to unconstitutional strikes even though they tend to have shorter and quicker grievance procedures (Ibid.; 128).

The foreign multi-national company has, however, been more capable of responding forcefully, autonomously and effectively to the 'challenge from below' posed by shop floor bargaining power. Most of the innovations in industrial relations that arose in the 1960s emerged from the practice of foreign multi-national companies, most notably productivity bargaining (Ibid.; 101 and 108-10). Such bargaining involved companies like Esso, Mobil Oil, Alcan and Shell, and their lead tended to be followed by leading British firms, like British Oxygen, BP, ICI as well as the CEGB, while also being supported and encouraged by the state, building it into government prices and incomes policies (Ibid.; 107-10).

In order to plan more effectively the overall nature and continuity of production and to counter the influence and demands of labour and unions upon this, foreign multi-nationals have also taken the lead in making fixed term company agreements. Many employers have complained about the unpredictability and consumption of time and effort taken by collective bargaining in the annual round of wage negotiations. But foreign, and especially American, capital has secured agreements with unions such that what has been agreed over wages and conditions applies for fixed term periods of two to three years (Ibid.; 105-107 and 113). The determination of wages has likewise figured in the control foreign multi-nationals have attempted to exercise over their conditions of accumulation and circulation. In the motor industry, the three US firms, Ford, Vauxhall and Chrysler, were the first to move to measured day work and away from payment by results systems like piece-work rates (Ibid.; 110-12) in order to stabilise the amount and pre-dictability of the wage effort bargain secured by workers. Gennard argues that 'there is some crude evidence to suggest that the foreign multi-national might be the determinant of the size of wage settlements' (1972; 33), not just in conced-ing high rates of pay but in setting the pace and size of wage settlements for the rest of the industries in which they operate, and indeed for the private sector of the economy as a whole (Ibid.; 29-33).

The initiation, sponsorship, and encouragement of inno-vations in industrial relations practice, like those detailed above, which foreign multi-nationals began to introduce into Britain in the 1960s brings to light a number of features. They are, first of all, demonstrative of the power of capital that characterises this fraction in its capacity to control labour. They also show, as a consequence, the extent to which this power can be exercised in a way relatively autonomous from any requirement for the state to intervene. It is, like-wise, the case that many of the practices and objectives of foreign multi-nationals have contributed to the processes and conflicts marking the economic and political crises which other fractions of capital have berated and framed their political demands upon the state to eliminate. Thus, in areas such as the concession of wage increases and local plant bargaining generally, foreign multi-nationals played a secondary but contributory role in encouraging or tolerating the devolution of collective bargaining to the shop floor and to the shop steward led work group, likewise fuelling or at least eliciting increases in money wages and so extending workers' wage expect-ations.

Compounding the effects of the industrial relations prac-tices of foreign multi-nationals on the UK economy, British capital and the state has been the dissociation of foreign multi-nationals from, if not their opposition to, indigenous employers' organisations. The policy of either not joining, or leaving employers' organisations in order to conduct collective bargaining has tended to be characteristic of foreign multi-nationals in general, and American multi-nationals in parti-cular (Steuer and Gennard: 1971; 95). The aim of enhancing autonomy and the capacity to make innovations in the organisa-tion of work and industrial relations has been the major, ostensible reason for this policy. In view of this and the fact that 'the foreign firms that have deliberately opted for plant bargaining are predominantly American owned' (Ibid.; 95) it can be claimed that these trends have both divided foreign multi-nationals somewhat from the interests of other fractions of capital in the formulation of programmes for the reform of industrial relations, while at the same time increasing their power and autonomy in the conduct of their own internal industrial struggles and economic production (Gennard: 1972; 22).

This is not to suggest that it could afford to eschew considerations of the state nor that its practices did not have influential implications for the state's role. There are some important instances in which foreign multi-nationals as well as responding to state initiatives, presaged, encouraged, established precedents for and even possibly precipitated more sustained changes in state policy and action towards industrial relations in the direction of the use of the law. These instances, however, clearly indicate the limitations for capital of independent initiatives to control the working class at work and how a role for the state in all this is essential and pressing for capital, even if it is not always continuously or unambiguously expressive of the interests of capital or of its respective fractions.

The examples I have in mind concern attempts by North American multi-national companies to introduce the law into industrial relations. Both Ford and Henry Wiggins, a subsidiary of the Canadian based International Nickel Company, tried to introduce penalty clauses and legal enforceability of agreements, the latter company meeting with some success. Both cases occurred against the background of the penalty clauses at one time included in prices and incomes statute, the debate over the provision of legal sanctions for unofficial strikers and the subsequent inclusion of legal controls on such strikers in the Labour Government's White Paper 'In Place of Strife' in 1969. And they also both entailed the novel approach to the problem of unconstitutional and unofficial strikes of offering financial inducements to workers to adhere to disputes procedure (Ibid.; 112). In 1967 and 1968 Henry Wiggins succeeded in gaining an agreement which was regarded as being legally enforceable (Henry Wiggins and Co. Ltd., RC, WE, 390, 1967). In order to conclude the agreement the company felt it necessary to leave the EEF (Ibid.; pp.1-2). This had, though, coercive attractions: 'if a union were to commit a flagrant breach of an agreement which is likely to have serious consequences, we should certainly like to be in a position to apply for an injunction' (Ibid.; p.5). But a similar initiative elsewhere by the same company encountered successful strike resistance (Collins: 1970; 96-7) and showed the limitations for capital of individual employer initiatives in this area.

The other example which can be cited of this process before the relevant legislation contained in the I.R. Act became law, that of the Ford strike of 1969, further illustrates the extent to which capital can by no means rely fully or confidently on the introduction of legalism into industrial relations. Judges are normally thought to conform to the interests of capital but they do not always do so. What as a consequence came to be required therefore was a more systematic and co-ordinated policy on the part of the state which the recourse of employers to the existing courts did not provide. In February 1969, just after the publication of 'In Place of Strife', Fords obtained majority union agreement to a settlement granting pay increases, a quicker disputes procedure, increased holiday pay, and guaranteed pay for lay-offs while providing for the loss of holiday bonus payments and guaranteed lay-off pay for involvement in unconstitutional strike action. This led to the results it was intended to preclude, namely an unofficial strike led by shop stewards, which the TGWU and AEU eventually declared official. Fords insisted that the procedure agreement be observed and applied for a mandatory injunction ordering the unions to withdraw their official support for the strike, arguing that the official action constituted a breach of the procedure agreement. The judge decided against Fords, concluding that the procedure agreements were not legal contracts since it had not been the intention of either side to enter into legally binding contracts. Fords withdrew its intention to appeal or proceed to a full trial, and the penalty clauses more or less disappeared from the final agreement, as a result of union opposition, the stand of the courts on the issue, and pressure from the DOE (Benyon: 1975; Chapter 10. Panitch: 1976; 179-81).

It has been noted that both of these cases represented a new challenge to the prevailing norms of the industrial relations system in the UK since if they had been successful, or rather more successful as independent employer initiatives, they would have undermined the norm of voluntarism (Steuer and Gennard: 1971; 113) by the forthright introduction of legalism into industrial relations on the basis of the action of individual and powerful capital units. Equally, there occurred an important reciprocation of state and employer tactics. Not only did the policy of the state begin to provide a basis for legal initiatives like that of Ford, but its experience made it more imperative to urge the government to do something (Benyon: 1975; 275. Panitch: 1976; 169 and 302). The result of Fords' use of the courts highlighted the need for the state to intervene in the face of the failure of the endeavours of individual capitals to effectively utilise the law as a means of control. While it became more and more usual in the 1960s for capitalists to make public their demands for the use of legal coercion and a worked-out legal framework for industrial relations, notably through the CBI and EEF, it was mainly the capital discussed above which went beyond the bounds of ideological mobilisation. The mutually reinforcing actions of capital and the state though similarly drew attention to the limitations of the initiatives of particular capitals in isolation, no matter how powerful they may appear to be. To have been successful these legal initiatives would have needed to have been conducted within a wider and more elaborate form of law and with more effective means of countering the collective resistance the union movement mounted, things which the state is better able to provide.

110

Foreign Multi-National Capital and the Donovan Commission

In detailing the general structural and more overtly ideological mainsprings of the specific interventions of foreign multinationals in the politics of industrial relations in Britain, attention needs to be paid both to the role charted out for trade unions and to the type of state action called for. The interests and orientations espoused by Henry Wiggins proved to be one of the most explicit in urging the use of law in industrial relations as we have seen (op. cit). But while it envisaged very clearly a legally coercive role for the state, this depended much more upon the mechanism of private initiative than the bureaucratic pre-emption of the interventionist state. Varying shades of conviction conforming to this strand of ideology and political policy can be found amongst the ranks of foreign multi-nationals, though in view of the contradictions involved, there are inevitably slippages in the direction of alternative forms in reacting to the changing nature of industrial conflict. An essential ingredient of the liberalist strategy adopted by foreign multi-nationals has been the emphasis placed upon the responsibility and initiative of management, but usually with the co-opted acquiescence of trade unions. This is seen not only in the attempts to use the law, but in the more usual pre-emption of collective bargaining practices and the commitment to innovations that we have detailed. In the face of the need for increased economic productivity, international competition and pressure from its US HQ, this formed, according to Esso, the mechanism for the establishment of productivity bargaining (WE, 143, 1966, p.1645). This has led to the buying-off of trade unions, which has been most feasible in capital intensive production where labour costs form a small percentage of overall running costs and do so progressively as productivity and output increases, thereby enhancing further the need to ensure that the initiative for change, innovation and control rests with management (Mobil Oil, ME, 49, 1966, pp.2145-8). This often entails as a consequence of the requirement of greater autonomy, withdrawing from or not joining employers' organisations and renouncing the principle of employer solidarity precisely in order to ensure control (Ibid.; pp.2132-3 and 2156-7. Esso, WE, 143, pp.1647-8 and 1650-3) even to the extent of being prepared to act as pace-maker for the respective industry in such matters as pay rates and thus to the explicit detriment of national and industry-wide collective bargaining structures (Ibid. Kodak, ME, 67, pp.2898-2902). This strategy has even been extended to hostile opposition to existing employer organisations and to the nature and type of support offered by other employers: 'We now find that more and more pressure is exerted upon us, as a company ... to make some concessions to avoid breaking the industrial peace, and this pressure comes not from the unions, but from fellow employers' (Phillips Industries, WE, 102, p.1688).[10] What was needed was to re-assert the role and authority of management rather than introduce the state, since much of what was thought to be wrong was seen to be the fault of management. The failure of management to actually manage and thereby to contribute almost by default to the breakdown of industrial relations institutions was emphatically stated (Ibid.; p.1088).

This orientation is by no means generic to nor firmly and statically established amongst foreign multi-nationals. Contradictory pulls resulting from the influence of class struggles, needless to say, exert their influence. Hence, for example, Kodak veered much more closely to the alternative of paternalism. This has been exemplified most clearly by its development of Workers' Representative Committees as internal carbon copies of trade unions. This has gone along with non-membership of employers' federations and a refusal to recognise trade unions. The major stress is placed on internal control with internal committees, high pay rates and generous fringe benefits - what it viewed as the 'welfare state privatised' - being geared to this end (ME, 67, 1967).

Corporatism as well as paternalism has competed with liberalism as the dominant strategy of this capital. But before identifying this let me clarify what such liberalism entails. It involves, first of all, the implied or de facto recognition of the autonomy and independence of trade unions. This rests on the assumption that it is management's responsibility to provide leadership, to manage and take decisions, to take action and innovate, and that in the face of this, it is up to the unions to accommodate themselves and to bargain unhindered on the basis of their own resources, and to obtain the best results from their point of view, given the successful assertion of managerial rights. There exists no need to coerce unions other than by means of the free market, relying upon the power of management to secure an appropriate role for trade unions by the mere assertion of the proper role of management in collective bargaining, leaving by default if not by design, a normatively autonomous role for trade unions (Phillips, op.cit., pp.1091-1100. Esso, op. cit., pp.1677 and passim). Connected with this has been support for political laissez-faire since conditions offered this as a feasible and available form of social control. The whole problem of the reform of industrial relations is seen as one in which management's job is to change its own attitudes and then persuade others to change theirs, securing co-operation by managerial leadership and not by legislation and the use of the law (Ibid.; pp.1657 and 1664-5).But it is equally possible if the principle of legal intervention is accepted as a last resort, to begin to adopt elements of the corporatist strategy for industrial relations.

Multi-National Capital in the Motor Industry
An example of the strategy of corporatism in this context is that urged by multi-nationals in the Motor Car Industry, whose

proposals, objectives and interests conform very much to those
offered by the CBI and EEF. Unofficial strikes, in which the
role of shop steward was dominant, were seen as having a highly
damaging and costly effect on the exports and efficiency of the
industry, producing wage drift and the unproductive use of labour. This arose, it was argued, from the power given to workers
by the highly complex interdependent nature of the industry,
with a strike by a small number of workers leading to large-
scale lay-offs (ME, 23, 1966. pp.833-4, 839-44 and 889-93).
While supporting voluntarism as the more desirable alternative,
they had, nonetheless, made a number of efforts to get the
state to introduce legal sanctions on unofficial strikes
(Panitch: 1976; 169 and 302), and clearly felt that voluntarism
was no longer a feasible or practical solution (ME, 23, pp.
835-6). On the contrary, the answer was sought in legal coercion of a corporatist kind. They supported the CBI and EEF
proposals on the registration of trade unions and the supervision of their rules, and the principle that the onus for disciplining their members be placed upon the unions themselves,
turning them into agencies of social control, since 'the authority of properly organised unions requires some measure of
legal support' (Ibid.; p.844). It was, therefore, thought that
'legal sanctions will be required if unofficial strikes are to
be effectively curbed' (Ibid.; 845), and a number of legal
changes to this end were proposed. Procedure agreements were
to be legally enforceable, the right to strike only operating
when procedures had been exhausted, thereby making the suggested sanctions, fines deducted from wages on the authority of
labour courts, similarly legally binding. In return for these
legal controls on strikes, it was proposed that the law accept
the closed shop. Both of these changes were seen as ways of
inducing trade unions themselves to discipline their rank and
file, and secure adherence to agreements. This stress on the
use of union rules likewise introduced outside intervention in
the form of the proposed surveillance of the unions' rules by
the Registrar to ensure that unions endeavoured to curtail unofficial strikes (Ibid.; pp.836-8). These employers stated
their willingness to take proceedings to an independent body,
such as a labour court or industrial tribunal, and argued that
such external support for the employers' role by the state, as
well as the social control exercised by trade unions, was essential, since the traditional sanctions available to employers
such as the sack or the removal of fringe benefits from strikers
no longer formed effective deterrents (Ibid.; pp.889, 895 and
902-903).

Conclusions
I have attempted to identify what I have seen as the predominantly liberalistic policy adopted by foreign multi-nationals
towards controlling industrial conflict. This has been associated with some examples of paternalism and a strong and important

impetus towards the adoption of corporatism as the last example above shows. The very economic existence of multi-national companies has, in part, been dependent upon liberal state policies towards trade and international economic relationships (Warren: 1971; 85). And it is this as much as anything else which may explain this fraction of capital's commitment to liberalism as well as its vacillation between this and the alternative strategy of corporatism. We have, likewise, argued that even as powerful a capital as this depends on the intervention of the state to control class conflict. Moreover, my intention has been to identify strategies towards the state's role in industrial relations in order to chart changes in the positions of classes, class fractions and political groups over time, and this is based upon the assumption that such changes will occur as the socio-economic structure and the nature of class conflict and political conflict change. With this in mind, it can be suggested that in the late 1950s, and the 1960s, the superior economic base of foreign multi-nationals in terms of capital intensity, technological advance, higher profits, the capacity to 'buy industrial peace' and to innovate in industrial relations, was conducive to a strategy of liberalism.

4. Money Capital, Paternalism and the Control of Industrial Relations

The last major group of owners and controllers of private capital that I wish to consider in this section of the study are those concentrated in the financial sector of the UK economy. In the main with respect to money capital I shall be concerned with the major clearing banks, insurance companies and building societies, and their structure of industrial relations control, their conceptions and ideologies of class interests in containing industrial conflict, and their view of and influence on and by the role of the state in the ordering of such relations. I shall argue that the structure of interests represented in and by the City conform most closely to the system of state control of industrial relations which I have termed paternalism.

Industrial Relations in the Money Capital Sector: the ideology and structure of paternalism

Interestingly enough, employers in banking as compared with manufacturing industry have been singled out by one staff association as being characterised by 'paternal benevolence' (National Provincial Bank Staff Association, WE, 87, 1965). This is certainly the image the financial sector likes to present of itself. But it is difficult to argue with Bain's conclusion: 'The most widespread use of company sponsored staff associations to hinder the growth of unionism has occurred in banking ... the employers took the initiative in founding them and still encourage them largely to hinder the growth of the

114

National Union of Bank Employees' (Bain: 1967; pp. 93-4).[11]
However, the banks have found it increasingly difficult to prevent the intrusion of trade unionism into the financial sector.
In many ways, the 'crisis' for money capital entails denying
the existence of unions rather than using them as a form of
social control. In the evidence submitted to the Donovan Commission, only two banks made significant contributions, both of
which imply support for staff associations and the general opposition to - if not absence of - collective bargaining. Lloyds
said it recognised its staff association rather than NUBE because it was more representative (Lloyds Bank Ltd., WE, 88,
1965, pp. 1 and 5). It expressed its opposition to the closed
shop and though it accepted in principle the need for a strong
organisation to represent employees' 'opinions', it had to use
this power, as did the employer, with 'moderation and responsibility' (Ibid.; pp. 4 and 7). The National Provincial Bank said
it did not recognise NUBE and pointed to the fact that it had
not experienced strikes, lock-outs, industrial action or any
form of disruption throughout its history (WE, 44, 1965; pp.
3-4 and 6). In a very informative account it attributed these
harmonious industrial relations to a number of different reasons. Firstly, the established tradition of high status that
characterises staff employed in banking. Secondly, the unhindered and considered recognition by management and staff of
the mutuality of their long-term interests, that profitability
is in the longer-term interests of both sides of industry.
Thirdly, 'the readiness of the management to recognise the
incidence of inflation by salary revisions from time to time'
(Ibid.; pp. 9 and 5). Fourthly, it pointed to the very generous
pensions and other fringe benefits it provided. Fifthly, it
stressed the small-scale organisation of the actual labour process in banking, which conforms more to the conditions experienced by wage labour employed by petit-bourgeois rather than
industrial monopoly capital. The work organisation of banking
in small units gave staff and their representatives immediate
and informal access to management. Lastly, it argued that only
recognising the staff association avoided the 'competitive
bidding of extravagant claims by rival staff bodies to the
detriment of good relations' (Ibid.; p.10).

The features analysed above can also be found in other
parts of the financial sector. For example, on 17th February,
1972, the Council of the Building Societies' Association issued
what was initially a strictly confidential letter to its members on the question of trade union recognition and in response
to the requirements of the IR Act. It stressed that 'no society
can afford to behave as though the Industrial Relations Act had
never been passed', and argued 'each society will need (if it
does not already exist) some form of formal staff representation, whether through a consultative committee, a staff association or a trade union'. It therefore suggested that the formation, recognition of and negotiations with a staff association

115

might be an appropriate policy and that 'Collective bargaining is not an exclusive boon to employees and there is nothing to stop a society from spelling out the disadvantages. Other societies may feel that unionisation is inevitable so that they would be wise to encourage the union of their choice' (see CIR: No. 86, 1974, pp. 48-50).

These objectives, interests and ideology did not change appreciably when they gradually came to accept some limited forms of collective bargaining involving a trade union. In their evidence, submitted in November 1978, to the Wilson Committee, the Committee of London Clearing Banks, comprising Barclays, Coutts and Co., Lloyds, Midland, Nat. West and Williams and Glyn, devoted a chapter to their industrial relations (1978, chapter 14). In view of their support for one negotiating body for employees (a by now general objective of capital), the banks noted that 'efforts to bring about a merger between the staff associations and NUBE have so far been unsuccessful' (Ibid.; Pa. 14.15, p.160). As alternative strategies to this, Midland had started to negotiate with NUBE and ASTMS, while Williams and Glyn had given sole bargaining rights to NUBE, as a result of CIR intervention (see below). It pointed out how good its industrial relations were especially when compared with the standards of industry and commerce at large. It said that the banks as employers had recognised the need for more effective consultations and communications with staff and was accordingly strengthening its links with trade unions and staff associations, experimenting with consultative committees and developing or announcing profit sharing schemes.

The policy of incorporating the staff associations and NUBE into one organisation to represent financial sector workers in collective bargaining was one which the CIR in point of fact urged upon money capital in the early 1970s. A number of points need to be noted regarding this evidence.[12] Considering the role of the CIR we can note how it more or less consistently supported in these and other cases the principle of union recognition and the role of unions as strong, authoritative organisations in controlled and disciplined collective bargaining and industrial relations. The evidence also shows very clearly the support within the financial sector for staff associations as a type of internal, heteronomous employee organisation and its opposition to the recognition of externally based and independent trade unions. This was, however, a policy which could no longer be countenanced by the state as these, admittedly limited, data indicate. Indeed, much of the support of financial institutions for staff associations derived from the passing of the IR Act and its emphasis upon orderly industrial relations, effective collective bargaining and representative employee organisations. That is to say, the stipulations of the IR Act made such employers aware of the failings of their own industrial relations and prompted them to consider organisational changes, staff associations, if not already existent,

116

emerging as the preferred mode of conducting such relations as opposed to the conventional pattern in most of manufacturing industry involving trade unions (see e.g. CIR: No. 42: 1973, p.2. Idem: No. 79; pp. 7-9).

The general tenor of the evidence is indicative of the paternalism that characterises the objectives of money capital in its drive for control of its work relations. On the basis of the CIR's own findings in these surveys, it can be argued that the formation, development, and support of staff associations by employers in the financial sector, has functioned mainly as a means of precluding or curtailing the unionisation of their employees. Money capital still insisted that the correctness of its policy of not accepting the very principle of recognising trade unions in all instances was borne out by its low labour turnover and lack of overt conflict (CIR: No.78; 1974, p.5), and that trade unions had positive disadvantages: 'it was felt ... that recognition of trade unions introduced an undesirable "them and us" atmosphere' (CIR: No. 52; 1973, p.7). The CIR therefore found extensive evidence of sustained attempts by money capital to pre-empt trade unionism by fostering staff associations. This was represented by such varying and discriminatory practices as providing finance for staff association salaries and activities, providing premises and time off for association meetings, providing typing, postal and other services, the check off for subscriptions, giving relevant information to the association but not the union, giving judiciously timed wage increases to blunt union appeals for membership and claims regarding their effectiveness, and insisting that management representatives be present at all union meetings. These practices went along with the denial of services and assistance and even token recognition to trade unions.

I think that the evidence analysed above clearly highlights the structure of control that money capital has aimed for in organising its internal industrial relations and the inflexion it has placed upon the ideological conception of such relations. This overall structure has been designated by the concept of paternalism. But two main features have so far been omitted from this picture which we shall now consider in turn. The first concerns the role of money capital within British capital and British capitalism, and the second concerns the relationship between money capital and the state in the ordering of industrial relations.

Money capital and British capitalism

Those institutions concerned with capital as money,[13] commonly referred to as, though by no means coterminous with, 'the City', are a central and dominant if not obvious feature of British capitalism. The global role of the City in the international financing of world capitalism underpins this dominance and very much undermines the relevance of the distinction between

nationalism and internationalism for this particular fraction
of capital (Cohen: 1971; especially Chapters 4 and 6). In the
past this international dominance has depended in large part
on the use of sterling as an international currency and this
was associated with the growth and stabilisation of British
imperialism during the nineteenth and twentieth centuries and
the export of capital overseas (Feis: 1961; 83-117. Strange:
1971; Chapters 2 and 4). The City has adapted to the decline
of sterling by moving 'ever increasingly from the use of sterling to the use of dollars' (Strange: 1971; 71 and 25). Thus,
as Glyn and Sutcliffe note, for the City 'its prosperity no
longer depends on sterling's role as an international currency',
since 'the growth of the need for international financing and
the City's expertise in this field meant that it became the
centre of borrowing and lending operations which were not conducted in sterling at all' (1972; 171 and 169-72).

Associated with and both buttressing and deriving from
this position is the generally profitable (notably as compared
with domestic industrial capital) nature of the City's earnings
from its financial services which further serve to secure its
dominant and influential position within British capital and
British capitalism. The overseas earnings of the City have
remained high and have increased over the years even if inflation is taken into account.[14] There is evidence to suggest that
money capital has not been nearly so affected by the profitability crisis which has afflicted much of British manufacturing
industry since the 1950s: property investment, financing and
managing takeovers, and investment of liquid assets overseas
have formed major ways by which the profit levels of financial
concerns have been reasonably well protected. And this has gone
along with the fact that declining profitability makes manufacturing companies more dependent on credit and borrowing; and
with interest rates increasing and the growth of public expenditure the state has become another profitable outlet for the
funds held by financial institutions (Glyn and Sutcliffe: 1972;
122-6 and 147-56. Pollard: 1969; 449. NEDO: 1975). This in itself does not prevent or preclude the City from being concerned
about profits and profit levels. In its evidence to the Wilson
Committee, the Committee of London Clearing Banks stressed the
banks' need for adequate profits to maintain confidence, accommodate losses and retain a realistic capital base. It stated
that when inflation was accounted for the rate of return for
finance was now lower than for industry as a whole. It therefore saw the banks as suffering the decline in profitability
that had affected UK industry as a whole. It argued that
especially since 1973 the profits of the banks had not matched
the rate of inflation, leading to a fall in the real value of
the funds in the banks' capital base (Committee of London
Clearing Banks: 1978; Chapter 7).

This indicates the kind of problem faced by money capital
which occasions and is accompanied by state intervention in

the economy in order to attempt to maintain the profitability
of the operations of financial institutions. It has been noted
that the economic policy of governments in Britain, because of
the commitment to the maintenance of the international role of
sterling (and after 1967 to general currency stability) and
consequently due to successive governments' deflationary mcnet-
ary and fiscal policies, has tended to favour the interests of
the City at the expense of building up Britain's productive,
industrial base (Thompson: 1977. Idem: 1978. Longstreth: 1977.
Idem: 1979). As a result, leading sections of industrial capital
have petitioned the state for the institution of more stable,
and long-term, corporatist planning mechanisms aimed at re-
invigorating the conditions of existence of productive, industrial capital (Longstreth: 1977. Idem: 1979). Thus, although
both fractions of capital share a general class interest in
the reproduction of capital accumulation and the state's role
in this, differences and conflicts arise over the content and
specific policies entailed in this process. What this illustrates is the influence of the division between fractions of
capital upon the policy of the state and the reciprocal impact
of that policy upon the varying fortunes and interests of the
different fractions of capital. Hence, what we now need to
determine is the relationship between money capital and the
features of its structure and practice, analysed above, on the
one hand, and its part in and its policies towards the role of
the state, on the other, with reference to the social control
of industrial relations.

Money Capital, the State and the Politics of Industrial Conflict

The interests defining the objectives of money capital towards
the role of the state in the economy and industrial relations
in a very general sense echo the interests of capital as a
class. Thus the Committee of London Clearing Banks affirmed
'the need to maintain a stable political and economic environment so as to preserve the confidence on which banking so cru-
cially depends. The clearing banks hope that the importance of
this is fully recognised in official circles' (1978; p. 128).
As we have seen with the other fractions of capital studied,
there exists a universal concern that for capitalism and the
power of capital to be reproduced state power is required to
ensure order in the polity and the economy. But the question
then becomes how is this state power to be shaped and used?

It is possible to identify interests specific to money
capital which make it view the role of the state in a more
particular manner and attempt to steer it in certain clearly
marked out directions. These derive partly from the nature of
the capital controlled which because it exists in a money form
needs to operate under conditions which allow for its flexible
and unimpeded use as with all capital, and also partly from
the international basis of its operations which accentuates
the former requirements and does not require in the same way

as industrial capital a specific urban and production location.
The Committee of London Clearing Banks expressed concern over
the restrictive effects of exchange controls on capital move-
ments (Ibid.; pp.126-8). But the particular interest of money
capital is with London's position as a banking and financial
centre, even though this is seen as being in the interests of
everybody because of the revenue brought into the UK economy
by the City (Ibid.; p. 128). What this means is that financial
institutions have their interests primarily in ensuring that
state intervention takes a liberal form. The British Bankers'
Association[15] make this clear: 'Amongst the main advantages
which London must seek to maintain is its excellent reputation
as the most liberal of major banking centres. Foreign banks
are able to open offices without undue formalities and, once
established, there are few restrictions on the business that
they may do.... The BBA advocates the continuance of the liberal policies which have been a major factor in the development
of London as an international banking centre' (Ibid.; p. 249).
This has direct implications for the role of the state in the
financial sector: 'Confidence in London has been undermined to
some extent in the past by the precipitate fall in the value
of sterling, by threats of bank nationalization, and by suggestions that the authorities should attempt to direct the investment of banks' deposits. The BBA hopes that the authorities
will ... ensure that the banks in London can continue to operate
in an atmosphere of stability and reasonable independence from
political direction of their activities' (Ibid.; p. 250).
Accordingly, liberalism implying a laissez-faire role for the
state in preserving the conditions of accumulation for money
capital constitutes a major political orientation and objective
of the City.
    This, in itself, raises an interesting point for it sug-
gests that money capital will be opposed to the kinds of controls on economic transactions and exchange, particularly those
conducted on an international basis, that would be entailed in
the autarchic and dirigiste policies of a corporatist state. As
Winkler (1976) has pointed out, corporatism would entail economic nationalism and state controls on the movement of capital
and goods both domestically and internationally and this would
clearly conflict with the interests of the financial sector by
putting constraints upon the free movement of money capital.
This would tend to lead it to support state liberalism rather
than the controls entailed in corporatism. This is especially
accurate if one recognises the potential links between incomes
policies and other forms of economic controls. While it can
conceivably be granted that the City may favour incomes policies to reduce inflation, they have usually involved quid pro
quos with trade unions and this has presaged, even if only on
paper, the possibility of corporatist (although they are often
seen as socialist) controls, such as economic planning and the
direction of investment (Longstreth: 1977. Corina: 1975).

120

The strength and dominance of the City and its maintenance of a laissez-faire conception of the state derive in large part from the close links established between itself and key agencies of the state. We have considered this briefly in the early part of this chapter when we distinguished the CBI and the City in terms of the latter's 'hegemonic' ties with state power which rest upon the established, institutional and representational relationship between the City, the Bank of England and the Treasury, and their general overall influence on the framework and content of economic policy making (see Grant and Marsh: 1977. Longstreth: 1979. Jessop: 1980). This relationship is very much appreciated by the City itself. It has rested upon the City being able either to deal directly with government departments or make its influence felt on state policy through the Bank of England. Such direct contact results from the growth of state interventionism and forms an appropriate way of handling this development from the City's point of view (Committee of London Clearing Banks: 1978; p. 179). This has meant that the City has ceased to rely on the Bank of England as its sole link with government and the Treasury, though it is still regarded as its most important one. There has also grown up a series of direct contacts between the hierarchical levels of authority in the bureaucracies of the banks and the state from the chairmen to the chief executives of banks on the one hand and the Chancellor of the Exchequer, the Governor of the Bank of England, its chief cashier and civil servants on the other. The Bank of England still deals with issues which concern the City as a financial market, while contacts with government departments handle issues concerning the status of financial institutions as large companies (Ibid.; Chapter 17). As such, the financial sector has set itself against the excessive external pressure entailed in state regulation and interventionism, and supported the maintenance of a liberal state. This reflects the class dominance of the City in British capitalism and its power within the structures of the state (cf. Longstreth: 1979).

Conclusions

I have argued that the most characteristic form of control which money capital has attempted to exert over its industrial relations has been paternalism. On the basis of the available evidence I argued that this could be seen, in one important respect, in its support for labour collectivities which had been internally generated and regulated by employers and could be maintained under employer control, so resisting the spread of externally based, autonomous trade unions. This attempt to ensure the heteronomy of labour organisations was said to be prevalent in the financial sector in the face of the challenge of trade unionism which has been increasingly posed since the 1960s. This heteronomy was then argued to be associated with money capital's support for the laissez-faire form of state mediation of economic and industrial relations, which derived both from the liberalism that it required to operate in economic relations as a consequence of the international structure and basis of its functions as a form of capital in the context of British capitalism, and also from the secure and influential hold that it·had managed to attain within the state itself such that any significant re-orientation of the state had not been considered necessary nor desirable (cf. Longstreth: 1979). This paternalism tends further to characterise its practices and ideology regarding the role of the state in industrial relations inasmuch as, say, its support for the Economic League[16] can be seen as a corollary of this very paternalism. The League is a good example of the powerful organisational initiatives that can be taken up and maintained by dominant groups of capital (cf. Whitt: 1980). Many theoretical discussions have missed the fact that what so often are seen as ineradicable functions of the state can be performed by private capital.

NOTES

1. Discussion of subsequent developments and changes in the CBI's objectives, policy and practices will be left to later chapters when they can be considered directly in relation to the course of state policy. I have not discussed incomes policies in detail in this study. But see for more elaborate considerations, Strinati: 1981. Crouch: 1977. Panitch: 1976.
2. The CBI did, however, also endorse the Ministry of Labour suggestion for a legally interventionist tribunal. See CBI, ME, 22, 1966, pp. 812 and 816; ME, 9, 1965, p.286; and the analysis of the Ministry of Labour's evidence below.
3. Registration was also to entail advantages such as the right to strike, tax exemptions, etc.
4. Lack of space prevents me from discussing the other organisations of capital which, like the CBI and EEF, represented domestic, industrial monopoly capital, shared their interests, and began to support the adoption of a corporatist strategy for controlling industrial conflict. On this see NFBTE, WE, 1968. ME, 16, 1966. (This evidence is particularly interesting in providing details of the day-to-day struggles occurring in the labour process.) NPA, WE, 261, 1965. IPC, ME, 59, 1966. WE, 318, 1966. Cocoa, Chocolate and Confectionery Alliance, WE, 135, 1965. Soap, Candle, and Edible Fat Trades Employers' Federation, WE, 239, 1966. Unilever, ME, 46, 1966. British Iron and Steel Federation, WE, 268, 1966. One notable exception to this was the Shipbuilding Employers' Federation, ME, 48, 1966. WE, 311, 1966. See also the EEF, ME, No.20, 1966. Idem: WE in Selected Written Evidence, 1968. Idem: 1969. For a discussion of the EEF see Strinati: 1981.
5. It has to be noted that Wright (1978) in fact uses the term petit-bourgeoisie instead of the more usual concept of 'middle class': his conception of the contradictory class

location of small employers places them between this class and the bourgeoisie (see, e.g., 1978; 63 and 86).

6. Years of almost unprecedentedly high levels of industrial conflict.

7. This company was a medium-sized rather than a small-scale capital unit whose plants and labour process rather than overall corporate structure are more representative of this capital. But both in terms of the size of its labour process and the ideological constructions of its chairman it has much more in common with this capital. Only 200-250 workers were employed at each works and it was claimed that this small number and small plant size meant that management would know most workers personally (Sir Halford Reddish, RC, ME, 68, 1967, p. 2931).

8. Stanworth and Curran (1973; 161-4) have also found that in line with their opposition to trade unionism small businessmen tend to support, if anything, internal employee representative councils or committees.

9. The example of Kodak is instructive on union non-recognition. See ACTT, RC, WE, 391, 1967. Kodak, RC, ME, 67, 1967. See also CIR: No.26; 1972. No.55; 1973. No.1, Cmnd.4246, 1969, and No.68; 1974. Numerous other surveys reported on by the CIR on union recognition reveal that this practice of non-recognition of unions is by no means specific to foreign multi-nationals.

10. Phillips admits that it tried to get a number of big companies to leave the EEF and form a breakaway association but to no avail.

11. In fact, many of the white collar unions who gave evidence to the Donovan Commission complained of this. In particular they cited the confidential letters, expressing clear sentiments of opposition to white collar unionism, sent to their members by the BEC in 1964 and the CBI in 1965. For the text of these letters see, for example, ASSET, RC, ME, 53, 1966, pp. 2253-4.

12. On this see, e.g., CIR reports No.2: 1969. No.16: 1971. No.35. No.42. No.52: 1973. No.57. No.58. No.75. No.78. No.79. No.82. No.84: 1974. See also Chapter 9 below. It has to be pointed out of course that some of the reports, i.e. Nos. 2 and 16, were prepared before the Act was passed and came into operation. This is discussed at greater length in Strinati: 1981.

13. I shall not enter into the wider issue of the theoretical nature and relevance of the distinction between industrial and bank or finance capital nor its specific manifestation in Britain in relation to the economic policy of the state. See Thompson: 1977. Idem: 1978. Longstreth: 1977. Idem: 1979. Jessop: 1980.

14. For the statistical details of the earnings of 'the City' which are provided separately by the government, see Central Statistical Office, United Kingdom Balance of Payments

1965-1975, HMSO, 1976, p. 48. And, Idem, <u>United Kingdom Balance</u> <u>of Payments</u> various years.

15. This is another organisation of bankers which includes those in the Committee and also foreign banks: it 'represents the interests of practically all recognised banks - both British and foreign - operating in the United Kingdom' (Committee of London Clearing Banks: 1978; p. 246).

16. On the League's origins, development, campaigns and organisational structure see State Research: 1978; 135-7. <u>The</u> <u>Observer</u>, 19.10.1969, p. 9. This is discussed at greater length in Strinati: 1981.

Chapter 6

CORPORATISM, SOCIAL DEMOCRACY AND ORGANISED LABOUR

In this chapter I shall be concerned with the structure, objectives, ideologies, and impact of sections of the organised labour movement in response to the crisis of capital accumulation, increasing industrial conflict and the extension of the state's role in the economy. These ideologies and relationships will be linked to the social-structural divisions within organised labour (outlined in Chapters 3 and 4) between shop floor, rank and file union members, and the official bureaucratic leaderships of trade unions. And, particularly in view of the pressures developing within British capital and the state towards corporatism, special and separate attention will be paid to the role of the TUC. I am not trying to argue that this is indicative simply of a split between the class militancy of workers at the point of production and the bureaucratic conservatism of union executives and the TUC. Apart from anything else this would not allow us to understand fully the reasons why, and the nature of the ways in which, the state mediates industrial relations for union leaders and the TUC are not merely subject to the state's pressure to force through corporatist institutions upon their members nor are they always readily incorporated into state administration. They have also for reasons of election and legitimacy if not as a result of more aggressive and coercive pressure to take heed of their memberships' demands and policies. After all, the wave of unofficial strikes in the 1960s was followed in the early 1970s by the re-emergence of large-scale official strikes through which the executives of unions attempted to regain the initiative from the shop floor and by so doing had necessarily to articulate certain of its demands rather than those of the state (Hyman: 1973). This is precisely one of the major structural dilemmas in which the executive leaderships of the major unions have been caught and warns us against the danger of over-simplification as does the fact that rank-and-file militancy is a variable phenomenon. But we are still nonetheless concerned with how this structural division worked itself out within the ranks of organised labour in the context of the burgeoning crisis of British capitalism and the increasingly interventionist part played by state power in the economy and in industrial relations.

We can, if we look at the actions of organised labour in Britain, see a similar kind of social contradiction to that characterising the practice of capital, between the simultaneous support for and opposition to the intervention of the state in the economy and industrial relations. This, however, has very different sources. For capital it derives from an ideological acceptance of the market rationality of capitalism, the 'free' economic exchange of equivalents as defined in contract law, while the reproduction of capitalism and the control of capital at the work place depends directly on the state. For organised labour it derives from the ideological appeal that the use of the state has in redressing and reversing the balance of power that favours capital, coupled with the factually grounded fear that the state cannot be trusted to really represent the interests of labour, either because it is controlled by powerful businessmen together with secretive bureaucrats and/or in its dealings with the affairs of labour it has consistently shown that it does not really favour its interests. In other words, organised labour has a contradictory and contingent, rather than a stable, and confident, belief in the ideologies of liberal-democracy and social-democracy.[1]

This means that I need to say a brief word about this ideology before proceeding to consider the role of organised labour in Britain from the middle 1960s onwards. The relatively successful struggle of the working class for political, legal and civil rights and its securement of a form of political party representation in a central institution of the state, namely parliament, encouraged its commitment to the values of liberal democracy. This entailed belief in and support for parliamentary sovereignty, an equal and propertyless franchise, party competition, the inviolability of elections, equality before the law and the universality of the application of the law (the rule of law) and the separation of powers. Needless to say, these have been extended on the basis of struggle by working class organisations and can therefore be regarded as contingent and unstable rather than firmly guaranteed; and their validity has been continually questioned by the practical class experiences of workers. But, emerging as it has from the way in which political class conflict in Britain has been working itself out over time, the liberal-democratic component of bourgeois ideology has gained an important consensual hold within the working class mainly because it has a secure basis in fact and is not merely a deception or a mystification successfully put about by an omniscient and omnipotent bourgeoisie.[2] This means that it has become a central political feature of the modern state that it faces a process of delegitimation if it transgresses the rights given by liberal democracy to the working class and organised labour. Thus, an

126

important even a conditioning aspect that has to be borne in
mind when considering the state's intervention in industrial
relations is that this is not merely reducible to economic
determinants or the impact of class conflict and class interests but is also structured by political factors and these
include not only the role of state agencies but the very way
in which the state seeks to legitimate its intervention. In a
very significant sense, it can be argued that the British state
in the 1960s and 1970s has not achieved an appropriate and
ideologically accepted mode of legitimation with respect to
its interventionism; this is, in itself, a leading feature of
the political crisis (cf. Habermas: 1976).

In this it has not been helped a great deal by the re-
formulation or extension of liberal-democracy into social democracy (cf. Parkin: 1979; Chapter 9) for its interventions can
by no means be adequately legitimated by the latter even though
it legitimates state intervention per se by suggesting it favours the working class. What I mean by social democracy is the
ideological complexion given to the further extension of the
incorporation of the working class into the state by way of
the emergence and consolidation of the welfare state (particularly after 1945), the nationalisation of basic and service
industries, the development of Keynesian techniques of economic
management to secure growth and full employment combined with
taxation measures to re-distribute income and wealth, i.e.
welfarism and Keynesianism = Social Democracy. The reality of
these measures - whether they really favoured the working class
as a whole is open to contention - and the emergence of a
social democratic consciousness within the organised labour
movement at least suggests that benefits were gained by workers
although the gains worked in the interests of capital as well
by assisting accumulation, by securing a post-war 'settlement'
with the working class and by further providing a form of legitimation for capital accumulation at a time when it came to be
assisted by welfare and Keynesian measures and when labour had
become more organised and more powerful (Jessop: 1980).

In a way, in terms of the extent to which any consensus
could be said to characterise class relations in Britain before
they came under the visible strain of declining accumulation,
escalating industrial conflict, and the crisis of state intervention, they can much more be said to have been marked by this
liberal-cum-social democracy than by the more nebulous notion
of a 'compromise'.[3] Capital, the state and the Tory Party may
have stressed the 'liberal' component more while organised
labour and the Labour Party may have stressed the 'social'
component more, but it formed a kind of modus vivendi for
class relations in politics and industry. It thus provides an
important back-cloth to our discussion of organised labour in
demonstrating what happened as the crisis began to bite. We
have already seen how in response some fractions of capital
began to favour state intervention and to support the sub-

version of liberal and social-democratic norms while liberal-democratic ideology lingered on in the guise of 'voluntarism'. Let us now consider organised labour.

1. The Role of the TUC: Social Democracy versus Corporatism

I wish to argue that the TUC has been caught in a contradiction between social democracy and corporatism. In so far as the incorporation of trade union leaders into state administration is conducive to their more secure and de facto participation in public policy making then it can be conceived of and argued for as an extension of the social democratic state. In other words, it can be construed as a logical and legitimate extension of the social democratic advances made by the organised working class. But when, as is the case, it turns out that this participation is more symbolic than factual and that it exacts its price by way of the TUC having to commit itself to ensuring that the union hierarchies will effectively constrain if not obviate the wage demands and strike actions of their rank and file members - the corporatist alternative - then the role of the TUC becomes ambiguous and subject to tension precisely because it is caught up in this contradiction and its co-operation with the state is thus by no means ensured.

The TUC's initial commitment to incomes policy initiatives, such as that introduced by the incoming Labour Government in 1964[4] was based in large part on its voluntary nature and the possibilities it offered for participation in policy-making (Panitch: 1976; 67). What the Labour Government's attempt to introduce an incomes policy meant was that the TUC became systematically involved in discussions and negotiations over the shape, criteria, machinery and application of the policy. In the first instance this entailed the government's reliance upon obtaining the voluntary co-operation of the trade unions though legal sanctions were very much on the agenda. In response, in order to delay if not prevent legislation, the TUC set up on its own initiative an Incomes Policy Committee to vet wage claims, loosely operating on the basis of criteria laid down in previous White Papers (TUC, WE, 1968, p.103). Eventually, by late 1966, without its consent or agreement, tacit or otherwise, the government had introduced statutory incomes legislation including the legal sanction of fines for failure to notify claims and for strikes to obtain pay increases contrary to the wage freeze imposed by the provisions of the Act (Panitch: 1976; 106-16. Crouch: 1977; Chapter 12). Thus, at the time at which the TUC gave evidence to the Donovan Commission it was very evidently caught up in the structural contradiction between social democracy and corporatism and the attendant vacillation of state policy between consensus and coercion in its relationship to the organised trade union movement and the TUC.

The TUC and the Donovan Commission

I shall therefore now attempt to illustrate empirically these contradictions and the manner in which the TUC was pushed towards support for the corporatist control of industrial relations and industrial conflict. This also provides a clear example of one of the ways in which attempts to institutionalise trade union support for state policies, be it in the form of social democracy or corporatism, mean that class conflict becomes built into the structure of the state itself. It is in this sense that we need to understand not only how such conflict limits and contradicts state policy but how crucial the management of such conflict is to the activity and objectives of the state.

The TUC's proposals have to be seen in the context of its conception of the sources, status and aims of trade unionism. This is very firmly set <u>within</u> and guided by the limits laid down by the labour contract. As it affirmed the first principles entailed in making a case for trade unionism: 'The individual contract between an employee and an employer does not reflect a position of equal strength on the two sides. Equality before the law is only relevant to the observance of the contract and not to its terms or to the procedure by which it is made' (TUC: WE, 1968, p.116). The limits of the labour contract defined in respect of the observance of its conditions are assumed because they are predicated upon the equality of both parties before the law, even if they may be unequal in other ways. Thus, the role of trade unions is constructed on this basis and aimed at determining the terms of the contract and the means by which it is arrived at (collective bargaining) but not at its limits and nature in so far as these confer on workers their status as the commodity of labour, and define the rights of ownership of capital.[5] Following on from this, the TUC argued that as a consequence of the nature of the employment relationship employees have legitimate interests which need to be represented. Trade unions provide the means whereby these interests are represented, safeguarded and extended. For this, equal and representative bargaining within the confines of the labour contract is required (Ibid.). Accordingly, the TUC conceived of the roots of trade unionism as follows: 'Whilst the position of the individual employee, both in law and in practice, is one of subordination, individual employees together recognise that it is through combination that they can develop a means, the essential means which they possess, to harness their own potential strength' (Ibid.; p.117).

This is reflected likewise in the definition of the objectives of trade unions, which are thereby distinguished as follows: improved terms of employment, in particular higher wages, arising from the bargain between payment and work, and thought of as having the highest priority for trade unions; improved physical environment at work involving a role for government; full employment and national prosperity, objectives deriving from the social democratic consensus; security of employment and income; improved social security, conceived of

as the extension of the welfare state in terms of further improvements in health, education and housing outside the immediate sphere of employment; fair shares in national income and
wealth, concerning the re-distribution of wealth and thus a
move away from the gross inequalities to be found in a 'laissez-
faire' free market economy, with this policy securing both re-
distribution away from capital and greater equality between the
incomes of workers; industrial democracy, defined as allowing
workers a greater say in all the things that affect them at
their place of work and as involving opposition to unilateral
decision-making by the employer; a voice in government which
is made necessary by the increased role and scope of government
and the consequent need for trade unions to make their views
known to governments; improved social and public services;
public control and planning of industry which is not so much
concerned with the ownership or management of industry but
with its performance and efficiency and public ownership is
seen as one means among many - the EDC's and the National Plan
are cited with approval - whereby this may be achieved: it is
clearly not conceived of as an assault on the private ownership
of capital (Ibid.; pp.118-24).

The emphasis upon the role of trade unions, their co-operation with the state and the benefits that can flow from
state action for trade unionists that is evidently to be found
in this picture, provides the basis for the state's co-optation
of trade unions as agents of social control to police incomes
policies and industrial militancy. But this stress upon etatisme
in social democracy is contradicted by the equal   if not more
important stress upon the autonomous economic demands of unions
in collective bargaining. After all, in the above list the TUC
regards the improvement of the terms of employment for their
members, rather than co-operation with government, as the fundamental priority and objective of trade unions and this will
very obviously not rest easily with the claims of the state to
minimise or over-ride this aim.

Inextricably bound up with its conception of the objectives of trade unions and with the contradictions as well as
opportunities for social control afforded by social democracy
has been the TUC's stipulation of the legitimate methods of
trade unionism to achieve its stated objectives. These can
again be listed and commented upon for their appropriate fit
with the tenets of social democracy and their conflicting
implications for the rule of capital. The methodology of trade
unionism rests fundamentally upon collective bargaining, 'the
most important trade union method' (Ibid.; p.127). It is, in
a sense, trade unionism par excellence and ineluctably demands
the recognition of trade unions. It is thus only when the
mutual recognition of the two sides to the labour contract has
been achieved that sanctions such as strikes are resorted to
in a minority of cases: 'the right not to work under specific
conditions is matched by the power of the employer not to

employ men under specific conditions' (Ibid.; pp.127-9). Likewise, the scope of collective bargaining is contained within
the limits of 'improved terms and conditions of employment'
(Ibid.; pp.129-30). Other methods which derive from this fundamental one are: joint consultation, negotiation on issues of
concern to workers but not included in the ambit of collective
bargaining; autonomous job regulation, work rules unilaterally
determined by trade unions themselves which reflect the organisational strength of a trade union at the work place; influencing government, which is based upon the government's reliance
on trade unions to represent the views of people in employment
and upon the legitimacy and use of pressure group politics; and,
especially given the historically contentious nature of trade
union involvement in politics, political action which is rooted
in the 'creation of the Labour Party as the political arm of
the trade union movement' (Ibid.; p.133 and pp.130-35). Again,
the social democratic emphasis upon the primacy of collective
bargaining gives rise to the same contradiction in that it
accords with the stability of capitalism by usually confining
the organised working class to economistic, corporate interests
and needs but is thereby relatively intractable to the pressures
of capital and the state when such bargaining itself comes to
constitute a barrier to capital accumulation.

According to this view, it is not even conceivable for the
state to perform the functions of trade unions. This stand
arises from the cardinal principle of free trade unions – their
responsibility to their members without direction by an external agency: 'This general attitude of abstention on the part
of the State arises ... from the competence of trade unions to
safeguard the interests of their members. In other words, it is
where this necessary protection is lacking that the State intervenes, because free collective bargaining is absent' (Ibid.;
p.140). The very criterion of what is thus state assistance as
opposed to state interference is the extent to which the complementary functions of the state, including legislation, undermine the independence of the trade union movement (Ibid.; pp.
140-42).

With respect to the role of trade unions in the economy,
more particularly the distribution of income, the drive of
trade unionism towards increased pay is legitimated by the
amelioration of unequal income distribution: 'Demands made by
trade unionists for wage increases at the expense of profits
reflect their attitude to this grossly unfair distribution of
income and wealth' (Ibid.; p.145). Trade union agreement on
wage restraint has therefore to depend upon at least equal if
not positively discriminatory treatment against capital (Ibid.).
The TUC likewise accepted the Labour Government's incomes policy
initiatives – precisely because they did not single out wages
for attention but located an incomes policy within a wider,
overall national economic plan. This provided the basis for
the TUC's vetting of wage claims by the establishment and

operation of an Incomes Policy Committee, which entailed the
voluntary persuasion of unions to recognise the incomes policy
and productivity guidelines, and if necessary to alter their
claims and practices accordingly (Ibid.; Pas. 213, pp.147-9).
In the light of these considerations it in general accepted the
role of the NBPI but, very importantly, urged that if the principle of voluntarism, rather than statutory intervention, was
to be observed it was essential that the TUC's role was enhanced
in supervising wage claims rather than allowing government
intervention through the work of an outside agency (Ibid.;
pp.149-51).

The TUC's policy deliberations on industrial conflict begin both by arguing that trade unions often support unofficial
strikes and that, not infrequently, unconstitutional strikes
are illegitimately condemned either because the union concerned
is not recognised or the procedure agreement is non-existent
or inadequate (Ibid.; pp.169-70). Trade union recognition has
indeed been a main concern of the TUC for it is an indispensable condition for the legitimate functioning of trade unionism
and collective bargaining – the fundamental rights to organise
and bargain – since it entails the employer recognising the
authority and representative nature of the union. But it has
only been through union struggles that employers have been
forced to accept this situation. The history of this issue
again supports the factual and normative autonomy of trade
unions from the state: 'The fact that trade unions in Britain
have succeeded through their own efforts in strengthening their
organisation and in obtaining recognition, not relying on the
assistance of Government through legislation, is one of the
most important factors sustaining their strength and independence. Trade unions have not been given privileges ... Trade
union strength has been developed without the help of any
external agency' (WE, 1968, p.171). Thus the roots of trade
union autonomy coalesce with social democracy in a way that is
ideologically if not always factually inimical to corporatism.

It has therefore been a clear implication of the TUC's
position to oppose the development of a system of labour courts
if this involved the use of a judicial approach to industrial
relations (Ibid.; pp.176-7). It similarly and vehemently
opposed the CBI's proposal to make collective agreements enforceable at law because it did not suit the overall climate
of British industrial relations and because the formal legal
equality between employer and employee contrasted with their
substantive economic inequality (Ibid.; pp.178-9). These themes
emerge in the TUC's specific consideration of the law on industrial conflict, concentrating upon the seemingly precarious
legal nature of the right to take industrial action. Of grave
concern here for the TUC has been 'the problem of judge-made
law', that is, the power of the judges to interpret existing
statutes without being constrained by them in order to pass
judgements detrimental to the interests of trade unionism.

This analysis adds great weight to the TUC's opposition to state (especially legal) interventionism in industrial relations (Ibid.; pp.179-83).

Conclusions

The above analysis has tried to take stock of the TUC's ideological conception of itself at a particularly crucial point in time: when class conflict was becoming more clearly accentuated; when the courts were again more legally coercive of unions and when such coercion was also on the agenda of governments; when capital had reached the point at which it deemed reform imperative and when a Royal Commission was to report in order to highlight this need further; and when trade unions were themselves becoming mechanisms for controlling industrial conflict and when the TUC's part in all this was becoming more and more prominent. The argument has therefore identified the social democratic ideology espoused by the TUC and pointed out how this is, in one regard, highly conducive to close collaboration between the state and the TUC in controlling industrial conflict since the involvement of trade unions with the state can be seen as a social-democratic extension of the power of trade unions within the state. But it was also pointed out that this very ideology and practice likewise poses severe contradictions for the state because its stress on the fundamental primacy of trade union autonomy and trade union rights to organise, to free collective bargaining and to strike free from external surveillance and coercion, has formed an often overriding constraint on the state's attempt to use trade unions and the TUC as agencies of social control. In other words, both for the unions and the state there are crucial contradictions as well as complementarities between social democracy and corporatism.

As far as the internal contradictions of social democratic practice and ideology are concerned in terms of its normative relationship to capitalism, the analysis endeavoured to extract a significant contradiction of the same order as that already outlined in that it refers to the relationship between trade unionism and British capitalism. On the one hand, trade unionism always has been inimical to key institutional features of capitalism and has suggested the possibility of alternative forms of organisation. As the TUC itself recognised, 'trade unionists do not believe in competition as the main driving force in society. Trade unions have always been in this sense "in restraint of trade" ... Trade Unionists believe in co-operation' (Ibid.; p.184). However, on the other hand, the specific social democratic inflexion given to this kind of argument has to be noted - co-operation, after all, clearly means co-operation with employers as well. Accordingly, the analysis above also tried to identify how the TUC's conception of trade unionism confined it very much within the contours of capitalist society by defining its rights and objectives from within rather than outside the framework set for the property rights of capital by the labour contract which legally structures relations of production between capital and labour. In this sense, trade unionism is incorporated within the constraints of capitalism but in a contradictory rather than in a functional manner and it is this which in turn imposes constraints upon capital and upon the state.

The initial establishment of the incomes policy vetting machinery, the stipulation that incomes policies also cover profits and dividends, the growing disenchantment with incomes policies, the concerted bargaining over the dropping of the penal clauses in 'In Place of Strife', the outright opposition to the IR Act, the explicit reluctance to acknowledge the Heath Government's incomes policies, the enthusiastic support for the Labour Government's 'social contract', incomes guidelines and the Employment Protection Act, and the relatively unrestrained hostility to Thatcherism can all be explained, in part, in terms of such contradictions and their roots in the material nature of class conflict. Clearly the rank and file militancy of powerful shop floor groups has not merely made itself felt on capital accumulation but has had its influential effects within the councils of the TUC itself and has constrained TUC policy in so far as it has been forced to recognise its consti-tuency, the interests of workers at their place of work, as well as the demands of class co-operation or the interests of the state as the fundamental axis of social democratic practice. Thus, the opposition to incomes policies and 'In Place of Strife' in the last two years of the 1964-1970 Labour Govern-ment and to the IR Act, in particular, can be traced to this causal factor which has its structural analogue in the way in which trade unionism is inimical to British capitalism.

However, the TUC has collaborated closely, usually of course with Labour Governments, over the imposition of incomes policy guidelines and TUC rather than Government formulated codes of practice for the conduct of industrial relations,[6] more tentatively and spasmodically with the 1964-1970 Labour Government, more systematically and more consistently with the 1974-1979 Labour Government's 'social contract'. This has, in an important respect, derived from what the TUC has seen as a quid pro quo - namely, trade union (mainly TUC supervised) participation in economic policy-making and the adoption of policies more favourable to the interests of trade unions. Thus, in return for incomes policy vetting in 1965 and 1966, as we have already noted, the TUC saw itself as being given a leading role in the machinery of economic planning. The national plan was in fact scuppered and the trade unions were left with a subordinate place in the NEDC and on the EDC's while successive incomes policies became more repressive (see Panitch: 1976). Again, the TUC's voluntary agreement to the pay criteria established by the last Labour Government was dep-endent upon the role it seemed to be promised in the industrial

134

strategy, and the legislative support that would be engendered
for TUC policies and trade union interests by the Employment
Protection Act and the intention, stated but never fulfilled,
to legislate on industrial democracy. In this case, the social
contract ultimately was undermined by rank and file opposition
to the 5 per cent pay norm in the winter of 1978. But the very
fact that such co-operation has been possible and has been welcomed by trade unionists and has for some periods actually
worked - in the latter case, incomes policy guidelines were
more or less adhered to from 1975 to 1977 - requires some
explanation.

I think this can be attempted, partially at least, precisely in terms of the reasons why the TUC thought fit to par-
ticipate with government, namely the extension of trade union
power within the state. This is the etatist side of social
democratic ideology and one thing which distinguishes it from
liberal democracy. As part of its underlying ideology the TUC
has sought not merely protection by and from the state but
also a position of influence within it, such as is afforded by
participation in the process of economic planning. Thus the
quid pro quos offered for TUC - and indeed trade union - support
for incomes and industrial relations policies offered a fulfilment of this ideology, the social democratic extension of trade
union influence within the state and the beneficial effects of
state intervention. This has its structural analogue in the way
in which trade unionism is accommodated to British capitalism.

The corporatist policies of the state are therefore subjected to the constraints of the opposition of the organised
working class not only when they come up against union rank
and file hostility to such policies but also when the co-operation of trade unions with the policies of the state is thwarted
because TUC and trade union leaders recoil from the corporatist
consequences of social democratic ideology and politics. Corporatism is not, as Jessop has it, 'the highest form of social
democracy' (1978), but is, because it treats trade unions as
more or less explicit agencies of social control and finds its
greatest opposition from the working class at the point of production, in crucial contradiction with social democracy as far
as trade unionism and its relation to the state is concerned.
After all, social democracy is not merely the contrivance of
the state and the trade union bureaucracy but also has very
strong and extensive social and historical roots within the
British working class itself, including its most militant sectors, in a way that its corporatist overtones and implications
with regard to the role of trade unionism within the state have
never had. The contradiction that social democracy therefore
holds for trade unionism - support for trade union industrial
autonomy within the labour contract and the separation of politics and industrial relations in contrast with its corporatist
consequence for trade unions as agents of the state in virtue
of its goal of trade union involvement with the state in

135

economic planning - forms the specific political distillation
of the way in which, in general, trade unionism is both incorporated in but hostile to the dictates and constraints of
British capitalism.

2. Official Unionism, Trade Union Leadership and Shop Steward Organisation

It is necessary here to consider also the ideologies and structures of interests characterising the leadership strata of the
major trade unions and shop steward led rank and file work
groups and how these and their relationship to the state have
changed in the period under consideration. In particular men-
tion has to be made of the attempts by both capital and the
state to incorporate and institutionalise the role of shop
floor leaders of powerful work groups in order to enforce
policy more effectively at the work place.

Although they have been very much involved in the committees and General Council of the TUC and in bargaining with
governments the leaderships of official trade unionism have
remained firmly wedded to the tenets of social democracy.[7]
However, it is essential to note here that there have been
important exceptions. At the time of the Donovan Commission
it is possible to discern corporatist leanings in some unions.
The Amalgamated Engineering Union (AEU - later the AUEW), for
example, implied that if legislation were introduced enforcing
the closed shop - a sine qua non of effective unionism - then
it would itself consider penalising and outlawing the unofficial strike (ME, 24, 1966, pp.935-7). It has to be remarked
that this proposal was made in the context of indicating the
increasingly important role of economic planning and the increasing need for trade unions to play a full and effective
part in this development (Ibid.). The Union of Shop, Distributive and Allied Workers sketched in a very similar background
to its claim for a legal right for unions to organise, to be
recognised and to be granted the closed shop. In return for
these statutory provisions it said that unions would be prepared to 'eliminate' the 'trouble-makers' (ME, 29, 1966, pp.
1120-23 and 1128-45).[8]

However, this stand on legal corporatism has been hardly
characteristic of the union movement in Britain. Even the AEU
and, to a lesser extent USDAW, in effect came out against the
use of the law and legal sanctions in industrial relations,
relying rather on the autonomy of trade unions buttressed
where essential by limiting and limited government intervention (AEU, op. cit., pp.960-6. USDAW, op. cit., pp.1126-7).
Both these examples exhibit some degree of ambiguity to say
the least over the use of the law in industrial relations, in
terms of wholesale and principled opposition to it on the one
hand combined with, on the other, the quid pro quo of legal

136

corporatism - the legalisation of unions in exchange for the
expulsion of unofficial strikers. However, it would be consistent with the pressure group conception of parliamentary democracy - the law can be used to cure problems that unions by
means of collective bargaining alone cannot alleviate and it
therefore becomes in their interest to pursue this course, the
legalising of union recognition and the closed shop, even if
the basic principle of legalism is opposed. But since pressure
group politics is also a process of bargaining, something must
be given in return - union surveillance of unofficial strikes.
This parliamentarism, a leading political motif in the more
all-embracing ideology of social democracy, in fact characterises the great majority of the examples of trade union interests
and objectives that can be brought to light and analysed. Such
major unions were, of course, also subject to pressures from
the shop floor similar to those affecting the TUC, as well as
capital and the state, which likewise thwarted to varying extents their capacity to act as agents of social control
(Panitch: 1977a; 500).

We may take the TGWU as our archetypal example here. The
basic theme of its evidence was the claim, 'we must make our
contribution as a trade union, and not as agents of even the
most enlightened Government' (TGWU, ME, 30, 1966, p.1160). Any
government limitation on free collective bargaining had therefore to be made part of a planned economy, otherwise unions
should maintain sole responsibility for the interests of their
members, and for the contribution they could make to the economic advancement both of their membership and of the economy as
a whole (Ibid.; pp.1161-2). In its espousal of the cause of
trade unionism the TGWU made plain its support for the closed
shop, which was seen as the responsibility of the trade union
and which was not to be achieved by legislation but by means
of free collective bargaining (Ibid.; pp.1163-4 and 1221-7).
However, the TGWU saw the need for legislation to impose a
statutory obligation on employers to recognise unions and engage in collective bargaining (Ibid.; pp.1164-5 and 1203-1206).

The TGWU stressed the importance of the strike weapon,
including unofficial strikes, for the defence of the interests
of labour. Employers were seen as much if not more responsible
for most disputes and so legal sanctions on strikes were seen
as harmful and unwarranted transgressions of a fundamental
right. Also, it pointed out that unions often gave official
backing to what were initially unofficial strikes if investigation concluded that the strikers had a fair case (Ibid.; pp.
1178-80 and pp.1227-33). Associated with this, the TGWU mentioned the value to orderly industrial relations of the role
of the shop steward, pointing to its effect in preventing
industrial disputes. It recognised the increased factual
importance of the shop steward in local bargaining and supported
the formal recognition of this role but stewards had frequently
to deal with hostile, self-assertive or inert managements who

137

consequently did not recognise the contribution that the steward had to make to the management of industrial conflict.
Recognition of the role of shop stewards was seen in the first
instance as a task for voluntary negotiations but if this
failed the possibility of legal provision was openly embraced,
including such things as special protection for shop stewards
against dismissal purely because they were stewards and the
use of an independent authority to judge such dismissals as
part of a much broader machinery to deal with dismissals (Ibid.;
pp.1180-2 and pp.1236-8). Clearly the TGWU, and the then ETU
and GMWU (see GMWU, ME, 42, 1966. ETU, ME, 57, 1966) represented early examples of the process of incorporating the leaders
of workplace power and pre-figured even the more formalised
recommendations made by the Donovan Commission.

On the question of the use of the law in industrial relations, save for what has already been said about recognition,
dismissal and shop stewards, the TGWU set itself firmly against
its use.[9] It rejected legal sanctions on strikes because this
conflicted with the fundamental right of workers to withdraw
their labour, a right essential to counter the power of employers and to ensure effective collective bargaining. Legal
sanctions did not deal with the source of strikes, workers'
grievances, and were seen as being most likely to inflame
rather than pacify industrial relations. What it saw as most
needed in this regard was more effective de facto joint regulation of industrial relations rather than the employer being
'judge and jury'. It saw this as being possible without state
intervention. It thus rejected employers' proposals regarding
the registration of trade unions. It was not compulsory registration nor the Registrar's powers to see that trade unions
properly applied their rules per se that it objected to, but
the fact that the proposals meant that the Registrar would do
the job of the trade union in the administration of its constitution, restricting the rights of autonomous trade unionism
(ME, op. cit., p.1234).

The general ambivalence of the union movement towards the
role of the state in industrial relations has been continued
with varying degrees of accentuation ever since. The early
years of the Wilson government and the middle years of the
Callaghan Government elicited union support and co-operation
however grudging and tenuous may have been its basis, while
'In Place of Strife', the latter phase of the Wilson government's incomes policies and the Heath Government, 1970-1974,
were generally characterised by union opposition and hostility
to state intervention. However, within these historical trends
some variations and distinctions within and between unions
have to be noted as the above analysis has indicated. While
most unions have generally remained within the framework of
social democracy, some have gravitated towards corporatism as
this has begun to be favoured and adopted by certain sections
of the state and capital as a means of controlling industrial

conflict, and which probably reached its institutional high-point during the maintenance of the 'social contract' by the last Labour Government. Conversely, throughout most of this period the rank-and-file, shop floor movement has tended to stress most strongly in its actions the structure of free collective bargaining and the ineradicably autonomous nature of union bargaining at the work place, untrammelled by controls imposed by either the state or the official union bureaucracy. The rank-and-file revolt against the 5 per cent voluntary incomes policy, in the winter of 1978, exemplifies the continuation of this source of working class militancy and hostility to the corporate state.

But important and far-reaching qualifications need to be entertained regarding this conclusion. The scope for, and the extent of, the incorporation of shop stewards and other rank-and-file leaderships into the official, bureaucratic hierarchy of their unions and their recognition and role within the more institutionalised frameworks of collective bargaining at company and plant level that had begun to be developed post-Donovan, has to be underlined as an important phenomenon. But we have also seen earlier, more emergent signs of this process in the way in which some major unions were already prepared in the mid-1960s to recognise, institutionalise and more consciously make use of the role of the shop steward. This in itself as well as the way in which the strategies of some employers invited plant-level bargaining, e.g. productivity bargaining, thereby carving out a more formalised place for the on-the-spot representatives of local work groups, has paved the way for the incorporation of shop steward organisations. And this was subsequently articulated as a policy by the Donovan Commission (1968; pp.185-9). It is by no means suggested that this is an even, accomplished or necessarily very extensive process but its strategic significance and effect have to be recognised in that it provides for capital and the state an appealing way of directly meeting the source of the threat that working class militancy has come to pose to capital accumulation since the late 1950s (see Hyman: 1978. Idem: 1979).

With the increased recognition of shop stewards by management in the post-Donovan era, coupled with more formalised collective bargaining and the further growth of monopoly, multi-plant companies, the 1960s pattern of highly localised, shop-steward led workplace bargaining has begun to give way to more centralised bargaining and a formalised role for shop stewards.[10] There has therefore occurred in parts of industry the entrenchment of a hierarchical centralisation of control within shop steward organisation and its formalised involvement in collective bargaining. It has also become more integrated into the structures of official unionism and company bargaining,[11] and where this process has been adopted and fostered it has been found beneficial by capital and been strengthened by state legislation to further collective bargaining and 'institutionalise' workplace representation (e.g. the EP Act, 1975).

NOTES

1.   Although I cannot enter into an extensive discussion here, such an observation obviously derives from what has been said to characterise working class consciousness as a whole, namely simultaneous and conflicting support for and opposition to capitalism; accordingly, the contradiction I have identified can be seen as a more specific and definite manifestation of this in the realm of political values. See, e.g., Mann: 1970. Idem: 1973. Giddens: 1973.

2.   Much of the evidence for the above can be found in Chapter 2. But see especially Miliband: 1972. Idem: 1973. Bendix: 1969.

3.   As is suggested by Crouch: 1977.

4.   A major if not overriding influence on this as well as the fostering of social democracy in general has been that exercised by the Labour Party. See Panitch: 1976.

5.   These and subsequent formulations on the nature of the labour contract are derived from (and elaborated upon) the work of B. Edelman (see B. Edelman: 1980).

6.   Cf. Labour Government - TUC Joint Statement: February 1979.

7.   For more details of the policies of the leaderships of the major unions see Panitch: 1976. Idem: 1977a. Crouch: 1977. Idem: 1978.

8.   See also for a union proposal on the need for legislative action to ensure the rights to organise, to recognition and to collective bargaining, ASSET (later ASTMS), ME, 53,1966.

9.   For other examples amongst trade unions of this stand other than those cited in the main text see, e.g., ETU, ME, 57, 1966. NALGO, ME, 26, 1966. NUR, ME, 17, 1966.

10.   One estimate suggests that the number of full-time shop stewards in private manufacturing industry rose from approximately 1,000 in 1966 to approximately 5,000 in 1976 (Brown and Terry: 1978; 659. Cf. Brown et al.: 1978. Terry: 1978).

11.   The best, overall, detailed analyses of this process are Hyman: 1979. Benyon: 1975. Terry: 1978.

Chapter 7

THE STATE, POLITICAL CONFLICT AND THE ROLE OF THE LAW IN
INDUSTRIAL RELATIONS POLICY, 1957-1968

In analysing the role of the state in industrial relations in
Britain from 1960 onwards I wish mainly to do two things; first
in this chapter I shall concentrate upon some of the political
factions and conflicts directly associated with this role and,
in the next, upon the course and nature of the policy and legislation of the state as it evolved during this conjuncture,
where in both the main emphasis will be placed upon class conflict and class interests, political conflict, existing state
agencies and the development of state policies. In the subsequent and penultimate chapter I shall concentrate upon the
implications of what has been said so far for the institutions
of the state, the actual re-organisation of the structures of
the state for the purpose of intervening in industrial relations and the actual forms of such intervention; here the main
emphasis will be placed upon class conflict and class interests,
political conflict and the re-structuring of state apparatuses
- how the state itself has had to be changed to intervene in
industrial relations. As such, the first theme will be oriented
towards changes in state policies, while the second will be
more closely involved with examples of changes in state institutions. Thus in this chapter and the next I shall consider
the structural process defined by the involvement of political
groupings and state agencies in the elaboration of policies for
reforming industrial relations in the light of the industrial
relations crisis, the role of the courts in attempting to introduce the legal coercion of paternalism into industrial relations, the Donovan Commission and its recommendations, 'In
Place of Strife', the IR Act of 1971, the EP Act of 1975, and
industrial democracy. It is not, of course, always easy or
possible to separate policy from institutional issues and no
attempt will be made to do so in an artificial manner. But in
so far as it is possible the penultimate chapter will detail
the changing interventionist role of the state in terms of the
transformation - or, more correctly, attempted transformations
- of state apparatuses and the relationship between Government,
Parliament and the Courts by analysing in historical sequence

the role of the Ministry of Labour, the NIRC and the CIR and the advent of ACAS.

The Law, Tory Lawyers and Corporatism

This study has placed great emphasis upon the endeavours of capital in developing strategic responses to the challenges posed to its control by the re-assertion of working class power at the productive base and the consequent escalation of industrial conflict. One central policy in this respect has relied upon the introduction of corporatism into industrial relations by means of radical changes in trade union law. And as we have seen this has drawn the support of leading representatives of UK based monopoly and multi-national capital, particularly as it has been expressed by the CBI and EEF. It was not, however, with this fraction of capital that this strategy found one of its first and most systematic, coherent and elaborate public and propagandist declarations. It was later to be enshrined as official Tory policy with the publication of 'Fair Deal at Work' in 1968. But its major rationale and themes were propagated ten years earlier in a sophisticated manner, appropriately enough by a leading group of lawyers within the Conservative Party, what was then called 'The Inns of Court Conservative and Unionist Society' (ICCUS), in a publication entitled 'A Giant's Strength: Some Thoughts on the Constitutional and the Legal Position of Trade Unions in England'.

This argued that the origin of the problem of trade union power was to be found in the fallacy of laissez-faire. The philosophy of laissez-faire, as it developed along with industrial capitalism in the nineteenth century, assumed that the contractual relationship at work of capital and labour was an equal one, governed by the market laws of supply and demand. Therefore it argued that free bargaining between an individual employer and an individual worker was the most efficient economic arrangement, so combinations of workers, trade unions, were seen by economic theory, the law and employers alike as acting 'in restraint of trade'. This, however, was a fallacy for the labour contract was not based on free and equal terms; the worker was not only not as mobile as capital but was 'at a disadvantage in comparison with the employer who has greater knowledge and resources at his disposal' (1958: 9). For those Tories in the nineteenth century who could not accept nor rely upon the economic rationality of the commodity status of labour and the deprived position of the worker with respect to the employer something had to be done: 'without the right to combine and without, when necessary, the right to strike, the workman could not bargain fairly with his employer' (Ibid.;10). Hence, Conservative governments legislated these rights into existence. The result of this achievement, however, has 'meant that the trade union and its members of today occupy a privileged position under the law.... These privileges put them in a position of great power' (Ibid.; 11). The Tory lawyers[1] thus

142

saw individual freedom being threatened and since the law ensures this freedom then there had to be something wrong with
its influence over trade union power. This is seen as having
its detrimental repercussions both on the national economic
interest and on the liberty of the individual: with respect to
the national economic interest trade union power had given rise
to strikes and restrictive practices, while the liberty of the
individual had been basically infringed by the closed shop
(Ibid.; 14-16).

The Tory lawyers, however, did not dispute in their recommendation the right of individuals to withdraw their own labour
since this constituted a 'fundamental civil liberty' (Ibid.;
17). What they wanted to get at was the concerted nature of
the strike for this was viewed as infringing individual liberty
and contributing to low productivity and disruptions in production (Ibid.; 20). However, there was deemed to be a minimum
level of collective strike action that ought to be available to
the worker to counteract the power of the employer (Ibid.; 19).

In proposing a solution to the strike problem ICCUS saw a
well-informed public opinion as the most effective sanction
that could be employed against strikes, dismissing as impracti-
cal because of the potentially large numbers involved the use
of the normal sanctions of the law courts. Therefore, to allow
information on a dispute to be gathered and disseminated and
public opinion to have its say, unilateral reference of a dispute to a fact finding independent tribunal was suggested. The
sanction that was to be applied to strikes called in breach of
the operations and report of the tribunal was to be the removal
of the protection given to the strikers by the 1875 and 1906
Acts. And this protection was to be further restricted to registered unions. The latter meant that the proposals dealt adep-
tly with the problem of unofficial strikes for these by definition could not be called by a registered union, unofficial
strikes being subject to the possibility of civil and criminal
proceedings since it was thought that 'this would do much to
strengthen the position of the trade unions: in effect it would
ensure that only an official strike backed by a registered
union could ever legally take place' (Ibid.; 23, my emphasis).
In fact, unofficial rather than official strikes were already
seen as the major problem for, since 1945, they had 'far exceeded official strikes in numbers and in the damage they have
caused' (Ibid.; 24).

In many ways the problem of trade unionism was seen mainly
as one of how to bring the power that it wielded within the
constitution and the rule of law for it was only if this was
achieved that this power would become beneficial to its members
and be in keeping with the national interest, while the unions
would become 'the new estate of the realm'. The Acts of 1871,
1875 and 1906 had placed the unions beyond the rule of law so
the ICCUS sought 'to suggest ways in which a settlement might
be reached that would regulate the relationship of trade unions

143

with the state by bringing them under the rule of law' (Ibid.;
53). And indeed this was seen as equally as problematic and as
equally as pressing as the economic problems that trade union
power was seen to engender.

What, in effect, the ICCUS did was to set the ball rolling
on the need to reform the trade unions and to set it rolling in
the direction of a legalised corporatism which relied on increased state intervention in the affairs and rules of trade
unions, through the Registrar and independent tribunals, providing for strong, responsible, official trade union organisation. And we can likewise note in this context how it supported
the buttressing of the authority of the TUC. These reforms were
put forward in response to what was seen as a combined legal
and economic crisis and set the framework for the debate over
subsequent policies and factional support for the corporatisation of trade unions. The ICCUS's intervention was one of the
first in the 'orchestration' by a particular grouping of interests with this aim in view; and this 'bloc' also included the
Conservative Party, the CBI, and the EEF. It was not a conspiracy by any means but it was an attempt to construct a particular response to a crisis, to mobilise popular and class based
(i.e. capital) political support and to attempt to ensure that
it became state policy. The policy of legal corporatism for
industrial relations was thus as much a result of political
practice and the strategy of policy construction as it was of
systematic, structural constraints and economic class interests,
although it was formulated within such limits.

In this sense it is interesting to note how many groups
of lawyers[2] elaborated and supported similar sets of reforms
to those worked out by the ICCUS, which itself put forward a
similar line of approach in the evidence it presented to the
Donovan Commission. It now explicitly suggested the setting up
of a National Industrial Relations Court, presided over by a
high court judge, to rule on union rules and appeals from the
Registrar and the Ministry of Labour, to grant injunctions and
to award damages in order to secure the cessation of strikes
or the continuation of work. Appeal was possible to the House
of Lords and thus the jurisdiction of the NIRC was to be judicial rather than executive (ME, 35, 1966, pp.1478-80). It retained its views of the closed shop, and supported a narrow
definition of peaceful picketing which had been established
in the Tynan case (Ibid.; pp.1480-4 and 1502-1506).

One of the things the new Court would have to do would be
to consider collective agreements for a suggested provision
was to be made for them to be legally enforceable if both sides
were so willing. Allowing in the rules of a union as a basis
for registration the authorisation for making such agreements
was seen as a way of strengthening 'the central leadership of
all unions' (Ibid.; 1484-5). The idea here was that employers
would have rights over unions to enforce collective agreements
and unions would have rights against any of their members in

144

breach of agreements thereby increasing the strength and responsibility of trade union leaders, ensuring the codification
of the chain of authority within unions, and securing adherence
to collective agreements: breaches of such agreements were no
longer to be protected by the 1906 Act (Ibid.; pp. 1484-7 and
1496-1502). It also proposed that with a dispute giving rise to
grave national economic loss or widespread hindrance to public
·health and safety, i.e. national emergencies, the NIRC be empowered to order the suspension of a strike or lock-out for 60
days so as to assert the national interest (Ibid.; pp.1479 and
1510).

The ICCUS in effect saw its aim as being to bring trade
union power under the rule of law (Ibid.; pp. 1490-1).
It thus wanted to redefine the terrain of class conflict: it
saw unofficial, unconstitutional and sympathetic strikes,
blacking etc., as the main battles and wanted to see them
fought on a different basis, one defined by the legal reforms
it had constructed - 'they are the battles that take place on
the present frontier. We should like to shift the frontier'
(Ibid.; p.1509). And it wanted to make trade unions agents of
social control in the field of industrial relations. Hence, it
saw its proposals on the removal of protection of sections 1
and 3 of the 1906 Act for unofficial strikes, the inducement
of trade unions not to support members in breach of collective
agreements, and encouraging trade unions to establish definite
rules either disciplining or recovering damages from recalcitrant members, serving to 'greatly strengthen the hands of both
the union leadership and of the employer in dealing with unofficial trouble makers acting contrary to union policy'
·(Ibid.; p.1512).

The Courts, Paternalism and the Control of Industrial Conflict
At about the same time the judiciary was similarly engaged in
dealing with the trade union problem in cases involving them
which came within their jurisdiction. In a series of decisions
from the late 1950s onwards the Courts, and in particular the
House of Lords, reversed what had previously been thought to
be the proper legal status for unions to engage in what had
come to be regarded as normal union activities. The courts
attempted to change this as we shall see when we look in detail
at a number of major decisions which have been considered by
some as indications of a return to legal interventionism or
coercion. But I want to dispute at the outset this lack of
conceptual precision for I shall contend that the strategy of
the judiciary is best designated as paternalism. By this I mean
that the intent and implication of the judiciary's decisions
has been to heteronomise trade unions, to restrict their autonomy by external, regulatory laws placing their ultimate source
of authority outside their own organisation, but to do this
within the rule of law, the existing statutes and institutions
and not by placing trade unions under the tutelage and direction

of an external agency, the state and a new system of industrial relations courts. The court's mediation of industrial relations has thus been of a laissez-faire rather than an interventionist kind; it has not been designed to increase state intervention into industrial relations at all but rather to minimise it by confining it to the strictly defined limits under which the courts can actually interfere in industrial relations. It differs very markedly in this respect from the IR Act whose objective was the more detailed intervention of the state. The existing rule of law has been the thing the decisions of the courts have been upholding and this does not sanction wholesale and extensive intervention: hence, in some part, the resort to corporatism.

We saw in Chapter 2 how after the very noticeable phase of judicial opposition to trade unionism, which lasted from roughly the 1890s to the early 1920s, a more liberal and accepting view began to be taken by the courts of what constituted the legitimate aims and functions of trade unions. However, this trend was reversed in the 1960s as the judiciary once again began to impose legal controls on trade unions, illustrating again the constrained character of the legal incorporation of organised labour. The ending of the liberal orientation of the courts towards trade unions, which recognised collective organisation and action as legitimate objectives, was marked most notably by the House cf Lords' decision in Rookes v Barnard, 1964. But other cases were also indicative of a change in the approach of the courts. The call for legislation to control strikes was thus being voiced in a context in which the diminution of trade union rights had begun to be effected by the judiciary (Wedderburn: 1971; 387). The recognition of the collective legitimacy of unions was therefore succeeded by paternalism, organised by the judiciary by means of its mediatory and cohering functions which are implicit in the notion of judge-made law (Ibid.; 480-481).

Beginning with the question of picketing, it is possible to argue that certain judicial decisions raised great doubts about the legality of peaceful picketing previously established by statute law. In Piddlington v Bates (1960) and Tynan v Bulmer (1966) picketing workers were found guilty of obstruction, notwithstanding the provision of section 2 of the 1906 Act, in that 'their conduct in sealing off a part of the highway by this moving circle' constituted 'a nuisance at common law as an unreasonable use of the highway'. This meant that the right to picket became uncertain due to the fact that section 2 of the 1906 Act does not apply if there is an actual or prospective common law 'nuisance'. While picketing is usually more effective in practice than these judgements allow and the police do not normally intervene (as they did in these two cases), except when violence or serious obstruction occurs, these decisions are indicative of the change noted in the judicial orientation towards trade union cases (Ibid.; 324-7).

146

The actual definition of a trade dispute and the legal immunities associated with it as provided for by the 1906 Act, were similarly called into question by the courts. As such 'before 1920 and after 1956 the courts have shown tendencies to restrict the area covered' (Ibid.; 330-1 and 374). In Stratford v Lindley (1964), for example, the decision of a company to negotiate an agreement on employment conditions with the TGWU only, led the Waterman's Union (which also had workers in the company) to place an embargo on barges hired out and repaired by another of Stratford's companies. Its officials were therefore sued and the House of Lords found against them, in part, on the ground that the union was not involved in a trade dispute: the Law Lords held that the case concerned 'mere inter-union rivalry and [was] just a matter of prestige for the Watermen'(Ibid.; 332-4). This change in judicial interpretation was confirmed by Torquay Hotel Co. v Cousins, in 1969 (Ibid.; 334-7).

It is, however, the attitude of the courts to the very right to strike that assumes the greatest significance in terms of the re-appearance of the imposition of legal controls by the judiciary over trade union activities. One means by which judicial intervention can penalise strikers is given by the fact that the 1906 Act only protects inducements of breaches of contracts of employment, and not breaches of other types of contract (Ibid.; 351). This would appear to depend on the law breaker's knowledge of such contracts, but in Emerald Construction Ltd. v Lowthian (1966), which was decided against the union officials, Lord Denning delivered the following judgement: 'it is unlawful for a third person to procure a breach of contract knowingly, or recklessly, indifferent whether it is a breach or not' (Quoted, ibid.; 351). A similar view was taken by the Law Lords in Stratford v Lindley (1964); although previous cases had demanded actual knowledge and intent, 'recklessness had begun to be enough' (Ibid.). The notion of inducements in respect of breaches of contract also came to be given wider connotations. In Thomson v Deakin (1952), Lord Justice Jenkins decided that calls by union officials for the 'blacking' of a company and its goods were not inducements to unlawful action (Ibid.; 375). But by the 1960s judicial attitudes had changed, and this decision was reversed in Stratford v Lindley (1964), while in the Torquay hotel case, although the Imperial hotel did not have a contract with Alternative Fuels, the union's intention to 'black' supplies led to an injunction being granted by the courts against the officials concerned because 'the officials sued had shown an intention to prevent supplies being delivered if any such contract were made' (Ibid.; 375 and 353-7). The ramifications of this case extended even further, however. Union officials had also managed to prevent delivery of supplies of fuel from Esso, with whom the Imperial did have a contract. This contract contained a clause removing liability from either party for non-fulfilment of the terms as

147

a result of, among other things, labour disputes. Thus, 'the
judicial extension of this tort of inducing "breach" of commercial contracts (contracts of supply, hire, repair, sale, etc.,
regularly made by employers) is a most effective weapon to
shrink the legality of union action in trade disputes' (Ibid.;
357-8. cf. 337-79).

The case that in a way most characterised this transitional
process was Rookes v Barnard (1964), 'the most important decision on trade disputes since the passing of the 1906 Act, undermining as it did the protection given to trade union officials
and members by creating or developing the tort of intimidation'
(Citrine: 1967; 28).[3] Rookes was employed as a draughtsman by
BOAC at London Airport where the Association of Engineering and
Shipbuilding Draughtsmen had an informal 100 per cent membership agreement. He resigned from the union in November 1955.
The union resolved to inform BOAC that they would strike if
Rookes were not removed from his post. He was dismissed from
duty on 16 March 1956, BOAC having given him due notice to
quit. Rookes had no legal remedy against BOAC since it had not
committed a breach of contract or tort. Therefore in 1957 he
sued the union instead, Rookes claiming that he was damaged by
'civil intimidation'. The union's threat to strike, if effected,
would have involved a breach of the contract of employment, for
an undertaking that no strike or lock-out would take place had
been written into the contract.

In the initial case, Mr. Justice Sachs decided Rookes had
a good cause for action and the jury awarded him £7,500 damages.
The Court of Appeal unanimously reversed this decision, holding
that Rookes had no cause of action at common law, and that anyway the defendants were protected by the 1906 Act. The House
of Lords, in turn, upheld the original decision. This meant
that 'the threat to strike in breach of contract was held to
constitute the tort of intimidation, and since this tort is
actionable, independently of the element of combination it fell
outside the protection given by section 1 of the 1906 Act'
(Ibid.; 29). The justificatory precedent that was used concerned a case in 1793, in which a sea captain had had to pay
damages for intimidation to a rival trader because he had
fired cannons near the canoes of customers in order to scare
them away from trading with his rival. It was argued by Rookes
that he had been placed in a similar position to that of the
rival trader, save that he was damaged by the threat to strike
in breach of contract rather than by his proximity to cannon
fire. The case therefore hinged upon whether a breach of contract is unlawful for the purpose of intimidation in the same
way that violence is unlawful. In reaching their decision, the
House of Lords, 'for the first time ... classified breach of
contract as similar to violence ... a coercive threat of a
breach of contract gave a cause of action just like a coercive
threat of violence' (Wedderburn: 1971; 364). There is little
doubt that, here, as with other cases, judicial intervention

148

formed a way of extending legal control over strikes. For example, Lord Hodson remarked, 'The injury and suffering caused by strike action is very often widespread as well as devastating and a threat to strike would be expected to be certainly no less serious than a threat of violence'; and Lord Devlin found 'nothing to differentiate a threat of a breach of contract from a threat of physical violence' (Quoted, Wedderburn: 1971; 364. Cf.Citrine: 1967; 624). The Lords, in effect, evolved a general common law doctrine that was applicable to all breaches of contract, embracing go-slows and acts of disobedience as well as strikes. As in the past, this served to antagonise the trade union movement, inducing it to obtain a political remedy. The anxiety of trade unionists turned out to be well founded in fact since as in the past, the Rookes decision was followed, in the short time before it was repealed by an Act of Parliament, by a series of actions brought against trade unions (Citrine: 1967; 30. Cf. Wedderburn: 1971, 370-1).[4]

The political solution argued for by trade unions was fairly quickly provided, albeit in a highly limited fashion, by the Labour Government in 1965. It did little however to abate the development of innovatory legal controls by the courts over union activities, as has been described above. The Trade Disputes Act of 1965 denoted the re-emergence of the social structural process associated with cases, such as Taff Vale: judicial coercion evoking a political response on the part of organised labour in the face of which the government adopts a limited, legislative compromise. The Act itself stipulated that action 'in contemplation or furtherance of a trade dispute' was not to be actionable in tort if it entailed a threat that a contract of employment would be broken, or a threat to induce a breach of a contract of employment (Wedderburn: 1971; 371. Citrine: 1967; 30 and 623-9). It was designed to restore the legal situation which was thought to exist before Rookes v Barnard and thus as a holding operation to restore the status quo pending the report of the Royal Commission on Trade Unions and Employers Associations on the whole ambit of issues involved in trade union law and practice.

A number of points in respect of this Act must be noted. Firstly, even in 1964, the trade unions' 'right to strike' was by no means secure in law, illustrating the controlled nature of organised labour's legal incorporation. This is related to a second feature of the Act, the constraints built into it as a result of the manufactured compromise effected by the government. As such, the Act did 'not strike at the central common law issue in that [Rookes v Barnard] case, namely, that a threat to break a contract may amount to the tort of intimidation' (Citrine: 1967; 625). Concomitantly, 'it [applied] ... only to contracts of employment' (Wedderburn: 1971; 372). The statutory protections afforded to trade unions by the 1965 Act were to be short-lived, not merely because of the limitations of the Act itself, not merely because of the continued coercive

approach of the courts, but also as a result of attempts by
both Labour and Conservative Governments to control trade unions and strikes by statute law. It is interesting to note that
the examples of judicial intervention which we have considered
here, and evidence of which continues right throughout the
1970s (see e.g. Davies et al.: 1979) have clearly not been considered to be enough by successive governments, otherwise why
else the attempt to legislate? The reason for this is simple:
the lead given by the courts in legally controlling trade unions has been of a paternalist character and this does not allow
for the institution of effective, systematic and continuous
means of state intervention under the control of government.
For this, more corporatist institutions are required. The kind
of control that governments and some sections of capital thought
was required could not in fact be left to the judiciary to
implement. Indeed, in his proposals for the establishment of
a corporatist set of formal constitutional rules for trade unions, Shonfield pointed to the unpredictable effects, from the
point of view of adequate control, of allowing this system to
be administered by the judiciary: he thus complained of 'the
vagaries of judge-made law' (The Times, 19.10.77. Cf. Winkler:
1977). We have also seen how the implications of the proposals
for reforming industrial relations put forward by the CBI have
similarly tended in this direction. The courts thus, at least
potentially, can be a thorn in the side of corporatist governments.

The Royal Commission on Industrial Relations
It is something of a commonplace to regard the work of a Royal
Commission as a form of non-decision making, allowing governments a formal and symbolic way of delaying or not taking a
decision on a contentious issue. And there is some basis for
this view in the Labour Government's decision to defer legislation on industrial relations by setting up a Royal Commission
in the wake of the 1965 Act discussed above. But while a Royal
Commission shows the legitimatory and ideological aspects of
the state's role at work in displaying its self-assumed impartial, referee-like qualities in a very open way, it also provides a concentrated, exhaustive and wide-ranging way of analysing in depth, and making considered recommendations about,
the problem it has been set. And in this respect its overall
organisation - the appointing of 'expert' and representative
lay members to the Commission, its calling of written and oral
evidence from all the interests involved and affected irrespective of their position on the political spectrum, its inquisi-
tional style of questioning witnesses, its authoritative capacity to gather evidence and to lay claim to the efficacious
nature of its proposals - make it suitable as a means of analytically developing strategic responses to problems. As Hyman
has pointed out, 'its importance was in expressing the key problems confronting British capital in its relations with organized

150

labour, and in suggesting guidelines for strategy' (1978; 462).

What then can we make of this importance of the Donovan Commission? Some have suggested that it put forward an essentially liberal policy. Crouch, for example, argues that 'the Report emerges as a managerial interpretation of liberal collectivism' (1977; 160 and 160-2). This entailed a programme of institutional reform which, primarily, was to be the responsibility of strong and autonomous unions and management to implement, with only a limited part being played by the state in providing an adequate framework for voluntary collective bargaining. Again, Goldthorpe has argued that the Donovan Report represents 'the most detailed working blueprint thus far prepared for the reconstruction of British industrial relations on liberal-pluralist lines' (1977; 207). However, while not denying the voluntaristic and liberal emphases in the Report, Panitch has suggested that 'the Commission was not in principle opposed to legal sanctions' not only in that sanctions could be introduced after employers and unions had voluntarily reformed collective bargaining procedures, so that they could be directed at those directly responsible for subverting such procedures (1976; 168), but also in that a majority of the Commission proposed that legal immunities be confined to registered trade unions (Ibid.; 168-9). And both Crouch and Panitch note that the Report supported incomes policy (Panitch: 1976; 168. Crouch: 1977; 161-2) while Crouch sees in it elements of a voluntary corporatist strategy in its plans for union integration of shop stewards in the interests of managerial control (Ibid.; 162).

What is one to make of these divergent interpretations? It seems to me to be the case that the Donovan Commission was not in the business of elaborating one strategy but in assessing a limited number of strategies while (1) attempting to integrate the useful controls the by then fragmenting industrial relations system had contained with new reforms to meet the effects of this fragmentation by means of a workable policy, and which (2), unlike those advanced by fractions of capital themselves, tried explicitly to conciliate and accommodate the demands and organisational power of work place and official trade unionism in order thereby to incorporate them into the controls exercised by an institutionally re-structured system of industrial relations.[5]

The main diagnostic point made by the Report[5] was its famous indication of the existence of two systems of industrial relations in Britain: 'The formal system assumes industry-wide organisations capable of imposing their decisions on their members. The informal system rests on the wide autonomy of managers in individual companies and factories, and the power of industrial work groups' (1968; p.36). The problem was that these systems were in conflict: 'the practices of the formal system have become increasingly empty, while the practices of the informal system have come to exert an ever greater influence on the conduct of industrial relations throughout the country' (Ibid.; p.37). If this was the problem, what were the cures to be administered?

In the first place and with a very definite view to re-structuring collective bargaining on an orderly and voluntaristic basis it proposed that unions and employers establish factory-wide agreements and institutionalise the role of the shop steward, thereby in effect 'formalising' and regulating the informal system (Ibid.; pp.40-66). An Industrial Relations Act was proposed providing for the registration of collective agreements with the D of E, the explanation of why such agreements had not been reached and for the establishment of an Industrial Relations Commission (later to become the CIR) to investigate and report on these agreements and to inquire into the general state of industrial relations in a particular industry or factory (Ibid.; pp.46-50). If a company failed to register its agreements or to report on its lack of agreements and the reasons for this it was to be liable to a monetary penalty (Ibid.; pp.50-1). The Commission was to assist the operations of incomes policies by opening up work place, pay settlement structures to the influence of public policy (Ibid.; pp.52-3). But a crucial distinction was drawn between the nature of an Industrial Relations Act and an incomes policy: 'The Industrial Relations Act will be concerned with the long-term reconstruction of British industrial relations, whereas incomes policy is concerned with the short-run improvement of the country's economic position' (Ibid.; p.52). This has, in fact, been a leading consideration in the process of developing an effective strategy for dealing with the crisis of capital accumulation. So, for example, the changes proposed in collective bargaining were seen, by way of the factory agreement, as allowing for the more efficient use of manpower and increased productivity, pace incomes policy (Ibid.; p.85).

The Donovan Commission was also highly instrumental in extending and concentrating public awareness on the problem of unofficial strikes, pointing to the way in which they derived from the two systems of industrial relations and the way in which their unpredictability and their capacity to indirectly halt production elsewhere harmed both managerial control and the fortunes of the economy (Ibid.; pp.97-112). It was suggested that the statutory powers of a Minister to inquire into industrial relations cases then available under the Conciliation Act of 1896 and the Industrial Courts Act of 1919 be extended so that 'statutory inquiries may be conducted under terms of reference wide enough to enable them to investigate long-term problems, irrespective of whether a dispute or difference exists or is threatened' (Ibid.; pp.116-17). However, since it argued that institutional breakdown was the real cause and that unofficial strikes were merely a symptom of this, the real answer was seen as being the reforms put forward to overcome the conflict between the two systems of industrial relations (Ibid.; pp.120-1). For this reason and for reasons of

152

irrelevance and impracticality the legal enforcement of procedure agreements was rejected. But if institutional reforms were introduced and adequate procedures were provided, legal sanctions would then become appropriate and the Industrial Relations Commission was to keep this under review and to advise the Secretary of State when legislation to enforce procedure agreements was needed[6] (Ibid.; Chapter 8). The Report also pointed out how reluctant employers tended to be to apply legal sanctions (Ibid.; p.131). Trade unions themselves were urged to institutionalise the role of the shop steward, integrating it much more into the structure of official unionism by changes in their rules and by providing 'constitutionally recognised committees' to replace unofficial shop stewards' committees (Ibid.; pp.186-91). The TUC was seen as being able to play a leading role in encouraging the institutionalisation of collective bargaining at the workplace so as to make it more orderly and more contained (Ibid.; pp.193-5).

The registration of unions with the then prevailing advantages was supported. A majority of the Commission (7 to 5) recommended that section 3 of the 1906 Act preventing action for breach of a contract of employment if induced in the context of a trade dispute should only apply to unions and employers' associations included on the new register (Ibid.; pp. 211-16).[7] A majority also recommended the repeal of section 4 of the 1871 Act which prevents the direct legal enforcement of trade union agreements (Ibid.; pp.218-19). It recommended that the protection afforded to unions by section 3 of the 1906 Act be extended to cover the breach of any contract, but a majority (again 7 to 5) said this should be restricted to registered trade unions (Ibid.; p.235). Lastly, it urged that the immunity given to unions against actions in tort by section 4 of the 1906 Act should be clearly confined to torts committed in the context of a trade dispute (Ibid.; p.238).

The Report throughout laid great stress on the invaluable effectiveness of a voluntaristic approach to industrial relations reform. In this respect, for example, it saw the government supporting rather than intervening in industrial relations and thought its proposals continued rather than broke with this tradition (Ibid.; p.35). But in, for example, the proposals on the institutionalisation of the role of the shop steward and its formal incorporation into collective bargaining and union structures, the registration of unions and the restriction of certain legal immunities to registered unions, the statutory provision for wide-ranging state inquiries into long-term problems of industrial relations organisation and reform, the legislated registration of agreements with the possibility of monetary penalties, the idea that sanctions become the second stage of reform after reformed procedure agreements had been voluntarily negotiated to deal with those workers who would not even adhere to the latter procedures (Ibid.; pp.137-40) and in its support for incomes policy (Ibid.; pp.52-3), we can

see clear signs of an emergent corporatist strategy. And, as
Panitch has noted, this was enhanced by the tenor and details
of the supplementary and dissenting notes appended to the body
of the main report (1976; 168-9. Donovan Report: 1968; pp.284-
302).

It should not come as a surprise to see the Report of the
Donovan Commission torn between pluralist and corporatist strategies. In the first place it developed different but somewhat
complementary strategies rather than one which was perfectly
coherent, thereby reflecting and adding to as well as sharpen-
ing the conflict over industrial relations reform that was well
under way. But it gave this conflict over proposed strategy a
more reasoned and concentrated form in bringing many matters
to public attention and in systematically addressing itself to
a wide range of proposals. It served as a debating forum as
well as a creator of strategies and a prelude to legislation.
Also, as much of its deliberation shows, it was at pains to
meet the crisis in industrial relations while retaining what
was seen as the still beating heart of those industrial relations - the principle of voluntarism. The point was to trans-
plant it to a more regulated system which institutionalised
shop floor power and state interventionism. At the same time
it recognised the need to conciliate and incorporate and so
control the trade union movement. Of course to do all these
things was impossible but being aware of them allows us to
understand just how the Report was marked by a surface and
explicit commitment to voluntaristic pluralism which was subject to the strains and contradictions arising out of an underlying and implicit corporatism.

Conclusion

In this chapter I have considered certain aspects of the political conflicts deriving from the crises of capital accumulation and industrial relations, since the late 1950s, which
served as a prelude to the inception of interventionist legislation by the state with the IR Act in 1971. In particular, I
have drawn attention to (1) the specificity of the political
conflict between the strategy of paternalism of the judiciary
and the strategy of corporatism formulated by legal and political factions outside the state, including those within the
Conservative Party; (2) the leading and constructive role of
the latter in politically constituting the class interests of
a particular capital fraction, namely industrial and national-
based monopoly capital, by formulating a corporatist strategy
for industrial relations; and (3) the central role played by
the Royal Commission as part of the processes of the state in
furthering the development and implications of this and other
options for state policy, as well as in analysing further the
problems requiring such solutions for capital and the state.

NOTES

1. I should perhaps point out that this designation is one the ICCUS applied to itself. See ICCUS: 1958; 12. The ICCUS's proposals are summarised on pp.54-6 of their book.

2. See also, e.g., Bar Council, ME, 43, 1966. Law Society, Selected Written Evidence, 1968 and ME, 52, 1966.

3. The following account of this case is based upon Wedderburn: 1971; 347-8, 361-74 and 377; and Citrine: 1967, 28-30 and 623-9.

4. For a list of such cases see Citrine: 1967; 30n. And for a discussion of a number of them see Wedderburn: 1971; 365-6.

5. For a very effective critique of the underlying socio-logical and theoretical bases of the Report see Goldthorpe: 1977.

6. Two members of the Commission went further in wanting powers for the Secretary of State to impose adequate procedure agreements in cases where agreement on their substance could not be reached. See Donovan Report: 1968; p.140.

7. The minority, including the two trade union members of the Commission, suggested instead that 'the need for compulsory registration could be met by a provision that the members of the Executive Committee of a body which should, but does not, register as a union should be liable to a penalty for each day of default' (Ibid.; p.215).

Chapter 8

THE STATE AND INDUSTRIAL RELATIONS LEGISLATION, 1969-1979:
FROM THE INDUSTRIAL RELATIONS ACT TO INDUSTRIAL DEMOCRACY

In this chapter I wish to consider certain legislative changes
introduced by the state to re-structure industrial relations
in order to meet the growing crisis of British capitalism, and
the conjunctural escalation of class conflict. I thus consider
how and why certain policies, in particular the Industrial
Relations Act of 1971, were put into practice in legislative
form, and their consequences, as well as a case in which conflict precluded the possibility of state legislation, namely
'In Place of Strife'.

'In Place of Strife'[1]

As a more or less direct result of the breakdown of its economic and incomes policy and the attendant need to maintain control over industrial class conflict, the Wilson Government began to move towards more legalistic and corporatist measures to
re-structure the institutions of industrial relations, building
upon the foundation laid by Donovan (Panitch: 1976; 170-1 and
177). The White Paper, 'In Place of Strife', the aborted Industrial Relations Bill and the TUC's solemn and binding commitment to maintain the social democratic alliance, were the
immediate results. In fact, apart from working class opposition,
a kind of social democratic inhibition of the type discussed in
the chapter on Trade Unionism tied the Labour Government sufficiently closely to the organised working class movement to prevent it from moving too far in the direction of corporatism.

Although it has been claimed that the White Paper was not
unambiguously corporatist (Crouch: 1977; 163-5), it did make
explicit the utility of state interventionism for the purpose
of controlling strikes since the prevailing system of industrial relations was no longer considered adequate in that it
could not handle the disparities of power that had grown up
between distinct groups of employees, the inappropriate collective bargaining structures that had been nurtured, the securing
of trade union recognition where necessary and the effect of
the unofficial strike weapon in a socialised political economy
(Cmnd. 3888, 1969, pp.5-9). Thus, while in the past the state

156

had generally held the ring for industrial relations, state intervention had now become necessary since 'it could be shown that certain important economic or social objectives were not sufficiently furthered or were frustrated by collective bargaining'. But this need not be imposed for some kind of tripartite corporatist consensus was deemed possible (Ibid.; pp. 6-7).

This intervention was to take the form of an attempt to re-integrate what Donovan had identified as the formal and informal systems (Ibid.; pp.9-14). Likewise, registration of collective agreements with eventual statutory backing was proposed but it came out against the legalisation of collective agreements (Ibid.; pp.14-16). The White Paper also laid down rights for trade union recognition to extend collective bargaining, though the state was to refer inter-union disputes to the CIR if the TUC could not resolve them (Ibid.; pp.18-21).

However, perhaps the most important set of proposals from our point of view, involved the suggested safeguards against strikes. It proposed greater state initiative in the provision of conciliation services (Ibid.; p.26). And as short-term expedients to the ever-pressing problem of unofficial and unconstitutional strikes it proposed, firstly, giving the Secretary of State the discretionary power of imposing a 'conciliation pause' of 28 days in the event of unconstitutional strikes in order to 'encourage trade unions to intensify their efforts to see that procedures were observed by their members' (Ibid.; pp. 28-9). Secondly, the Secretary of State was empowered to order strike ballots when the threatened strike would involve serious damage to the economy and the national interest, the ballot being conducted under rules approved by the Registrar, for it did recognise that consistent, indiscriminate and widespread balloting might lead to conservative union leaders becoming tied to a more militant membership (Ibid.; pp.29-30). Consequently, it proposed the registration of trade unions and the supervision and screening of their rules by the Registrar, refusal to register being subject to a financial penalty (Ibid.; pp.32-3). These proposals and others were to be embodied in an Industrial Relations Bill which never became law.

The then Secretary of State for Employment, Barbara Castle, who played a major role in the drawing up of the White Paper, has said that 'the whole motivation behind "In Place of Strife" was to strengthen the trade unions, rather than weaken them' (Sunday Times, 13.1.80). However, John Davies, then Director-General of the CBI, accused the government of 'taking a nut cracker to crack a cannon ball' (cited in Jenkins: 1970; 49). But the stand taken by Ford in 1969 in attempting to use the law to counter an unofficial strike obviously strengthened the government's hand (see above). In its Annual Report for 1969 the CBI in fact recognised that while the White Paper was by no means what it wanted, it nonetheless 'represented a halting step in the right direction' (1969; 30), since penal sanctions went along with other recommendations, particularly on trade union recognition, to which the CBI was opposed (Ibid.).

As it happened the government decided to introduce a short, interim bill to deal specifically with the pressing problem of unofficial strikes, this being designed as an alternative to incomes policy legislation, especially to gain credit from international financial institutions (Panitch: 1976; 184-5. Jenkins: 1970; 85). The bill laid down the statutory right to belong to a union, empowered the government to enforce CIR recommendations for union recognition, and allowed unemployment benefit to be paid to workers indirectly laid off by strikes elsewhere in industry. However, it also gave the government the power to impose, (a) settlements in inter-union disputes in which TUC and CIR mediation had failed, and (b) a conciliation pause in unconstitutional strikes for a 28 day period while the status quo was restored (Industrial Relations Bill, 1969. Panitch: 1976, 185-6. Crouch: 1977; 164-5).

This bill and the White Paper never became law mainly because of concerted and united union opposition. The main bone of contention between the government and the organised labour movement as represented by the TUC was whether the latter would discipline its members voluntarily or whether this discipline was to be imposed by the state. The government was moving increasingly in the direction of the latter but it was a road which, in part because of the overarching social democratic ideology, it had to go down without much trade union support. The outcome, after much in-fighting, was the government's abandonment of the penal clauses and its acceptance of the TUC's case for voluntarism.

A major factor in the whole episode was the maintenance of social democratic unity and an important element in the subversion of the Labour Government's strategy was rank and file, working class opposition within the labour movement. But not only did the Labour Government fail to attract union support, it also failed to attract the backing of capital and, equally, its failure to effect the strategy it pursued may have had something to do with the contradictions within social democratic practice and ideology. After all, the integrative functions of an ideology which stresses the fundamental nature of the right to strike must be dubious to say the least and I think we can see and, in part, explain the conflict over 'In Place of Strife' and the subsequent bill and the eventual political impasse in the light of the contradictions that this 'economistic' right posed for the state's attempt to use trade union organisation as an agency of control, albeit couched in the framework and rhetoric of social democratic ideology.

The Industrial Relations Act, 1971-1974[2]

The Industrial Relations Act of 1971 represents the most prominent watershed in this process of developing an effective form of state control for industrial relations, being the first

legislative attempt to establish a comprehensive legal framework for industrial relations in Britain. The Act was not explicitly nor consistently corporatist in intent and design,
containing, as we shall see, elements of paternalism as well
as the usual genuflections in the direction of the norm of
liberal voluntarism, but this merely attests to its significance as a form of state policy. As such, it represents a very
clear expression of the autonomous operation of the state in
endeavouring to elaborate a strategy for the control of industrial conflict that draws upon the strategies formulated by
particular capitals but which is not determined by these but
rather by the need to construct a coherent and workable policy
to meet the prevailing crisis in class relations. One cannot
see the Act so much as the direct manifestation of the interests of capital or its particular fractions but more as the
manifestation of the operations and interests of the state in
managing capitalism and its class struggles. While the Act was
most clearly consistent with the CBI's strategy it also contained elements which conflicted with that strategy and was
bounded by political decisions, such as the refusal to establish state prosecution of unofficial strikers or to usurp civil
liberties, which directly confounded that strategy.

For this reason I think it wise not to minimise, as many
commentators are prone to do, the significance of the Act. We
have already seen its influence upon the behaviour of employers
in the financial sector. It was also what some employers wanted
and judging by present-day statements still want. It laid down
guidelines for the subsequent strategies of capital and pointed
to the limitations of various strategies, including, in the end,
that embodied in the Act itself, and so allowed strategies and
tactics to be re-formulated. The present attempt by the encum-
bent Conservative Government to sell their Employment Act
measures, which are similar in their consequences to the Industrial Relations Act, as 'moderate' proposals may be one graphic
example of the state's political learning process (Davies et
al.: 1979). But I think that most importantly the Act has shown
that if corporatism is to be instituted then there is no going
back: the ends of the Act are crucial to the establishment of
corporatist structures in industrial relations; and in showing
up the limitations as well as the possibilities of corporatism,
the Act has been significant, especially in highlighting the
practical issue of whether the legal control of strikers is to
be the responsibility of employers or the state. This has remained a contentious and unresolved focus of conflict between
capital and the state.

As the most far-reaching attempt we have encountered on
the part of the state to re-structure industrial relations what
did the Act look like? It should come as no surprise that the
general principles espoused in the Act covered free collective
bargaining and the independence of trade unions and that these
were coupled with the principle of order in industrial relations

and the institutionalised settlement of disputes (<u>Industrial Relations Act 1971</u>, Chapter 72, Section 1). The legislation thus endeavoured to marry these objectives in responding to the prevailing conditions of British capitalism with a view to laying down a coherent and systematic strategy as a resolution of the tensions in class struggle and the impediments to capital accumulation.

Particular aspects of the Act either went beyond or rejected prior proposals of both employers and the Conservative Party, but the main pillars of the Act reflected the strategy developed by the Tory lawyers, the CBI and EEF, and the Conservative Party. This can be seen firstly if we look at the Act's requirements on trade union registration. In the first place, the very term 'trade union' was confined to an organisation of workers which was registered (Section 61). A registrar of trade unions was to be set up (Section 62) to register organisations of workers as trade unions if their rules were approved (Sections 67 and 68). If the rules were deemed to be defective in, inter alia, arbitrarily excluding certain people from membership, not allowing for democratic elections, imposing unfair discipline particularly to engage in an unfair industrial practice (see below) and not having a proper appeal procedure, the Registrar could investigate and request an alteration of the rules or enforce de-registration (Sections 65, 75-77, 81-83). This was buttressed by the Act's definition and stipulations regarding 'unfair industrial practices'. These included the inducement of a breach of contract even 'in contemplation or furtherance of an industrial dispute' unless carried out by a registered trade union; industrial action to support an unfair industrial practice; industrial action against parties extraneous to a particular industrial dispute (Sections 96-98); and contravention of the model principles or rules of union organisation (Sections 65 and 66).

A National Industrial Relations Court was set up with the full powers of a court of law to adjudicate upon complaints of unfair industrial practice (Sections 99-110). Collective agreements were to be regarded as being legally enforceable unless explicitly excluded by the provisions of the agreement itself. It was to be an unfair industrial practice to break such a legally binding agreement <u>and</u> for any party to an agreement not to take all reasonably practicable steps to prevent its representatives or members from breaking that agreement (Sections 34-36). The powers of the state to intervene in other respects were likewise strengthened. The Secretary of State was to be enabled to apply to the Industrial Court in cases where procedure agreements were non-existent or defective and led to disorderly industrial relations and substantial loss of working time, to order an investigation by the CIR: the CIR was to report its proposals and to attempt to secure new or revised provisions, and if necessary it was left in the last instance to the Industrial Court to impose such provisions in the form of a legally enforceable contract (Sections 37-41 and 58-59).

One of the subsequently most notorious sections of the Act concerned the emergency procedure powers given to the Secretary of State, covering cooling-off periods and strike ballots. This part of the Act empowered the Secretary of State, in cases in which it appeared to him that an actual or threatened strike would harm the national economy, national security, public order, or endanger life or expose people to injury, to apply to the Court for an order preventing any industrial action for a specified period of not more than 60 days (Sections 138-140). The Secretary of State could also apply to the Court for an order requiring that a ballot be taken over the decision to undertake industrial action in cases where it appeared to him that there were reasons to suppose that the workers involved were not committed to the action and in which substantial damage would be done to the livelihood of large numbers of workers employed in that industry. During the period of the order and before the ballot was held industrial action was to be banned (Sections 141-145). These measures were clearly aimed at the unofficial strike, particularly those which had widespread consequences as a result of the integrated nature of the modern political economy, but in view of their designation as emergency procedures they did not establish the systematic legal sanctions against unofficial strikes that national, industrial monopoly capital had petitioned for; these were rather contained in the registration proposals but here the main emphasis was upon long-term reforms in union rules and union behaviour and, while allowing for state intervention, did not provide any short-term expedients against unofficial strikes.

The main tenor of the Act was corporatist but not wholly or consistently so in view of its liberalistic reliance upon employers and unions deciding if collective agreements were to be legally enforceable, and upon employers to bring cases of unfair industrial practices to the NIRC; and, in its provisions on union recognition and collective bargaining units and agents, and its emphasis upon the autonomy and independence of registered trade unions from employer control and tutelage it clearly went against the paternalism favoured and fostered by money and petit-bourgeois capital. To set this in context, it is necessary to look at the Act's requirements with regard to the closed shop. The Act made it clear that every worker had the right to belong or not to belong to a trade union and it was to be an unfair industrial practice to infringe those rights (Section 5). The only exception was to be where an agency shop agreement was in force: the pre-entry closed shop was outlawed (Sections 6-7). An agency shop agreement was to be one in which trade union membership or union contributions or charity payments in lieu of membership were to become a condition of employment. This had to be argued for through the Industrial Court, a CIR investigation and the holding of a ballot if necessary to decide the issue. If a majority of workers decided in favour the shop was a de facto reality for the employer (Sections 11-18).

With this in mind let us look at the Act's requirements regarding union recognition. These enabled registered trade unions, as well as employers and the Secretary of State, to apply to the Industrial Court to consider (the investigation was to be carried out by the CIR) whether a group of employees within which it had some membership should be regarded by the employer as a bargaining unit and whether the union itself should be regarded as the sole bargaining agent for that unit by the employer. In investigating and making recommendations in such cases the CIR was to take into account not only the resources and facilities of the union and whether the employees concerned actually wanted the union but also whether it was an independent organisation of workers. (This financial and organisational independence was a condition of registration.) The Industrial Court could subsequently make orders imposing the defined bargaining unit and agent (Sections 44-53 and 67). As we have seen, these requirements conflicted very much with the paternalistic control over labour organisation exercised by employers in the financial and petit-bourgeois sectors without providing in its place the alternative of a fully fledged, corporatist closed shop.

The divisions within capital and the differing strands of practice within the Act need to be stressed. We do not only find the Act predominantly conveying the corporatist strategy pursued by the CBI and EEF, e.g. registration, unfair industrial practices, etc., but also elements of the liberalism that characterised foreign multi-national capital, e.g. over legally enforceable agreements, as well as elements of the paternalism of both petit-bourgeois and money capital, e.g. leaving it up to the employer to sue. And it is instructive to note here that it was mainly small-scale employers or individual workers rather than big business which made use of the Act (Thomson and Engleman: 1975; 149. Weekes et al.: 1975; 185).[3] Moreover, in so far as each of these strategies were interwoven in the fabric of the Act they tended to contradict and work against each other, such as with the provisions strengthening collective union control and supporting individual liberties within unions (Thomson and Engleman: 1975; 145-6). But even more than this and other conflicts between liberalism and corporatism, the stress on independent trade unions and the need for collective bargaining representation thwarted paternalism, while the contradiction between the interventionism of the roles of the NIRC, CIR, Secretary of State and Registrar, and the laissez-faire mode of allowing (1) collective agreements to be legally binding only voluntarily, (2) employers rather than the state to take unions and strikers to court, and (3) union registration to be voluntary (cf. Ibid.; 146-7) served to place serious limitations upon the Act as an effective strategy for capital.

I would argue that these conflicting divisions within the Act between liberalism, corporatism and paternalism are linked to the material factors represented by the class interests of capital, the articulation of these interests by different fractions of capital, and the role played by the state. It is quite possible to see in the Act the main part taken by the corporatist strategy favoured by the CBI and EEF, and the lesser but nonetheless important parts taken by the paternalistic strategy favoured by money and petit-bourgeois capital and the liberalistic strategy favoured by foreign multi-national capital. This goes some way towards explaining the presence of distinct strategies within the Act, strategies which are not given as the general interests of capital but are articulated by specific fractions with specific interests in the course of political struggle; and it gives us some of the reasons why they have thus tended to contradict one another. But since no one interest or strategy is unambiguously reflected in the Act this means we also need to take account of the 'relatively autonomous' role of the state in fashioning policy. Given what has so far been argued, we cannot account for the strategies represented by the Industrial Relations Act as an expression of the interests of capital as a whole because of the divided nature of both, the existence of different fractions with distinct strategies, and the need to respect the nature of the political mode of representation as well as what it represents. This means that in an important sense we have to regard the Act not so much as the manifestation of ideas or an idea (as Moran does (1977)), nor the muddled expression of the interests of different fractions of capital, but much more as an attempt by the state, within the social constraints exercised by these interests and by the nature and rate of capital accumulation, class conflict, and the political system, to hammer out a strategy for capital as a whole. But it need not, given the nature of struggles, achieve this end; hence, the main emphasis on corporatism. The Act could, for example, be seen as an attempt to placate 'public opinion' as well as fractions of capital, while also trying to control class conflict, construct an institutionalised and orderly system of industrial relations in keeping with the more organised and planned nature of monopoly capitalism and still stay within the bounds of bourgeois democracy by not directly proscribing strikes or unions or removing from trade unionists the democratic liberties to organise against the Act. But, at the same time, those conditions which gave rise to the Act also served to confer on it its contradictory nature despite its role in the process of reconstructing an effective form of state control of industrial relations for capital in British society.

In illustrating these points further it is instructive to chart the reactions of the CBI, other capitals and the labour movement to the Industrial Relations Act. The CBI obviously found much of what it wanted in the Industrial Relations Act,

but at the consultative stage of the Bill it put forward two
reservations to the government: firstly that the Registrar
should be given powers, in addition to those proposed for employers, to take action against trade unions whose members consistently breached agreements; and, secondly, that it should be
possible to secure the legal enforcement of industry-level procedure agreements (CBI, Annual Report, 1971, p.33). Both aims
were rejected by the government (Open University, 1973. CBI,
Annual Report, 1971, pp.25-6). It has been noted by a number
of commentators that the Act was not really popular amongst
employers and not really used by them, mainly because of the
harm it would do to their own industrial relations, even though
it had been designed, in some part, in keeping with their requirements (Thomson and Engleman: 1975; 31-2. Weekes et al.:
1975; 158, 182 and 223). And part of the government's rationale
for rejection was its view that responsibility for reform was
to lie with the two sides of industry and that the legal framework provided by the long-term strategy entailed in the Act was
intended to support and not to replace this objective (Open
University, 1973). These features are symptomatic of a more
deep-seated aspect of the relationship between capital and
the state, which derives from the fact that capital looks to
the state in the first place to legislate for changes. This
therefore indicates the 'relative autonomy' of the state not
merely in refusing the demands of capital or meeting the demands of some capitals and not others but in actually deciding
what is best for capital. This episode thus can be used to
illustrate the fact that the state is an element of class
domination but is a constitutive and mediatory and not a subordinate and residual element in this process.

The CBI continued to think that the pay determination system was inflationary because the balance of power had swung too
far in favour of labour (CBI: 1976; 18). The CBI's proposals on
pay determination represented a novel departure in its tactics
but one in keeping with its overall corporatist strategy. In
order to meet the failings of the prevailing collective bargaining system and of previous attempts at reform (1977; 4-11),
the CBI proposed a system of 'free bargaining within monetary
discipline but with some central influence on the level of pay
claims and settlements ... a system based on market forces and
monetary discipline, but one in which central guidance influences pay claims and settlements' (Ibid.; 13-14). This entailed
a national, tri-partite economic forum to decide on general pay
levels and to generate consensus on problems and objectives
(Ibid.; 5, 6, 20-22). This was to entail greater employer solidarity and stricter control by unions of their members (CBI:
1977; 22, 32-3, 36). This was endorsed as official CBI policy
at its first ever national conference, by a majority vote with
some concern being expressed over its 'corporatist' and interventionist implications (CBI: 1977b; 62-80).

However, more because of these proposals than despite them,

the CBI remained concerned about the legal position of trade
unions and saw itself as attempting to counter the way in which
the Labour Government's industrial relations legislation had
become pro-trade union, pro-collective bargaining in its orientation (see 1977a; Chapter 6). This concerned in one respect
the role of ACAS (see below) but, overall, it entailed learning
from the experience of the Industrial Relations Act (Ibid.).
The CBI affirmed its opposition to the closed shop to the extent that it infringed individual freedom but accepted it as a
fact of life in some cases[4] (1977b; 83 and 100) and pointed to
the way in which the Industrial Relations Act had shown how
making the closed shop illegal without effective sanctions
meant that unions could still enforce it anyway[5] (1977a; 34).
Registration of unions and control over their rules were supported even though the Industrial Relations Act had shown how
difficult it was to legislate on these issues (Ibid.; 35). The
CBI maintained its opposition to the immunity enjoyed by trade
unions when taking industrial action which it now extended to
the way in which the TULR Acts of 1974 and 1976 gave immunity
to breaches of any kind of contract, thereby legalising secondary action. In consequence, the CBI urged that lawful industrial action be limited to the firm involved in the dispute and
aimed at the possibility of determining whether there were
majorities within unions in favour of industrial action and of
finding ways of forestalling the increase in unconstitutional
strikes (Ibid.; 35). The adoption by workers during the 1970s
of more varied and effective forms of picketing, such as the
mass and flying picket, on a more systematic basis (Crouch:
1978; 231. Dubois: 1978; 9-10) also had its effects on the CBI.
This problem, for the CBI, would have, in part, been dealt with
by making secondary industrial action illegal (CBI: 1977a; 35).
Less reliance, however, came to be placed on a rigid legal
framework and more on employer initiative and solidarity, while
the aim of a strong and disciplined trade unionism was retained
(see, e.g. 1977b; 84 and 99-102). Indeed, a theme to have
emerged from CBI conferences has been the increased stress
upon the need for greater employer solidarity in the face of
the failures of the imposition of a legal framework by the
Industrial Relations Act. This has gone to the extent of emphasising the need for employers to be willing to take civil legal
action in order to make the present Conservative Government's
legislation on industrial relations with respect to the closed
shop, secondary picketing and the secret ballot work as effective controls on industrial conflict and trade union power.

The stand taken by the organised working class movement
against the Industrial Relations Act is, of course, much better
known and, indeed, much better documented (Crouch: 1977. Moran:
1977. Weekes et al.: 1975. Thomson and Engleman: 1975). The
first major point that needs to be made in this respect is
that the TUC decided not to co-operate with the requirements
and institutions of the Act and advised its member unions, save

for certain heavily qualified cases, not to register under the provisions of the Act. This advice was quite widely taken so that few unions qualified for trade union status under the Act and most of these were expelled or resigned from the TUC by 1973 (Weekes et al.: 1975; 252-61). This meant that the Act, in some of its central provisions, was inoperable. A series of one-day strikes and marches against the Bill in 1970 and 1971 went ahead, with the backing of the TUC and some major unions, attracting the support of over 1½ million workers. And the stand taken by the TUC and a large number of trade unions in opposition to the Act and its institutions became more uncompromising over time with the organisation of 'political' strikes against the Act by the TUC and AUEW in 1972. Moreover, the TUC expelled member unions registered under the Act, union representatives refused to serve on or to have anything to do with institutions, like the CIR, included within the provisions of the Act, dockworkers, print workers and engineering workers went on strike in direct defiance of the Act and got away with it, unions like the AUEW and TGWU refused to recognise the NIRC and the legitimacy of its decisions, and the trade union movement lurched towards a general one-day strike over the issue of the five dock workers imprisoned for picketing and contempt of court. The latter possibility was forestalled to some degree by what was for the government the highly embarrassing use of the official solicitor and the House of Lords' decision, that it was the TGWU, and not the dockers, which was legally responsible for the fine, thereby securing the release of the dockers from prison (Weekes et al.: 1975. Barnett: 1973. Thomson and Engleman: 1975; Chapter 5).

The TUC legitimated its stand from within the confines of social democracy. Not only did it reject the practicality of introducing the law into industrial relations but, more importantly, accepted and argued for the inevitability but also the pluralism of industrial conflict, the need for the defence of workers' interests at work and hence the need for autonomous trade unions independent of the state and of capital (TUC: 1971a). Though there was more militant pressure both from the rank and file and some union leaderships to take a more direct, oppositional and unconstitutional approach to combating the Bill and the Act, by e.g. using the strike weapon to prevent the Bill being passed, the TUC acted to keep opposition within the confines of parliamentary democracy, relying upon the Act's repeal by a future Labour Government, though the Tory Government's coercive approach made the TUC itself take a more militant stand.

The introduction of an Act of Parliament with severe implications for union autonomy within a political system affording civil, democratic rights and liberties, such as the right to organise marches, demonstrations, petitions and publications against the Bill and the Act, placed serious prohibitions upon the actual objectives of the Act. Liberal democracy would have needed to have been abrogated for the Act to work (Panitch: 1977; 86. Cf. Kahn-Freund and Hepple: 1972; 60. Marx: 1973; 189). Thus, while the TUC's social democratic practice generally kept it within the confines of constitutional politics, this still gave it effective weapons for fighting the Act, though the expression of more militant, rank and file opposition also played a part in the organised and effective defeat of the Act.

It should not be forgotten that the Act also failed to work, as we have noted, because most employers did not co-operate with or use the Act either (Weekes et al.: 1975). In this sense, the voluntaristic emphasis in the Act upon unions agreeing to register and co-operate and upon employers being responsible and willing to use the sanctions in the Act infringed extensively upon its coercive and corporatist objectives (cf. Crouch: 1977; 181 and 238-9). The government could accordingly have set up a state agency to enforce sanctions against unofficial strikers as some employers wanted, but this would not have met the interests of all fractions of capital, would have involved the state in detailed intervention in industrial relations at a time in which it wanted to extricate itself from direct involvement in the economy, would have wrested some degree of control from private capital, and it would have undermined further the neutral picture of the state that trade unionists had by identifying it too closely and visibly with the interests of capital. However, at the same time the Act was also clearly interventionist in character.

In fact the state, including the government and the institutions founded by the Act, notably the NIRC, began to find itself caught in a contradiction: it needed to maintain legitimacy in the context of parliamentary democracy in order to act, i.e. be accorded constitutional legitimacy by trade unionists, while, at the same time, being constrained to intervene by the course of capital accumulation and class conflict, i.e. introduce coercive corporatist controls over shop-floor trade unionism, which served to undermine such legitimacy. This, and the general difficulties entailed in making the Act operable, were particularly evident on the relatively few occasions when the state was either involved or itself decided to act using the provisions of the Act. For example, in the one instance on which the government used the emergency powers in the Act in the guise of the maintenance of economic stability and constitutionalism it served to encourage rather than restrain industrial action when on the occasion of a pay dispute on the railways, the NIRC granted the Secretary of State's request for a cooling off period order and a secret ballot showed a greater than six to one majority in favour of the union's stand for industrial action. Union solidarity and confidence were thereby increased as was its pay demand, and the Act, although it forestalled industrial action, was deemed to have failed (Weekes et al.: 1975; 215-16 and 227. Barnett: 1973; 12-13.

Thomson and Engleman: 1975; 114-18).

This point is often seen as being symbolic of the impot-
ence of the Act overall and of its very limited influence cn
the conduct of industrial relations and on the behaviour of
management and unions (Weekes et al.: 1975. Thomson and
Engleman: 1975). But this should not obscure the obvious significance of the Act. It has become a reference point for subsequent debate on the reform of industrial relations, both aca-
demic and political, and a land mark in the history of the
labour movement. It was the first wide ranging and systematic
attempt to establish a legal corporatist framework for industrial relations in Britain, thereby breaking sharply with preceding practices and legislation. As a consequence both of
this and the willingness of a small minority of employers and
unions to use the Act, the NIRC began to develop a limited
body of case law which even attempted to corporatise the existing and relevant common law (Weekes et al.: 1975; Chapter 4).
And this is important because once established, decisions made
under the Act become and remain relevant precedents for future
cases (Thomson and Engleman: 1975; 145). It also provides a
very instructive case study of the extent of the militancy capable of being expressed by the organised trade union movement,
the parliamentary and social democratic nature of such militancy and the state's need to legitimate itself to trade unions
in the interests of reform, as well as trade unionism's more
noted defensive ability and power of veto. It is likewise instructive as a case study of the working out of a strategy for
industrial relations by the state, in relation to those prof-
fered by capital.

I have, furthermore, remarked above upon the effect of
the Act upon capital, not only in encouraging employers in the
financial sector to establish internal labour collectivities
but in showing to employers as a whole the strategic implications of trying to be over-ambitious and overly reliant on one
piece of legislation. Also, as McCarthy and Ellis point out,
one of the Act's 'most desirable effects so far has been to
focus the attention of top management on the need to have a
policy for industrial relations' (1973; 183-4). This is particularly apposite in the era of 'planned' capitalism. The Act
and its history provides for capital not only indications of
the limits of the use of the law (Weekes et al.: 1975) but
also, as a possibly unintended consequence, suggestions on the
need for the development of company level initiatives by employers (where they are powerful enough to take these) like
more institutionalised bargaining (see, e.g. Thomson and
Engleman: 1975; 132. Cuthbert and Hawkins: 1973) and the formal incorporation of shop stewards into company and plant bargaining which began to grow in the mid-1970s (Terry: 1978), as
alternatives to and stop-gaps for state intervention. Moreover,
the desire of employers for the Act and their unwillingness to
use it reflects both their unfulfilled aim of a state agency

to enforce the Act and the contradiction between the 'local' interests of employers in managing their own industrial relations and the national, societal-wide role of the state in providing an overall framework of control for the localised industrial relations structures of capital. These considerations suggest that the implications of the Act for capital have not been negligible and as we noted above many employers have retained the long-term objective of controlling industrial relations by means of a framework of law.

The Social Contract and Corporatism

In order to demonstrate the continued corporatist trend in the state's control of industrial relations, which the Industrial Relations Act in a legislative sense initiated, and the strains and opposition to which it has been subject, we can briefly survey the policy of the Labour Government which took office on the defeat of the Heath Government by the miners' strike of 1974. This government was much better able to make a reality of the tripartism that the Heath Government had pursued after the failure of the IR Act. Close collaboration had already begun to develop between the TUC and the Labour Party while the latter was in opposition (see, e.g. TUC-Labour Party liaison committee: 1973) and when it came to office it was pledged to repeal the IR Act amongst other things (Ibid.).

This was duly done by the TULR Act of 1974. The Act repealed the IR Act while re-enacting some sections such as the one on unfair dismissals (Section 1 and Schedule 1). Trade unions were not to be regarded as corporate bodies and the Act talked of the right to belong as opposed to the right not to belong to a trade union, though the closed shop principle was weakened by the broad basis upon which non-union membership could be claimed (Sections 2, 5 and 7). The Act had been forced to confine legal immunity to breaches of contracts of employment (Section 13) though collective agreements were no longer viewed as being capable of being legally binding (Section 18). The NIRC went and its pending cases reverted to the High Court (Section 21. Cf. Thomson and Engleman: 1975). The TULR(A) Act of 1976 met some of these earlier reversals: it, for example, extended legal immunity to commercial contracts (Section 3(2)); the definition of a trade dispute was extended to include areas outside the UK thereby covering multi-national companies (Section 1 (d)); and the ability of an individual to object to union membership where a closed shop existed purely on reasonable grounds was revoked (Section 1 (e)).

These legislative changes were introduced as part of the social contract in an endeavour to institute corporatist controls in industrial relations not under the rubric of the 'rule of law' or by direct legal controls as with the IR Act but under the mantle of administrative convenience and social democracy, and with, rather than without, the co-operation of union leaders. The 'social contract', the TULR Acts and the EP Act in

effect embodied support for union structures and for unions
and their activities, like collective bargaining, to make them
more dependent upon the state rather than their own autonomy,
one hall mark of corporatism. The 'social contract' developed
out of the closer contacts that arose between the TUC and
Labour Party leadership during the Heath Government (TUC-Labour
Party liaison committee: 1973) and rested on the unions' agreeing to voluntary wage restraint in return for the legislation
they wanted, particularly that which supported trade union
rights (TUC: 1975; and Idem: 1976). This entailed state guaran-
tees for trade unionism together with union agreement on the
level and form of a voluntary incomes policy (with TUC supervision and opposition in instances in which the policy was
flouted) within an overall consensus between the industrial
and political wings of the labour movement (see, e.g. Idem:
1976; 3-22). The consensus and continuing discussions covered
a wide range of social and economic reforms, not just union
rights, including the reduction of social and economic inequalities (see Ibid. and Idem: 1975). But the contract did commit
the TUC and trade unions generally to accept some political
responsibility for controlling the rate of inflation.

The effects of this strategy were realised in one regard
with the imposition of voluntary incomes policies between 1975
and 1977, which consisted of compensations for price increases
between 1974 and 1975, the flat rate £6 limit between 1975 (the
first year in which the Labour Government had an effective
policy) and 1976, a 5 per cent limit with a minimum of £2.50
and a maximum of £4 between 1976 and 1977, a 10 per cent ceil-
ing between 1977 and 1978 which the unions began to oppose,
with a 5 per cent limit after July 1978 which led to the demise
of the policy and the social contract (see, Cmnd. 6151, 1975.
Cmnd. 6882, 1977. Cmnd. 7293, 1978. And Tarling and Wilkinson:
1977). This overall policy entailed the explicit citation of
the TUC's political responsibility for the maintenance of pay
norms and their enforcement on its member unions (see, e.g.
Cmnd. 6151: 1975; Pa. 3, p.3). In the event of the failure of
these policies a clear threat was made by the government to
introduce legal powers of compulsion if necessary (see, e.g.
Cmnd. 6151: 1975; Pas. 25-6, pp.7-8), and the sanction of
government contract work was subsequently used against employers who exceeded the income guidelines. In any case, the government also moved towards using controls on public expenditure
as well as pay to control inflation (see, e.g. Ibid.; Pas.43-5,
pp.11-12. And Cmnd. 6882: 1977; Pas. 29-31, p.6) though both
of these White Papers, for example, also made genuflections in
the direction of other reforms such as the industrial strategy
and tried to assuage concern about the equitable nature of the
policy by pointing to controls on prices and dividends (see
Cmnd. 6151: 1975; and Cmnd. 6882: 1977).

One consequence of this retrenchment of a social democratic, ideological and political consensus, then, was a kind of

corporatist control of incomes. This was supplemented by legislative changes which not only were part of the exchange the
unions demanded for helping to run an incomes policy but led
to union structures and actions being more closely defined by
the state. The EP Act of 1975, in effect, established a new
set of legal rights for trade unions and collective bargaining.
It set up machinery on a statutory basis to improve industrial
relations, namely, ACAS, CAC, and a Certification Officer to
replace the Registrar with the job of giving, and also withdrawing, certificates to trade unions validating their independence (Sections 1-8). Trade unions were given the right to be
recognised with provision made, if necessary, for an ACAS inquiry and recommendation for recognition, backed up by, on
condition of a union complaint, the imposition of an award by
the CAC upon a reluctant and recalcitrant employer (Sections
11-16). The right to belong to a trade union and not be impeded
in this by an employer was established with provision made for
complaints to an industrial tribunal and appropriate compensation (Sections 53-6). Time off for trade union activities was
laid down by statute (Sections 57-8) and stringent remedies
were put forward to deal with unfair dismissals (Sections 70-80).
A duty was placed upon employers to consult trade unions over
redundancies and to notify the Secretary of State accordingly,
it again being made possible for a trade union to complain that
the employer had not consulted it and receiving an award in
consequence (Sections 99-107). Lastly, it enabled a trade union
to refer an employer to the CAC on the grounds that the terms
of employment of the union's members working for that employer
were below the general level for 'comparable' workers employed
by 'comparable' employers (Schedule 11). Now, although in practice some of these rights have not worked as originally thought,
as is shown, for example, by the failure of workers to gain
union recognition in the Grunwick case, the low rate of trade
union success in industrial tribunal cases, and the irrepres-
sible rise in the rate of unemployment, as we have seen many
employers bemoaned the existence of such rights on the statute
book, and our brief survey of them shows how certain trade
union activities could become dependent upon the institutions
and definitions of the state.

Another highly central 'clause' in the social contract
from the trade union movement's point of view and especially
in the light of its commitment to monitor and control incomes
was the Labour Government's agreement to institute industrial
democracy[6] (TUC-Labour Party liaison committee: 1973; 7-8).
The government accordingly set up a Committee of Inquiry on
Industrial Democracy under the chairmanship of Lord Bullock
which reported in 1977. Its terms of reference entailed examining how industrial democracy could best be achieved, presuming
acceptance of the need for its 'radical extension' through the
role of trade unions (Bullock Report, Cmnd. 6706: 1977; V).
The Committee framed its proposals for extending trade union

participation in the management of economic enterprises in the light of the increasing size and power of industrial companies, the growth and centralisation of trade unions and the need for unions to be represented in order to counter-balance the concentration in the economic power of business. It was also seen as necessary to respond to what was viewed as an increased demand for greater control at work by workers though meeting this demand was also seen as a way of increasing productivity and efficiency in industry, as, that is, a way of 'putting the relationship between capital and labour on to a new basis which will involve not just management but the whole work force in sharing responsibility for the success and profitability of the enterprise' (Ibid.; p.160). These corporatist overtones to be found in the Report need to be underlined since they provided the rationale and justification for the proposals made on industrial democracy, for trade union representation in management at enterprise level was seen as a way of complementing the development of corporatist policies and institutions at the level of the national economy and state (Ibid.; p.22).

In the light of the criterion of maintaining efficient management, the Report argued that industrial democracy had to be real and effective. To this end, a unitary - as opposed to the German style two-tier system - board of directors structure was proposed where the crucial managerial decisions would be taken and where, consequently, employees would be represented (Ibid.; Chapter 8). As for the democratic composition of this board, the Report proposed parity of representation, the familiar 2X + y formula: this entailed an equal number of employee and shareholder representatives plus a third group of directors co-opted by a majority of the other two groups, which was to total an uneven number of directors greater than one and to form less than one third of the total board. The constitution of this third group was to avoid deadlocks in the process of decision-making and to prevent it from reverting to de facto collective bargaining (Ibid.; Chapter 9). The proposals were only to apply to companies with over 2,000 employees because here the rationale for the reforms - economically strategic, large scale corporations and organised trade unions as effective channels of representation - was most relevant and applicable (Ibid.; p.103). The trade union was viewed as the most appropriate institutional form for channelling employee representation on boards of directors. To have suggested another form would have diluted the policy of encouraging and strengthening trade unionism, would have made having a single channel of representation impossible, would not have allowed for a smooth and integrated relationship between board level representation and collective bargaining, and would have ignored the most effective and legitimate channel of representation. The actual institution of employee representation was to be by a secret ballot of all employees at the request of a trade union (Ibid.; Chapter 10).

The trade union movement was divided in its view of these proposed reforms, especially since by this time cracks had begun to appear in the Social Contract. The TUC's proposals recognised the possibilities in industrial democracy for extending the influence of trade unions within industry, as a beneficial consequence of normal trade union activities (TUC: 1977; p.5). To assist this, board level representation of trade unions to influence decisions on things like investment, closures, takeovers, etc., was also thought to be required. This was not seen to conflict with the function of collective bargaining if it were based on trade union representation. Therefore the TUC proposed equal worker participation at board level in companies employing more than 2,000 workers and in nationalised industries and representation and election via trade union machinery guaranteed by enabling legislation (Ibid.; Chapters 4 and 5). Some major unions, however, like the AUEW and the EETPU, did not accept that board room representation was consistent with trade union collective bargaining. The EETPU, for example, rejected the idea of worker directors as the path to industrial democracy, and wanted instead 'to dramatically expand the scope and range of issues dealt with by the collective bargaining process' (EETPU, Evidence to Bullock, n.d., p.3). It did not think that collective bargaining could be integrated with board level representation because of the harmful effect such a 'corporatist' concentration of power was seen to have on the autonomy of trade unions and the fact that unions have been rooted in the conflict of interest between management and worker (Ibid.; p.6). However, the GMWU, for example, did in effect want more wide ranging and flexible legal powers than those proposed by Bullock, including a general legal requirement on all employers to subject board level issues and decisions, like corporate planning and investment, to joint control with trade union representatives, the Bullock 2X + y formula being merely one possible and optional way of achieving such joint control, the enforcement of which was to be ultimately dependent upon either withdrawing financial privileges from companies, such as taxation or investment allowances, or refusing price increases (GMWU: June and August 1977). In contrast, some unions on the left saw Bullock as a way of merely precluding the institution of workers' control (Passingham and Connor: 1977).

The Bullock Report and the intentions of the Labour Government attracted the vehement opposition of capital. In fact, a banker and two industrialists who were members of the Bullock Committee felt compelled to append a critical minority report to the main report (see Bullock Report: 1977; pp.V and 167-95). This, as the CBI and other employers' groups were also to do, criticised the Committee's very terms of reference for stipulating the need to consider how to achieve industrial democracy rather than whether it should be achieved (Ibid.; p.169). In contrast, it proposed employee participation which developed voluntarily from the grass roots upwards and from a more

173

'democratic' basis than trade union representation (participation only through unions was rejected) and the statutory imposition of trade union representatives at board level (Ibid.;
pp. 171 and 174-5). The last thing that it thought was needed
for efficient, wealth-creating companies was for there to exist
conflicts of interests on their boards of directors. The participation it thought eventually desirable was left to a nominal,
supervisory board (with the $2X + y$ formula for representation
on the basis of a secret ballot of all employees) rather than
a managerial board of directors concerned with day-to-day decision-making, thus reverting to a two-tier structure. It is
important to note that the supervisory board was not to parti-
cipate directly in the management of the company nor to initiate policy, that employee representation was to include management, that it was always to cover less than half of the supervisory board, and that such employee participation was not to
become operable until a specified number of years had seen
lower level developments within the company of forms of employee representation on issues closer to their immediate interests (Ibid.; pp. 172, 176-83 and 189-91). This kind of reform
was to be supplemented by the minimum amount necessary of back-
up, enabling legislation to allow employers to develop such
schemes voluntarily in companies with 2,000 or more employees
(Ibid.; pp. 186 and 177). Although these proposals might seem
limited and paternalistic in character, they were not to be
applied to the major financial institutions, clearing banks
and insurance companies. The immunity of money capital to even
highly attentuated and nominal forms of industrial democracy
was based upon a number of considerations: the highly confidential and complex nature of its business; the essentially secretive and market-sensitive nature of its investment policies;
the need to keep confidential the communication of the Bank of
England's wishes on monetary policy; and the dominant international role of the City in the functioning of money capital
(Ibid.; pp. 194-5).

The overall tenor and reach of this reaction was quite
consistent with the interests and objectives towards industrial
democracy of both money capital, as represented by the City,
and of industrial, monopoly capital. Very noticeably money
capital came out openly in defence of the property rights of
capital as well as of its own paternalistic form of employee
representation and participation. The Stock Exchange explicitly
defended the rights of property against possible trade union
control: 'ultimate control is inseparable from the right of
property which lies, and should continue to lie, with the
holders of the share capital of a company' (The Stock Exchange:
1976; 2 and passim, especially 6-7. Cf. Committee of London
Clearing Banks: 1978). Participation was not to mean control
and any step to reform work relations had to be subordinated
to the 'profit motive' (Stock Exchange: op.cit.; pp. 2-3).
Equally the City Company Law Committee argued: 'for share-

174

holders, the majority [Bullock] proposals entail an unambiguous expropriation of rights which they now possess' (1977: p.19).

The CBI played a central, and what it saw as a successful (CBI, Annual Report, 1977, pp.2-3 and 6) role in leading and orchestrating the opposition of capital, both industrial and financial, to the Bullock Report. This can be seen, in part, by the very endorsement of the CBI's policy by other representatives of capital. The CBI attempted to meet the possibility of reform on industrial democracy by putting forward its own moderate proposals and holding out the promise of back-up legislation if necessary. In its evidence to the Bullock Committee, which derived from an extensive survey of, and campaign within, its membership (CBI: 1976; p.1), this exercise in political management and balance was made apparent. The fragile state of the UK economy was not seen to warrant radical changes but the CBI's policy of a flexible, voluntary and practical approach to employee participation was viewed as a constructive way of improving industrial relations and increasing economic efficiency (Ibid.; p.2). Employees and employers were to be left free to devise schemes appropriate to their own circumstances, if they wanted them developed in the first place. Employee participation was seen as a way of gaining the acceptance of employees to decisions made with the objective of wealth creation in view, and thus as a way of justifying managerial priorities. It was to be developed on the basis of existing schemes, and initially to build upwards from the 'grass-roots' rather than be imposed from the state and the board room downwards. The CBI in fact did propose legislation on the issue even though this was not to be mandatory and not to lay down a uniform structure, such as the 2X + y formula. The back-up legislation proposed was to require companies employing more than 2,000 people in the UK to reach a Participation Agreement (PA) with their employees; this PA was to be reached after a four-year period but if no voluntary agreement had been reached an arbitration agency could enforce the PA on the basis of a unilateral reference and subject to (1) a secret ballot producing a clear majority, (2) its acceptance by the employer as well, (3) its being built upon and often just endorsing existing institutions for participation, and (4) its being consistent with the efficiency and profitability of the enterprise. This was coupled with a rejection of union only representation and employee representation at board room level, for reasons of impracticality and inefficiency.

Participation was not to mean control and it was thought vital that capital itself take a lead in developing such a policy in order to structure participation into manageable forms, reap what benefits it would present for efficiency and assuage and control what desire there was amongst workers for increased participation in the running of the places in which they worked (see Ibid.: March, 1976. Idem: May 1976. Idem: October 1976; Chapter 9). In this sense the CBI itself, as opposed to the state as such, determined to mobilise the class interests of employers in developing opposition to the Bullock Report and used this alternative policy as its basis. This enabled it to argue that its policy could stand 'in place of Bullock' and that the latter was not really about employee participation but about 'trade union control of industry', the confiscation of the property of shareholders, the undermining of confidence and thus investment in British industry, the denial of rights to non-unionists, intractable conflicts of interests for trade unions themselves, and collective bargaining in the board room. Consequently, the CBI's own policy could claim what credibility the Bullock Report may have had in suggesting a way of instituting industrial democracy; and it also meant that the CBI could take a lead in ensuring that companies developed employee participation schemes where necessary which they could control, thereby pre-empting both the organisation and the ideological debate about such schemes (see CBI: May 1977). There is more than a hint of the corporatist control of industrial democracy in the CBI policy in so far as, although it only stipulated back-up legislation, it entailed the co-opted use of industrial democracy for the purpose of control and some enforcement by an outside agency (cf. EEF: March 1976. ABCC: 1975).

We can thus see a coherent and agreed defensive posture against the 'social contract' version of industrial democracy emerging amongst sections of capital. In this context and given that the CBI began to play an objective role in cohering the interests of different capitals, it is interesting to note what happened to the CBI's policy at its national conferences. At its first conference, flush with its concerted campaign against Bullock, the conference floor supported the policy by an overwhelming majority (CBI: 1977b; 103-19). However, at its next conference, when the possibility of legislation on the basis of the Bullock proposals had subsided, things were quite different and more controversial. Indeed, much opposition was voiced to the CBI policy of limited legislation, even by the EEF, some seeing it as merely a sop to trade union leaders, while most would not accept it until trade unions were more democratic and made equal within and not placed above the law; and on a vote the conference jettisoned the CBI's commitment to back-up legislation (CBI: 1978b; Sessions 3A and 3B). In some part this derived from the fact that with Bullock out of the way there was less need to pre-empt the issue with alternative proposals for legislation although the re-election of a Labour Government may have altered this condition. There is also little doubt that, as with the issue of the closed shop, the small firm 'caucus' within the CBI made itself felt, possibly fearing a subsequent extension of the proposed policy to their own enterprises. Furthermore, the need for employers to take the initiative in involving their employees was seen to conflict in principle with the need to legislate, and if employee participation were to grow it would be best if it were not fostered by the state since this would directly conflict with the paternalistic structures inherent in the kind of employee participation envisaged (Ibid.).

The breakdown of the social contract, and the government's White Paper on Industrial Democracy (Cmnd. 7231, May 1978) must have allayed, in an immediate sense, many fears capital may have had of legislation on the issue. The White Paper re-affirmed the contribution that industrial democracy could make to increased industrial efficiency and the idea that the best way it could be developed was on a voluntary basis preferably drawing upon already existing schemes (Ibid.; pp.1-2). It proposed that the law should oblige companies employing more than 500 workers in the UK to discuss with their representatives major proposals affecting the business, like investment plans, before decisions on them had been made (Ibid.; pp. 3 and 13). Joint Representation Committees (JRC's) were to be set up, composed of employee, trade union representatives, which would have available a statutory fall-back right to require discussions with the company board in cases where the latter refused to consult, on appeal to ACAS or a similar body which could either recommend or impose the requirement (Ibid.; pp. 3-4). It proposed legislation allowing employees the right to board room representation so that, in cases where voluntary agreement could not be reached, employees in companies employing more than 2,000 people in the UK were to be able to claim the statutory right to representation on a two-tier board structure, initiated by a request from the JRC, and on the basis of a ballot of all employees leading to a majority in favour of such representation. Before this could occur the JRC was to have been established for three or four years (Ibid.; pp.6-7). Significantly enough, it did not directly come out in favour of (a) the 2X + y formula, suggesting instead one third employee representation on the policy board in a two-tier system as the preferable first step (Ibid.; p.8); nor (b) representation by means of trade unions, seeing the initiative lying rather with the JRC (Ibid.; pp. 8-9). These facts did not, however, dissipate the opposition of capital and the CBI still rejected the proposed form of legislation.[7]

What light does this discussion throw upon the major concerns of this study? First, it shows how potentially more united capital is in developing a defensive strategy against proposed state policy rather than in devising an offensive strategy to initiate state policy as with the IR Act. But we have still seen, in the strategies adopted not merely to defend but also to pre-empt the political conflict over industrial democracy, the leaning of money and petit-bourgeois capital towards paternalism and the CBI and EEF's corporatist gesture towards conciliatory, stand-by legislation and the use of state agencies. Second, we have noted the important co-ordinating, _political_ role that the CBI played in attempting to develop a strong and coherent opposition to state policy and in trying to mobilise all employers around the class interests of capital in property rights and the profit motive. Third, the analysis has, quite simply, shown the power that capital can exercise over the state. Fourth, it has nonetheless shown how the state can formulate a line of policy independent from the political claims and strategic interests of capital, though constrained by the conjunctural shape of the class struggle and capital accumulation, to restore industrial profitability and secure trade union co-operation by pursuing an incomes policy within the corporatist framework of the social contract (cf. Jessop: 1980. Coates: 1980). And, fifthly, it shows again the contradictions posed for the organised labour movement by the state's attempt to transform the social democratic entry into the state into the corporatist control of the working class.

Conclusion

I have attempted to provide a detailed account of the development of the policy and legislation of the state towards industrial relations, discussing the conditions, nature and consequences of specific policy programmes and legislation which have been designed to re-structure work relations to control industrial conflict. This was done particularly with respect to providing a case study of the relationship between capital, its varying fractions and its political organisations, and the state, in order to analyse the development of state policy. These processes were also examined against the background of the changing conjuncture of class conflict that British capitalism went through in the period under discussion. This conjuncture meant that the control of industrial conflict by the state entailed not only the re-structuring of work relations but also the re-structuring of state apparatuses, and it is to a consideration of this process that I shall now turn.

NOTES

1. For detailed accounts see Panitch: 1976; Chapter 7. Jenkins: 1970. Crouch: 1977; Chapters 9 and 13.
2. The best, detailed accounts of the Act available are Thomson and Engleman: 1975. Moran: 1977. For background to the Act see Conservative Political Centre, Fair Deal at Work, 1968.
3. The major exception to this was the case involving Midland Cold Storage who took picketing dock workers to the NIRC: it turned out that Midland Cold Storage 'was an offshoot of one of the country's biggest conglomerates, the Vestey group' (Ferris: 1972; 18).
4. As recent research has shown, employers tend not to be opposed to the closed shop in so far as it ensures that the respective union is representative, that the procedures cover all workers and that it helps to stabilise industrial relations, though it is also seen as a way of increasing the power of

trade unions (see M. Hart: 1979. Weekes et al.: 1975; Chapter 2).

5. For the most recent and detailed survey of the closed shop which tends to support the figure cited by the CBI see Gennard et al.: 1979 and 1980.

6. Useful discussions of industrial democracy can be found in Poole: 1978. Elliott: 1978, and Ramsay: 1977 and Idem: 1980.

7. On the fall of the Labour government and the role played by working class opposition in this, see Coates: 1980. Cf. Glyn and Harrison: 1980; Chapter 4. For one of the last vain attempts to maintain the corporatist direction of the government see Labour Government - TUC Joint Statement, February 1979.

Chapter 9

THE RE-STRUCTURING OF THE INSTITUTIONS OF THE STATE, 1965-1979

In this chapter I wish to consider some of the institutional
changes associated with the complex of factors I have thus far
examined. This means that I shall now analyse certain aspects
of the re-structuring of the state which the conjuncture of
class conflict and the process of capital accumulation and
state interventionism gave rise to as a result of their impact
upon the structure of industrial relations and the re-orientation of state policy towards such relations. In particular,
this will entail scrutiny of the institutional changes associated with this change in policy. In order, therefore, to provide a case study of this process I shall look at, respectively,
the roles of the Ministry of Labour, the NIRC, the CIR and ACAS.

The Ministry of Labour and State Intervention in Industrial Relations

In its evidence to the Donovan Commission the Ministry of
Labour not only commented upon and surveyed its own role, but
as a consequence of the monitoring of that role it began to
raise problems and offer as possibilities for reform, issues
of strategy and policy for industrial relations. It thus
offered, as an agency of the state concerned specifically with
the structuring of work relations and their ramifications, a
reasoned and cogent case for the fostering and buttressing of
well-organised, 'strong and responsible' trade unions, acting
in 'the national interest' (WE, 1965; 4. Cf. ME, 2, 1965; pp.
43-4).

The Ministry identified a need for trade unions to be
strongly organised to overcome their own sectional interests
and realise that their interests were ultimately bound up with
the national economic interest represented by government policy.
Shop steward led plant bargaining and unofficial strikes were
seen to lead to wage drift and harm economic prosperity and
weaken the authority of trade unions. It was thus seen as imperative that this authority be restored (Ibid.). Trade union
recognition, even if imposed on an employer, was thought to be
crucial here in restoring union authority and control over

180

members (WE, p.4). Some support, albeit limited, had therefore
to be given to the closed shop and this, especially in view of
the need to protect the individual, would allow for the registration of unions and the greater supervision of their rules
by government (Ibid.; pp. 5, 83-6 and 86-90). And to further
this process, and so control the level of unofficial strikes
and re-integrate industrial and local plant bargaining it further suggested the integration of shop stewards into the structure of official unionism (ME, 2, pp.50-1 and 62-4. ME, 3,
1965, pp. 88-9).

The Ministry adamantly rejected the use of penal and
financial sanctions against unofficial strikers, that is making
unofficial strikes illegal, because experience had shown this
to be impracticable, because unions might make more strikes
official, because financially undermining trade unions by
making their funds open to legal action was not the way to
foster strong and responsible trade unionism, and because 'the
law would be brought into contempt' (WE, pp. 7 and 78. ME,
2, pp. 57-61. ME, 3, pp. 100-103). This did not mean however
that the Ministry of Labour was opposed to legal remedies tout
court. The very nature of unofficial strikes gave trade unions
a key role in preventing them by taking disciplinary action
against unofficial strikers. In this context, legal coercion
to assist trade unions was possible if procedure agreements
were made legally enforceable (WE, op. cit., p.43). The onus
was thus to be placed on unions to observe agreements and they
were to be supervised by a system of labour courts (Ibid.; p.
93). This was one major way of redressing and reversing what
the Ministry saw as a shift in the balance of power in class
forces towards the working class and its de-stabilising consequences for capital accumulation (ME, 2, pp.51-7).

The Ministry also pointed out how the re-structuring of
industrial relations and the pacification of class conflict
were limited by the competition between capitals and the consequent lack of employer solidarity. It saw employers giving
in to unproductive wage demands both because of the labour
market constraint of full employment and the relative ease
with which they could raise prices (ME, 2, p.52). This seriously undermined the use of prices and incomes policies: 'if
an incomes policy is going to work there has got to be a good
deal more discipline among the employers' (ME, 3, pp. 93-4).
However, as far as the question of the institutional responsibility for taking legal action against strikers was concerned,
it was still seen to rest with the employer or employers'
organisation and not the state (Ibid.; pp. 99-100).

Despite this, the constraints of the growth of state interventionism began to show in the conceptions the Ministry had
of its own role. In response to the issue of the degree of control over class relations exercised by voluntary collective
bargaining and a laissez-faire form of state mediation of work
relations it remarked, 'The state now perhaps more than in the

past is looking at the end result and saying, here are gaps where we think something has to be done' (ME, 2, p.47). Hence. at that time such changes as the Contracts of Employment Act, 1963, and the Redundancy Payments Act, 1965. were seen to precipitate a change in the legal intervention of the state in laying down 'minimum' standards in areas where collective bargaining had failed (Ibid.). This was, however, seen to be consistent with the Ministry's role as an 'honest broker' in conciliating in industrial relations rather than asserting the interests of the government, on such issues as incomes policy, though the question of its independence from government policy was recognised as a problem (ME, 2, p. 81).

Its conciliation function was seen to be far more seriously undermined by the difficulty of intervening in and thereby legitimating unofficial strikes (WE, p. 43). For the ideological reasons of endeavouring to appear independent of government and not to give legitimacy and recognition to unofficial strikes, one of the main interventionist arms of the state was limited in what it could do to conciliate in industrial relations. The autonomy and impartiality of the state vis a vis the interests of employers and unions was crucial to the Ministry's position in conciliating in industrial disputes (WE, op. cit., p.95). Hence, the Ministry's powers to intervene, since conciliation was viewed merely as an extension of the process of collective bargaining, were not realised until the latter had broken down, so failing to invoke the full force of interventionism (Ibid.). Compounding this was the fact that the Minister, as part of the state, had to bring the general or national interest to bear upon work relations and make sure this prevailed in collective bargaining (ME, 2, pp.74-9). Consequently, in order for the Ministry to intervene effectively and secure industrial peace and to be able to legitimate that intervention it was necessary for it to be, or to appear to be, independent of government policy. This thus emerged as a problem in the political structuring of an interventionist form of state control of industrial relations which had arisen at that stage because of the development of incomes policies and the constraints this imposed on the Ministry's ability to secure settlements and to appear to be independent of the policy (WE, pp. 97-8. ME, 2, pp.74-9).

Similarly, the Ministry's powers to control strikes were constrained by the simple fact that most strikes were unofficial and unconstitutional, since consequently 'conciliation has commonly been inhibited by the concern that nothing should be done which might appear to condone or even encourage breaches of agreement ... intervention by the Ministry in such circumstances might also undermine the authority of the trade union official over his members' (WE, p.98). When a strike was sufficiently serious to threaten the national economy the Ministry did intervene but always dealt with trade union officials and never with unofficial strike leaders. The question

182

was therefore raised of whether the Ministry should be able to intervene more often in such situations (Ibid.). It is clear that the particular nature of the unofficial, unconstitutional strike problem posed contradictions of this order for the legitimacy of state intervention of the kind traditionally employed by the Ministry.

A further acute problem for the Ministry and its role was 'how to ensure that the normal processes of arbitration can be reconciled with the national interest' (WE, p. 109), since, previously, arbitration had been concerned solely with the interests of the employers and workers involved in a dispute, but had now been limited by the state of the economy and government economic and incomes policies. The Court of Inquiry procedure faced difficulties as a result of the fact that 'in the last few years, it has been increasingly recognised that the Government has an interest, not merely in ensuring that particular groups of employers and workers manage to settle their differences as best they can, but also in ensuring that situations where persistent labour problems exist should be remedied, in the interests both of efficiency and of better relations generally' (WE, p.109). Institutional change was required since this procedure tended to be ad hoc and had to be carried out with a sense of immediacy which did not allow more general and fundamental proposals for the long-term reconstruction of industrial relations to be made (Ibid.; p.110).

This analysis of the Ministry of Labour's monitoring of its role has brought to light a number of themes associated with the institutional re-structuring of the state in line with changes in the state's re-structuring of industrial relations. Firstly, it clearly provides us with further evidence of the transition in the form of state mediation from laissez-faire to interventionism, and how this transition has been constrained, even within the state, by the principle of voluntarism, the practice by which industrial relations issues are settled primarily by voluntary collective bargaining between the parties concerned. But, secondly, it has also demonstrated the impetus towards increasing state interventionism in industrial relations attendant upon the growth of unofficial strikes, a more interventionist role for the state generally, and declining capital accumulation. Thirdly, it has shown how such state interventionism comes up against the barrier of needing to appear to be independent of central government and its policies in order to maintain legitimacy and ensure industrial peace and how this has to be accounted for in any subsequent re-structuring of the state. Fourthly, the problematic nature of the legitimacy of the state's intervention in industrial relations has been brought out in terms of the problem of how the state can intervene to control unofficial strikes without giving legitimacy to such strikes, a political contradiction that was seen to lead in the direction of a corporatist rather than a conciliatory and pluralist style of intervention. Lastly, and fifthly. it showed how if the state was altering the way it was intervening in industrial relations it was also necessary to alter the means by which it did so, that is change the structure and role of the state institutions concerned with industrial relations, a trend which emerged. for example, not only as a result of points 3 and 4 above, but also as a result of the development of incomes policy and the need to provide for (as opposed to the ad hoc and contingent emergency) a more systematic, long-term and wide-ranging method of controlling industrial conflict.

The Establishment of the CIR

We have seen how the idea of a Commission on Industrial Relations was first put forward in the Donovan Report (1968, pp. 48-51), a proposal we can now argue to have emanated from the Ministry's monitoring of its own role; and we also made note of how the CIR was established and changed by 'In Place of Strife' and the Industrial Relations Act of 1971. For the Donovan Commission, such an institution was to 'carry out inquiries into the general state of industrial relations in a factory or an industry such as have previously been entrusted to ad hoc committees', including cases involving trade union recognition and inadequate collective agreements and procedures, with a view to furthering the development and strengthening of collective bargaining, trade union representation and, more generally, the normative regulation of industrial relations (Ibid.; pp.48-50).

The CIR was established in 1969 by 'In Place of Strife'. The institutional opening within the state was made very clear in the White Paper: 'The Government ... shares the responsibility of bringing about the necessary changes in our system of industrial relations ... as the Donovan Report pointed out, and as both the TUC and CBI recognise, there remains a major gap in the public apparatus for change. There is no institution primarily concerned with the reform of collective bargaining' (Cmnd. 3888: 1969; p.13). The CIR's role was to have three specific dimensions. It was, firstly, to be

> concerned with ways of improving and extending procedural arrangements, for example, how to promote suitable company wide procedures, how to develop acceptable rules governing disciplinary practices and dismissals, how to encourage effective and fair redundancy procedures, how to bring shop stewards within a proper framework of agreed rules in their firm, and how to ensure that they are provided with the right kind of facilities to do their job (Ibid.; p. 13).

Secondly, it was required,

> to tackle other problems that are not now the direct

184

responsibility of any public agency, so that its work
will represent a novel extension of public involvement
in industrial relations in this country. For example,
it will investigate trade union demands for recognition;
encourage reforms in trade union structure and services;
examine cases where companies or trade unions report
failure to negotiate satisfactory agreements; and ...
the effectiveness of existing procedures in an industry
or part of an industry (Ibid.; p. 13).

Thirdly, it was to secure the continuous co-operation and confidence of unions and employers in its work and for this reason
it was not given any legal sanctions, save for authority to obtain information. The CIR was to be 'a disseminator of good
practice and a focus for reform by example ... to bring about
a general move towards the reform and re-structuring of collective bargaining agreements' (Ibid.; p. 14).
On this basis, the CIR produced twenty four reports (see
below) before it was locked into the statutory machinery of the
IR Act which established the CIR as a statutory body (Section
120), working on the basis of references from the Secretary of
State. Within this framework, the questions referred to it were
to be related but not confined to the following problems: (a)
the way in which employers and workers were, or ought to be,
organised for collective bargaining, including the amalgamation
or co-operation of bodies representing either side; (b) the
nature and provisions of, and, where necessary, the need for,
procedure agreements; and (c) recognition and negotiating
rights for the purposes of collective bargaining (Section 121).
The CIR was to report to the government on these and other
cases, as well as providing an annual report giving a general
review of the development of collective bargaining and under-
lining problems of special importance (Sections 122 and 123).
The CIR was also, (a) to carry out research and ballots for
the Industrial Court in cases involving the agency shop provisions of the Act (Sections 11-16); (b) to make detailed proposals and secure discussions for the reform of, or the institution of, procedure agreements to make them more effective in
controlling industrial conflict, with a view to its recommendations taking the form of a legally enforceable contract, and
on the basis of a reference from the Secretary of State to the
Industrial Court (Sections 37-41); (c) to determine the validity of trade union claims to the Industrial Court for recognition with respect to both the numbers of workers and the
common occupational character of the bargaining unit represented in order to decide, on the basis of investigation and
balloting, whether a group of workers constituted a distinct
bargaining unit and whether the union or organisation of workers concerned should be recognised as the sole bargaining agent
for that unit (here, the Industrial Court could make an order
imposing the CIR's recommendations upon employers - see Sections

185

44-50); and (d) to report and carry out a ballot for the Industrial Court in response to a Secretary of State reference to the Court under the emergency procedures of the Act (Sections 138-145). It can thus be seen that one of the major ways in which the CIR became integrated into the legal machinery of the Act was the way in which the Act defined its relationship to the Industrial Court, the NIRC. This gave its work a certain inflection but also maintained a distinct continuity with its previous formation by 'In Place of Strife'. And though its incorporation into the institutional framework of the IR Act brought certain limitations to bear on its practice, such as union non-co-operation, it still developed a decisive contribution to the process of reforming industrial relations, most certainly at the ideological level, serving as a counter-weight to the 'anti-union' provisions of the IR Act.

Capital, the CIR and ACAS

Before proceeding to consider the role of the CIR let me consider its relationship, and that of its successor, ACAS, to capital, most specifically as the latter has been represented by the CBI. The CBI welcomed the proposal to establish the CIR because it represented a way of dealing with things like inquiring into disputes procedures and handling union recognition that accorded with the CBI's own policy, though the CBI questioned the idea of the statutory registration of agreements (CBI, Annual Report, 1968, p.35). The EEF actually went further and saw in the CIR a way of deciding whether specific reforms, like compulsory arbitration and legal enforceability of procedure agreements, could be applied in certain circumstances and not in others. This gave it a general role in controlling industrial relations for what was really required was that the CIR should be able to impose its own ideas upon unions and employers and so shape the form and content of the agreements made (EEF: 1969; 20-21).

Consequently, the CBI supported the setting-up of the CIR by 'In Place of Strife' and 'saw it as having an important function in investigating cases of bad industrial relations and trade union recognition questions, particularly inter-union disputes' (CBI, Annual Report, 1969, p.31). It did, however, come into conflict with certain features of the CIR's early work. It opposed the lack of any chance for employers to reply to the DOE on the CIR's terms of reference and proposals, and it argued that trade unions should become more of a central object of investigation, expressing the fear that the CIR's objective seemed to be to spread trade unionism, a fear that the government sought to placate. Subsequent cases referred to the CIR by the government, after the initial ten, tended to conform with the CBI's demands (Ibid.; pp. 32-3).

When the Labour Government of 1974 proposed to set up a new conciliation and arbitration service, it was supported by the CBI, provided it did not produce high wage settlements and maintained its independence (Idem, Annual Report, 1974, p. 13). However, partly because it was locked into the Labour Government's legislation on industrial relations and partly because of its terms of reference and actual work, the CBI did not see ACAS developing in the way it wanted. It thought that ACAS, in its questions and its consultative drafts on codes of practice, was biased in favour of trade unionism. The CBI also objected to ACAS's terms of reference which it argued conflated erroneously the extension of collective bargaining with the improvement of industrial relations. This did not mean that the CBI rejected ACAS. It saw it as playing a crucial role in providing long term stability for the reform of industrial relations, provided it remained impartial (CBI: 1977a; 34).

The National Industrial Relations Court, 1971-1974

Aside from our main concern with the CIR and ACAS, the other major innovation in state institutions in this phase of indusrial relations reform, which requires brief attention here, was the NIRC, introduced by the IR Act of 1971. The NIRC is an instructive case not least because of its failure to survive, unlike the CIR with its transmogrification into ACAS. It was, furthermore, a directly legal, interventionist agency unlike the CIR and ACAS, central to the corporatist strategy of the Act itself which may say something about its origins, and its eventual disappearance with the repeal of the Act in 1974. In this sense it represents the breakdown of corporatist interventions in industrial relations by legal means, an inappropriate re-structuring of the state to accommodate the growth of state interventionism, particularly as it identified, in an institutional form, state coercion of indigenous working class organisations with the rule of law, and so undermined the legitimacy of its interventions.

The NIRC constituted a response to the previous organisation of the state vis a vis its role in industrial relations. It formed a mode of coping with the structural process whereby the executive and judicial arms of the state contradicted one another in the administration and control of industrial relations. As I have argued above (see especially Chapter 2), the relationship between the state and the organised working class movement in terms of trade union law has been marked, in one important respect, by the way in which, in periods of heightened class conflict, the courts have endeavoured to circumscribe and over-ride the actions, rights and organisation of trade unions; and that these judicial decisions have been either revoked or remedied by parliament and the government in the face of sustained political pressure organised by the labour movement. This has posed a problem for the structure of the state in terms of how to co-ordinate the actions of the executive and judiciary towards industrial relations and trade unions since they have often constructed distinct and sometimes contradictory strategies and since it has been an intention of corporatist

reformers to curtail the autonomy of the judiciary within the
state and to rely on systematic, and predictable administrative
law. Making the NIRC a court responsible for industrial relations has formed one of the few and most notable responses to
this contradiction within the state. This, and its place in
the legal corporatist strategy of the Act, makes sense of the
setting up of the NIRC as a specifically political phenomenon
while still tying it to the re-structuring of industrial relations and the state in the overall interests of capital accumulation.

The NIRC was set up by the IR Act as the court which
applied the sanctions in the Act, e.g. compensation awards
against trade unions, to which complaints about unfair industrial practices could be made, to back up the Registrar's surveillance of trade union rules and practices and to decide upon
the provisions of legally enforceable collective agreements
(IR Act, 1971, Sections 99-119). It was established with the
powers of a normal court (Schedule 3, Part II, Section 114).

The NIRC failed in achieving its objectives, its fate
being bound up with the fate of the IR Act as a whole, floun-
dering, as did the Act, on union non-co-operation, and employer
and state reluctance to follow through the legal clauses in the
Act to their logical conclusions. But as some commentators have
noted, the NIRC had sufficient work to do to allow it to establish some kind of case law and to initiate changes in the law
as it applied to industrial relations, specifically in laying
down precedents for any subsequent and parallel cases which
arose or could arise even despite the subsequent repeal of the
Act (Thomson and Engleman: 1975; 145).

What then can we make of the line the NIRC developed in
the cases that were brought before it? Let us first consider
cases which came before the NIRC concerning trade union control
over their members.[1] In the Heatons Transport v TGWU case, the
NIRC decided that the union was responsible and so legally
liable for the actions of its shop stewards. Though initially
overturned by the Court of Appeal, this line was supported by
the House of Lords which found the union responsible for its
shop stewards' illegal actions of blacking and picketing, and
therefore made the union liable to financial penalties. The
only way for the union to avoid this, according to the House
of Lords, was for it to have disciplined its stewards to the
extent of withdrawing their union credentials. The precedent
then established by the House of Lords was followed by the
NIRC in subsequent cases, and re-affirmed the NIRC's resolve
in its policy of using the IR Act against the funds of unions
rather than against individual workers. In this way, the NIRC
developed the law to allow the courts to make the responsibilities of non-registered unions for the control of their members
comparable to those for registered unions (Weekes et al.: 1975;
97 and 100-113), a policy in keeping with the corporatist as
opposed to the liberal implications of the Act. This was

188

similarly the fact with the decisions reached in cases involving the closed shop which it tended to support in the interests
of good industrial relations as against the claims of individual workers (Ibid.; 55-61).

But in order to do this the NIRC had to be able to define
the leaders responsible for industrial action (Ibid.; 112).
This led to the NIRC fixing responsibility on union officials
since it believed industrial action had to be organised and led
and union officials were likely to be involved in some way.
This attribution of leadership and responsibility had two consequences: it opened up union funds to penalties rather than
risk the more disruptive and effective industrial action which
followed from the prosecution of individual workers or groups
of workers; and it enabled the NIRC to justify and further its
own policy of coercing unions to control their own members
(Ibid.; 112-13, 189 and 197), again in keeping with the corporatist strategy of the Act. The NIRC developed the common law
within a corporatist framework, particularly as the approach
it adopted in part served to overcome the practical problem of
prosecuting large numbers of workers (Ibid., and Crouch: 1977;
183).

What, then, of the NIRC's role with respect to cases involving strikes? This essentially entailed it, like other
courts, extending the legal liability of unions for industrial
action, a policy covering what it thought constituted irregular
industrial action short of a strike and illegal secondary action, all of which of course set important precedents. Accordingly, the former was deemed to include bans on overtime on
work which was not contractually binding, and the refusal to
do extra work, the latter to include, tout court, 'blacking'
irrespective of the registered status of the union, and peaceful 'secondary' picketing, which also re-affirmed the precarious nature of the legal right to picket (see Weekes et al.:
1975, 189-97, 199-200 and 213-19).

By its very presence the NIRC represented an attempt to
corporatise not merely the trade unions but also the paternalism of the courts for as a court directly responsible for
industrial relations cases it represented an interventionist
rather than a laissez-faire mediation of industrial relations.
However, the very ambiguities of its constitution mitigated
the leading role it could play in this process. The IR Act
restricted it quite obviously to recruitment from the benches
of other courts (Section 99) and it remained part of the appeal
arrangement whereby its decisions were open to scrutiny by the
court of appeal and the House of Lords. As a preliminary and
atypical institution of a state court for industrial relations,
it was highly circumscribed and a more developed corporatisation of the state would have entailed, at least, detaching it
from the normal court structure, giving it total autonomy from
the judicial arm of the state and making it much more a crea-
ture of the executive. This would have had severe political

and ideological repercussions for it would have undermined one
of the main institutional planks of the 'rule cf law' by which
the state was attempting to legitimate its intervention, namely
the separation of the executive and judiciary and the independence cf the courts.

The NIRC was likewise caught, in dealing with industrial
relations. between its role as a court of law and the need for
conciliation which arose from the cases it investigated. In
short, the Act required the NIRC to dc certain things by law
but this was not necessarily consistent with the need to remedy
the underlying causes of conflict, in particular cases, for
which a conciliatory function would have been more suited. In
some instances the NIRC did investigate before reaching decisions but it was limited by the law in what it could dc. This
was a contradiction which the procedure of the NIRC as a court
of law could not overcome (Ibid.; 197-200 and 217).[2]

The CIR and its Role in Ideology and Political Practice, 1969-1974

An important element of continuity in the work of the CIR was
its support for strong and well-organised trade unionism as
the key to industrial peace (Ibid.; 229, and cf. pp.183-4, 222
and 229). Although it would obviously be affected by its articulation with the wider dimensions of state interventionism,
the CIR can be seen as attempting to develop an approach to
industrial relations reform consistent with such interventionism and to make it appropriate to the large-scale multi-plant,
interdependent and planned structure of monopoly capital and
the increasingly centralised nature of labour representation,
as well as to the conjunctural escalation of class conflict.
And this approach consisted of support - by the state if
necessary - for a well-organised, efficient and representative
trade unionism as a form of social control for industrial relations, and, concomitantly, the systematic and planned rationalisation and bureaucratisation of the structures and procedures
of collective bargaining, the formalisation of industrial relations roles, most specifically that of the shop steward and the
industrial relations function within management, and the elaboration of the need for capitals to construct long-term structures and policies for their own internal industrial relations.
In this sense, its own ideology and practice under both Labour
and Conservative governments can be construed as exemplifying
an incipient expression of corporatism.

a) Trade unionism and collective bargaining. The import of the
CIR reports[3] I shall discuss under this heading bears most
closely on the issue of trade union recognition. In its very
first report the CIR affirmed the rights of association and
representation for employees, and the need to accept the growth
of white collar unionism and to make sure that it followed a
'sensible' and 'orderly' course, especially since such unionism

190

derived from basically similar occupational characteristics, such as, work conditions, skill, pay and authority structure (CIR: No. 1; 1969). An important consideration in this was the fact that, most notably in the financial sector, staff associations and other forms of heteronomous labour collectivities were not considered independent or effective enough for the purposes of collective bargaining. This meant supporting the growth of trade unionism for the CIR argued it was erroneous to suppose that management and employees shared the same interests in pay and conditions. And this support went to the extent of urging that even in cases where the percentage of trade union membership was low, employer recognition or at least employer accommodation was the best way to ensure its development and where necessary other types of independent organisations were suggested. (See No. 2, 1969. No. 16: 1971. No. 26: 1972. No. 35. No. 42. No. 52: 1973. No. 57. No. 58. No. 75. No. 78. No. 79. No. 82. No. 84. No. 86: 1974.)

In this way the CIR attempted, sometimes not without success, to foster the development of trade unionism, or at least single channel, independent organisations, within its remit both before and during the IR Act, not only for money capital per se, but for white collar occupations more generally, which have arisen out of the increased bureaucratisation of administration and the socialisation and differentiation of the labour process. We can see this at work in a number of cases, not only with respect to the nature of the occupations which claimed representation, but also in the fact that quite often the CIR had to deal with the industrial relations problems besetting multi-plant companies and corporate groups of companies. Trade union representation and recognition, and the planning by capital for union bargaining, were seen as ways of meeting the interests of such newly emergent occupational groups and preventing the fragmentation and local, sectional bargaining engendered by multi-plant structures. (See, e.g. No. 5. No. 12: 1970. No. 70. No. 74. No. 88: 1974.)[4] This position of the CIR's extended to the structure of company groups in which in one case the smaller companies in the group complained of the centralisation of industrial relations control and collective bargaining in the largest company in the group. This complaint the CIR rejected, arguing for the clear advantages of centralised industrial relations structures in preventing fragmentation and instability (No. 32: 1973).

b) Collective bargaining and industrial relations institutions. Not only was the CIR called upon to pass judgement on the role of trade unionism and collective bargaining in the management of industrial relations, but also on the relationship between the latter and the overall institutionalisation of work relations, in order to accommodate the changing structure of capital and the prevailing conditions of industrial conflict. In a number of cases the CIR was asked to report on instances of

companies and industries in which industrial relations seemed
to consist of a perpetual stream of disputes and strikes. It
was the job of the CIR to investigate and monitor and to recommend and encourage ways of reducing such conflict. What the CIR
did in these cases was to make one or more of the following
recommended changes in the structure and practice of industrial
relations: the development by management, especially in view of
the increasing complexity of the structure of the control of
capital, of long-term policies for the ordering of industrial
relations in companies; the specialisation of management in
handling and planning industrial relations; the establishment
of joint negotiation and consultation, formal and written domestic procedure agreements for collective bargaining and disputes;
the formal recognition of the positive role of the shop steward
in ensuring order; the level at which collective bargaining
would be most effectively institutionalised, be it company or
plant level, or a centralised amalgam of these within multi-
plant (sometimes also multi-national) companies; the fostering
of closer links between shop stewards and trade union officials
and the formal incorporation of shop stewards into the structure of official unionism; and the rationalisation of pay
structures to reduce points of conflict and bargaining, to
regularise the pattern of differentials and to establish clear,
measured, and agreed relationships between job characteristics
and levels of pay.[5]

c) General problems in UK industrial relations. While much of
what has been said above clearly has general relevance, the CIR
was also called upon to consider issues which were not directly
or immediately specific to a particular firm or industry. We
can now examine some of these 'general problem' areas.

i) Shop steward incorporation. As a continuation of the Donovan
Commission's recommendations, the CIR considered the formalisation of the shop stewards' role. Pointing to the growth of
workplace bargaining and shop steward organisation, the CIR
also indicated how the shop stewards' role had not really been
incorporated properly in industrial agreements, company and
plant level bargaining, and trade union structures. It therefore suggested that these things be remedied, that companies
recognise the functions performed by shop stewards and provide
facilities for this purpose, making sure their role was rule
governed, defined in writing and jointly agreed. Trade unions
were urged to do likewise with their own rules and the formal
collective bargaining role of the shop steward was to be negotiated into collective agreements. In this way the CIR asserted
for management the positive role that shop steward incorporation
could play in controlling industrial relations (No. 17: 1971).

ii) The role of management in industrial relations. In part,
the CIR in this reference summarised what it had to say on the

need for management to develop specialisation in industrial relations and formal, comprehensive, well-defined, integrated and written company policies leading to predictability, order, consistency and equitability in its control of industrial relations, 'enabling management to plan ahead, to anticipate events, and to secure and retain an initiative in changing situations' (No. 34: 1973; p.6). It found that legislation was having an effect in that nearly all of the companies it studied were considering the implications of the IR Act and the Code of Practice. In particular, the response of industrial relations policy formation, assisted by such encouragement from the state and as suggested by the CIR, was to be tailored to the structure of the company, being notably but not exclusively appropriate to the increasingly monopolistic and multi-plant character of the structure of capital (Ibid.; p.9).

iii) <u>Small firms and the code of industrial relations practice.</u> In this report, the CIR tended to confirm the findings of the Bolton Committee both on the nature of the small firm sector and its industrial relations, though it questioned whether the latter were quite as uniform as Bolton had implied (No. 69: 1974; chapters 1 and 2). However, in keeping with their paternalistic structure, it found that most small firms had taken no notice of the code for one or more of a number of reasons: they had no collective bargaining; they depended on good, informal 'human' relations to settle problems; the code was too 'legislative' and interventionist in character and favoured workers; the day to day operations of the business allowed no time for industrial relations specialisation; and trade unions had refused to co-operate with the code (Ibid.; chapter 3). The CIR rejected the petit-bourgeois claim that trade unionism was irrelevant to the small firm and saw the major obstacles to collective bargaining residing in the lack of employer organisation, the unwarranted hostility of employers and workers (though this hostility tended to subside as the size of the firm grew and to the extent that it was no longer run by an owner-manager) and the consequent constraints placed upon trade union recruitment. The CIR considered collective bargaining relevant to even very small firms because conflicts of interest still could arise. In effect, this implied that small firms did not have better industrial relations than large firms, that they should thus encourage trade union recognition and collective bargaining, and that they needed more not less external intervention by the state, trade unions and employers' organisations in order to achieve this (Ibid.; pp. 44-8).

iv) <u>Industrial relations in multi-plant undertakings.</u> Here the CIR dealt directly and specifically with the way in which economic concentration and centralisation had increased the size and complexity of capital units, had made large, multi-plant companies' industrial relations much more central to the

national structure of industrial relations, had produced a more
highly complicated managerial structure for capital, and thus
had generally changed while increasing the problem of industrial
relations control. This had to be dealt with, according to the
CIR, while allowing management to achieve adequate levels of
productivity and efficiency (No. 85: 1974; Chapter 2). Of major
significance here was the fact that the growth of capital by
mergers prevented the centralisation of the subsequent capital's
industrial relations since the acquired companies could and did
have widely varying systems. And, relatedly, it pointed to a
tendency for multi-plant companies to be prone to single plant
bargaining and to lack adequate industrial relations specialisation. Needless to say, there also existed a tendency for such
companies to have to bargain with a multiplicity of trade unions,
often with unofficial shop steward committees (Ibid.; Chapters
4, 5 and 6).
     The CIR emphasised the crucial role of management in the
process of reform and its need to develop a highly specialised
industrial relations function. It also urged the institutionalisation of information and communication channels, the formulation of some kind of collective agreement irrespective of the
degree of centralisation, and the integration of plant bargaining into the overall structure of company level bargaining. It
suggested that trade unions construct more effective organisational links between their representatives and the representatives of other unions in multi-plant companies, integrate plant
bargaining into the structure of official union bargaining, and
develop bargaining organisations based on inter-union co-operation (Ibid.; pp. 50-53).

The CIR and State Control of Industrial Relations
So far we have examined the corporatist strategy developed by
the CIR in response to the changing structure of capital and
the intensification of industrial conflict. This strategy has
consisted of the corporatist use of trade unions as a way of
socially controlling industrial relations, the more rationalised
normative regulation of such relations, together with, albeit
not ordered by, state intervention in so far as such features
could not be developed voluntarily: the state, for the CIR,
was not so much to intervene as to assist but the CIR clearly
envisaged close co-operation between capital, the state and
union leaders in this process.
     But what of the actual effectiveness of the ideology and
practice of the CIR? In a number of the cases on which it was
called to report, the CIR was able at the time or subsequently
to intervene to at least conciliate and to either resolve the
dispute, secure trade union recognition or agreement to move
towards recognition, or the acceptance of both unions and employers involved that its proposals served as a basis for negotiation and for institutionalising their industrial relations.
While perhaps the most striking aspect of this was the CIR's

success in securing the recognition of a trade union, or a joint body also containing staff associations, and the acceptance of collective bargaining by certain banks and other financial institutions, it was able to obtain, to varying extents, some form of acceptance of its ideology and practice in a number of other cases.[6] Despite some very notable failures,[7] this meant that out of the 60 directly relevant cases, that is those in which the CIR could have had a relatively immediate effect, it was able to secure some agreement with aspects of its strategy in only 17 of them.

However, on the basis of more long-term evidence it is possible to suggest that the effectiveness of the CIR's role in having its recommendations accepted was not as small as this would appear to indicate. James has concluded that there had been a move towards the recognition of independent trade unions in 21 of the 41 cases subject to a reference to the CIR and which were still available at the time of his survey (1977; 30-37). This is indicative both of its moderate effectiveness and also of its remaining weaknesses. For, as James also points out, its work illustrated the limitations of intervention on the premise of reasoned argument without adequate sanctions and without realising how fact-gathering investigations by a third party and the conclusions it reached could very quickly and easily become the focus of industrial struggle (Ibid.; pp. 38-9). These remarks have to be set against the conclusions of another follow-up survey by Purcell which attempted to assess the extent to which the reforms recommended by the CIR in the nine companies which it investigated in 1969-1970 had been achieved and maintained by 1976-1977 (1979; 4). This found the following: the fact that institutions and procedures suggested by Donovan and the CIR though not essential, had usually formed part of the reform process; the way in which shop steward incorporation and the extension of joint regulation formed part of the reform process; the role of a crisis in industrial relations in providing an opportunity for change to occur; and that while the role of the CIR was seen as secondary in inducing reform, except in possibly two companies (that is out of a total of nine), 'in leading the public debate on industrial relations reform after the Donovan Report, it undoubtedly influenced the ideas and attitudes of some key people in management and the trade unions' (Ibid.; p.18). In fact, Purcell sees ACAS as capable of playing a more effective interventionist role than the CIR since it combines simultaneously, in a way that the CIR did not, the capacity to provide both the diagnosis and analysis of the institutional changes required for reform and the ability to mediate and conciliate directly in the immediate industrial relations problems facing employers and unions (Ibid.; pp.18-21).

This evidence would seem to bear witness to the contradictory nature of the CIR's role, the way in which it began to fill the gap within the state for an interventionist agency on the one hand, but was limited, on the other hand, because its structure, practice and ideology did not allow it to become more properly and effectively interventionist in providing for a more unambiguously corporatist control of industrial relations. Another way of examining such a contradiction is to analyse the CIR's own monitoring over time of the general dimensions and limitations of its role, for in this it set out its own conception and an assessment of its effectiveness. The CIR thought that it could claim a measure of success but that it had not fulfilled its intentions which meant that its operations threw up a number of problems to be taken account of in any future re-organisation of the state vis a vis industrial relations (No. 90: 1974; pp.12-13).

Firstly, it thought that the scope of its inquiries had been too restricted in dealing only with industrial relations institutions and procedures and that any future agency like the CIR should be able to relate more directly and systematically the investigation of such issues with the economic, productive and distributive factors involved in the reference. For it had been, as we have seen, one of the major emphases of the CIR that for the purpose of controlling work relations it was necessary for industrial relations policies to be explicitly linked to the wider managerial policies of capital (Ibid.;p.13). Secondly, the CIR pointed out how such an agency as itself committed to fundamental reform by voluntary means required 'general acceptability both politically and by employers and unions' (Ibid.; p.14). To this end, the CIR suggested that 'it would be most valuable if representatives of employers and unions could have a participating role involving positive responsibility rather than the exercise of veto rights' (Ibid.; p.15). Finally, and very significantly, the CIR pointed to the need in future for any similar state agency to be clearly independent of government and of political conflict and capable of de-politicising industrial relations: '"Taking industrial relations out of politics" is a common aspiration' (Ibid.;p.15). We can see here the CIR, returning to some of the themes raised by the Ministry of Labour in the mid-1960s, contributing in its turn to the re-structuring of the state.

So far we have analysed how the CIR represented a transition towards a more interventionist role for the state in industrial relations, how its establishment was meant to fill the need for such an institution in reforming collective bargaining, how it inculcated the corporatist policy of using such bargaining together with trade unionism as means of socially controlling industrial conflict for capital but how this was constrained by an ideological if not a practical commitment to a liberal role for the state, albeit one moving in the direction of corporatism and more direct intervention by its very presence. Let us now consider, in conclusion, the effect of its own interventions and its monitoring of those interventions in the further re-structuring of the state's role in industrial

relations by considering how its proposals for the future of
this process were implemented with the institution of ACAS in
1975.

The Role of ACAS. 1975-1979: State Intervention and Corporatism

ACAS was set up by the Labour Government and became a statutory
body under the EP Act of 1975. Its main functions developed out
of the experience and proposals of the CIR, and represented the
centralisation of the industrial relations functions of the
state into one agency. As such, ACAS specialised in tasks previously carried out by the CIR, DOE, industrial courts and
courts of inquiry, while also co-ordinating them and incorporating the capacity to respond both to short-term crises and to
elaborate long-term strategies of reform (ACAS: 1975; pp.2-5).
        Another aspect of the re-structuring of the state which
ACAS represented and which derived from the process of state
intervention involving the CIR was the stress placed on the
independence of ACAS 'from the machinery of government'. This
was said to be ensured in three ways: first, the council which
has run ACAS has been responsible for the general conduct of
its work; second, it was laid down in the EP Act that ACAS was
'not to be subject to directions of any kind from any Minister
of the Crown as to the manner in which it is to exercise any
of its functions under any enactment' (Ibid.; p.2); third, it
has been the norm for ACAS itself, within its terms of reference, to determine when to intervene in the face of industrial
relations problems (Ibid.; p.4). Moreover, of equal significance has been the way in which ACAS has become a more explicitly tri-partite institution, incorporating into its administrative and policy council leading representatives of employers
and trade unions as well as government in marked contrast to
the lack of union co-operation which constrained much of the
work of the CIR (Ibid.; p.6).
        Also of particular interest has been the responsibility
of ACAS for trade union recognition cases brought under the EP
Act. In supporting trade union organisation and recognition
ACAS has balanced the principle of majority support with the
desire not to fragment existing bargaining arrangements nor
to usurp the TUC inter-union disputes procedure (ACAS: 1977;
Chapter 9). We can also single out for attention the actual
effectiveness of ACAS's interventions which will bring us on
to a consideration of its place within the state and its articulation with other agencies, most notably the courts. ACAS
laid great emphasis upon the extent of its effectiveness, significantly by comparison with the period prior to its formation,
in securing industrial order and peace in a high number of
cases (see, e.g. Idem: 1976; pp. 8-9 and Appendix A). This
conclusion seems to be borne out by follow-up evidence, even
in the most contentious area of ACAS's interventions, namely
trade union recognition. A survey in 1978 of the recognition
cases dealt with by ACAS under the EP Act found that in 30 per

cent of the cases in which ACAS recommended it, union recognition had been conceded by the employer, bringing over 11,000
of the 18,000 workers covered by such recommendations within
collective bargaining arrangements, an effectiveness highly
notable, the survey argues, given ACAS's power to recommend
but not to order or force recognition upon an employer (IRRR:
November 1978, No. 188; 13-17 and 19-24). The survey found that
ACAS tended to recommend union recognition where majority (50
per cent or more) support for it could be found and that even
support for union recognition above 40 per cent but below 50
per cent could lead to an ACAS recommendation for recognition
if the levels of current and potential (in the event of union
recognition) union membership were substantial. However, it
found that this was mitigated by ACAS's aim not to fragment
existing collective bargaining arrangements, even in cases also
involving a clear majority in favour of union recognition, as
well as in cases in which employers argued full recognition
'would fragment the company's country-wide payment system and
personnel policy' (Ibid.; pp.14-15).

It clearly becomes apparent, however, that a major restraint upon the effectiveness of ACAS's role has been employer
non-compliance with its recommendations, a form of opposition
which has been extended by some employers to taking ACAS to
court (Ibid.; pp. 15 and 17-18. ACAS: 1977; pp. 42-5. 1978;
pp. 27-30). The CBI opposed what it saw as its pro-union bias
while 'the National Federation of the Self-Employed has called
ACAS the "recruiting wing of the TUC" and has urged small businesses to steer well clear of involvement with the service'
(IRRR: 1978; 18). In fact, as ACAS indicates, most of its trade
union recognition cases have involved small and medium sized
companies (ACAS: 1977; p.20), and it complained of problems of
delay and non-co-operation in dealing with trade union recognition cases, mainly concerning small-scale capital (Idem:
1978; p.29). Though this did not impede too severely the ability of ACAS to extend trade unionism and collective bargaining
widely and consensually, it did entail, by virtue of a specific
and concentrated expression of the hostility of capital, conflict with the courts and their interpretations of ACAS's role
(Idem: 1978; pp.27-8. Idem: 1979; pp.28-30).

This brings us on to consider, as an aspect of the process
of forming a means for the state to intervene in industrial
relations, the nature of the contradiction within the state
between an agency like ACAS and the courts. I have tried to
emphasise the burgeoning corporatist character of ACAS in terms
of a number of factors: its formation, centralisation and specialisation as a state apparatus geared to intervening in industrial relations as a phase in the overall re-structuring of the
state and state intervention; the explicitly tri-partite character of its governing, administrative council; its quango status,
that is, its representation as an agency independent of government within the state; and its support of trade unionism and

198

collective bargaining as mechanisms for socially controlling
industrial relations and industrial conflict. However, such
changes are by no means automatic or trouble-free and ACAS came
up against not only the opposition of capital, particularly
petit-bourgeois capital, but also encountered the institutions
and norms of the laissez-faire state, the principle of voluntarism and the absence of sanctions to secure and enforce its
intervention. Its role has thus been marked by a contradiction,
one which it itself recognised as a consequence of its involvement in the trade union recognition procedures of the EP Act.
In effect, it thought that its statutory work on union recognition contradicted its independent, impartial, flexible, discretionary and voluntary role in conciliating, advising and
ensuring the effective resolution of industrial disputes and
of deep-seated problems of industrial relations structure
(Idem: 1978; p.30. 1979; p.30). Such a contradiction was made
manifest by the fact that some employers brought ACAS into contact with the courts. In a letter, sent on behalf of the Council
of ACAS to the Secretary of State for Employment, on 29 June
1979, the chairman of ACAS argued, 'legal decisions are now
having a serious effect on the way in which the Service carries
out its duties.... It might lead to the Service being required
to recommend the break up of existing negotiating machinery or
the fragmentation of the existing grouping of an employer's
work force' (Ibid.; pp.111-12). In effect, ACAS was caught in
a contradiction because it had not constructed an institutional
form appropriate to the ideology of voluntarism and the reality
of interventionism, nor had it been able to de-politicise
either itself or industrial relations, and it continued to be
restricted by its relationship to other agencies of the state.

Conclusion
We can see therefore that the process of re-structuring the
state's control of industrial relations involves not only an
articulated response to the structure and rate of capital accumulation, the intensification of class conflict and the growth
of the defensive economic power of sections of the working
class; that it arises not only as a result of the interests of
fractions of capital, their political organisation and their
relationship to the construction and mediation of state policy;
not only from the constitutive and relatively autonomous role
of the state and political organisations in forming policy and
legislation, out of the conflicting strategies and tactics of
fractions of capital and political agencies on the shape and
direction of industrial relations reform; but also, and very
importantly, from the connections and contradictions between
distinct apparatuses of the state. In concluding this latter
argument we can suggest that the continuing contradiction
between ACAS and the courts indicates that the re-structuring
of the state to re-assert its control over industrial relations
has not yet been able to align, as part of the logic of this

199

formation, the autonomy of the judiciary with the construction
and establishment of a corporatist form of state intervention
in industrial relations.

NOTES

1. The source I shall rely upon here, in the main, is
Weekes et al.: 1975. But see also Crouch: 1977; 180-84.
Westergaard and Resler: 1976: 228-36. Thomson and Engleman:
1975; passim.
2. The above account attempts to explain the NIRC within
the context of the institutional structure of the state rather
than only seeing it and its policy, as Westergaard and Resler
appear to do, as an expression of the strategy and opinion of
the ruling class. See Idem: op. cit.
3. I shall refer to the year of a set of reports and
not the year of individual reports and to the number of the
CIR reports in question. For a fuller discussion of the CIR
see Strinati: 1981.
4. It is interesting that in one such case, that of Con
Mech (Engineers) Ltd., No. 53: 1973, the CIR recommended union
recognition, while the NIRC penalised the union in question,
the AUEW, for failing to call off a strike at the company.
The matter was only resolved when the union's fine was paid
off by an anonymous group of businessmen. See Westergaard and
Resler: 1976; 233-4.
5. For examples of cases involving the above points see,
e.g., CIR reports No. 10. No. 11: 1970. No. 18. No. 19. No.
20. No. 22: 1971. No. 29: 1972. No. 45. No. 54: 1973. No. 62.
No. 76. No. 80. No. 86: 1974.
6. For examples see, e.g. CIR reports, No. 13: 1970.
No. 35. No. 43. No. 52. No. 56: 1973. No. 57. No. 60. No. 61.
No. 62. No. 67. No. 70. No. 75. No. 78. No. 82. No. 86: 1974.
7. See CIR reports, No. 24: 1971. No. 26: 1972. No. 59.
No. 79: 1974.

Chapter 10

CAPITALISM, THE STATE AND INDUSTRIAL RELATIONS: CONCLUSIONS

In this study I have attempted to provide a sociological account of some of the reasons why the state intervenes in industrial relations in order to contain industrial conflict, the nature and the structure of the interventions undertaken and some of their more notable consequences, by examining a specific, historical conjuncture, that of Britain from the late 1950s onwards.[1] It is now necessary to clarify the conclusions I have drawn from this analysis. This I shall do in two ways: first, I shall summarise each chapter in turn, setting out the details of its argument; then I shall identify certain theoretical and empirical points and indications for research strategy that emerge as plausible conclusions from the work as a whole.

In the first chapter, having defined the central concern of the study as being the sociology of the role of the modern state and its relationship to class structure and class conflict, I endeavoured to look at the existing stock of theories of the state to discover in what ways they would be of help in this project. The answer I arrived at was that unless amalgamated into a broader framework, their relevance would be limited for despite such insights as I have made extensive use of - like the importance of conceiving of capital as being divided or 'fractionalised' rather than forming a homogeneous, monolithic bloc - I argued that they either provided few conceptual clues for research or have been ultimately reductionist, assimilating the state to the economy and therefore obviating the study of politics almost by definition. More positively I did suggest that some of the threads of the various arguments could be drawn together, and argued that what was needed was a set of concepts specifically related to analysing the political structures of modern capitalism, and which accounted for their specificity as well as their relationship with the economy without at the same time reducing this specificity to economic factors. To this end and with the precise object in view of the state's involvement in industrial relations in Britain I drew up a typology of forms of state control of industrial conflict: liberalism, paternalism, pluralism, and corporatism. As conceptualisations, however, these types necessarily remain purely descriptive categories; they do not explain anything but are merely ways of describing the strategies adopted by classes, class fractions and political groupings in Britain over the form to be taken by the state's control of industrial conflict. In order to effect an explanation it is in fact essential to consider the social conditions allowing for such conflicts to arise, and this entails examining the historical development of British capitalism and the historical conjuncture within which such conflict takes place.

With this in mind, in chapter 2 I detailed the history of the law relating to industrial conflict between 1799 and the late 1950s. This was done for a number of reasons. It allows us not only to give an historical context to the use of legal controls over industrial conflict that re-emerged in the 1960s but it also, and more importantly, allows us to pose in a coherent fashion the historical specificity of the latter phase. Is the IR Act of 1971 and its judicial and statutory associates merely a case of plus ca change ... as many would have us believe, or are there peculiarly novel features of the historical conjuncture of the 1960s and 1970s which distinguish it from previous phases of legal control and which thus more adequately explain the present phase? Chapter 2 does in fact indicate how a class conflict model appears to be able to account for coercive legal controls on union actions in that it shows, in a number of cases, increasing industrial conflict leading to more coercive judicial controls which are subsequently removed or watered down by Acts of Parliament under political pressure from trade unions. This has obvious implications for the 'citizenship' rights granted to trade unions as well as for their legal status since, as chapter 2 has illustrated, this has been a very uneven, controlled and contingent process.[2] But it has also to be recognised that any class conflict model must have serious limitations in that it is a somewhat unargued assumption that such conflict always takes place under the same conditions. This has to be empirically established, and in this way it can be shown, as chapters 3 and 4 attempt to do, that British capitalism has changed very markedly such that the very notable escalation of industrial conflict that began to occur from the mid-1950s onwards and the subsequent moves towards legal controls have to be explained in structural and conjunctural terms and cannot be reduced solely to a class conflict model since the conditions under which the state's intervention in industrial relations occurs change over time. Aside from these points, chapter 2 also attempted to show the progressive transition in the state's role from laissez-faire to the burgeoning signs of interventionism in the policies of the government, parliament and the judiciary towards the legal status of trade unions, and their use of the rule of law as a means of de facto and symbolic social control in response to the assertion of union and working class militancy.

202

To thus provide an explanatory, historical and structural context for the emergence of state intervention in industrial relations in Britain in the 1960s, chapter 3 discussed in detail some of the key changes in the political economy of British capitalism, concentrating in particular upon the socialisation of the labour process and the political economy as a whole, the monopolisation of capital, the centralisation of trade unions, and the growth of planning and economic intervention by the state. It is the main contention of this chapter that such structural changes provided a basis for the enhancement of working class strike power, the marked intensity of capital's need for planning and the greater direct influence of state power in maintaining capitalism. But, while chapter 3 illustrated some major changes in the economic and political determinants of class structure and thus in the structural limits of class struggle, it by no means fore-closed on the analysis of the exercise of class <u>power</u> with which the rest of the study is concerned. Nor could it have done so since it is not possible to read off from a political economy of class structure a political sociology of class conflict even though the former provides important insights on the conditions which both limit and are shaped by the form and content of the latter.

It is therefore in chapter 4 that the specific, conjunctural features of class conflict in Britain from the 1950s onwards and the problems posed for capital accumulation, the state and the overall exercise of class power are set out. Thus, firstly, it identified a useful analytical distinction between class conflict in the sphere of production and in the sphere of distribution. This was seen as useful in analysing the empirical material and in pointing to the different targets of state intervention. It was then suggested that central to and structurally connecting both sets of conflicts has been the growth in the militancy of shop floor workers who possess powerful positions within the structure of the political economy and who are estranged from the control, influence and policies of the leadership of their official union hierarchies. This lack of control of union leaders over powerful rank and file work groups has in fact been seen as a major problem by both capital and the state. This, as well as the more general escalation of industrial conflict linking conflicts over production and distribution, plus declining profitability and low investment, low productivity and low growth, are empirically identified as the constitutive features of the economic crisis that has confronted British capitalism from the 1960s onwards. But, as chapter 4 goes on to point out in conclusion, an economic crisis has also to be at the same time a political crisis, given the state's responsibility for the economy; the failure of the economy is at the same time a failure of the state. If the structure of industrial relations has been producing conflict which is disrupting capital accumulation then the primary need for capital is for some kind of response by the state to re-order and control industrial relations.

The ways in which capital saw the problems confronting it and the forms it thought the response should take and the reasons for such responses being taken are the topic of analysis of the next section of the study. The state's reaction is not seen to follow solely from the needs of capital but also from the whole complex of factors that are outlined in chapters 3 and 4 as well as the specific features of the exercise of class power and the incidence of class, intra-class and political conflict that are discussed in subsequent chapters of the study. It had already been suggested in chapter 1 that crucial to an understanding of the relationship between capital and the state is the qualification that this is not a relationship between two monolithic entities: in practice important structural divisions exist within the ranks of both and this is central to an understanding of the role of the state. This theme is then taken up with respect to capital. It is suggested that in looking at capital's exercise of its power and influence over the state on the issue of industrial relations policy in the particular period under consideration, a four-fold division within the ranks of capital in terms of structure, interests, ideology and policy objectives has to be taken into account in any adequate understanding of the state's role in this process. The 'fractions of capital' empirically identified and discussed in turn were: national based, industrial monopoly capital (i.e. mainly the CBI and EEF); small-scale or petit-bourgeois capital; foreign (mainly American) multi-national capital; and money capital (i.e. the 'City'). It was accordingly suggested that the CBI and EEF have been the main proponents of a corporatist strategy for industrial relations, petit-bourgeois and money capital have tended to support paternalism, while liberalism has tended to characterise foreign multi-national corporations. It therefore follows from this that it is up to the state to develop a strategy or policy for capital since the strategy or amalgam of strategies to be adopted will depend as much if not more so on the support for each strategy within the state and on the part of political factions as it will on the interests of capital. For one thing the interests of capital in any particular conjuncture cannot be defined satisfactorily in abstract terms since what such interests are and what they are aimed at only emerge in the course of the actual conduct of class conflict and political struggle and cannot be defined in advance; for another they do not emerge in the form of the general interests of capital in any case but in the form of often widely differing and divided interests and strategies as to how to preserve (including re-structuring to preserve) the status quo. In this sense, it is as much the state as capital which defines what the interests of the system are which are to be respected and what political strategies for re-structuring and re-trenchment will be adopted.

204

Before proceeding to discuss the state. a chapter was devoted to the role of organised labour. This looked at the structural divisions within the organised labour movement between the TUC, the official leaderships of the major trade unions and shop steward led. rank and file work groups. It made the point that despite these divisions and some tactical and principled differences the labour movement as a whole has still been wedded to the ideology of social democracy though this was subject to but still capable of containing the split between union leaders and shop floor workers. It was also argued that social democracy is consistent with corporatism in the sense that it can be seen as furthering the influence of organised labour within the state but, at the same time, inconsistent with corporatism in so far as the latter undermines the autonomy of trade unions. It was thus found that none of the strategies put forward by capital and none of the strategies available to the state could be guaranteed to ensure the control of trade unions and industrial conflict and this is, of course, because any such strategy must be subject to the impact of class conflict, though a recent trend towards shop steward incorporation was noted.

In the remaining chapters I considered the structure of the state and the role of political conflicts in the determination of the industrial relations policy. notably corporatism, which began to emerge in the 1960s. I approached this discussion on the basis of a separation between issues of state policy and legislation on the one hand, and a consideration of the wider institutional changes in the state. on the other. Hence, firstly I detailed the development of a corporatist strategy for industrial relations by a leading group of Tory lawyers; the paternalistic nature of the major decisions handed down by the judiciary in trade union cases in the 1960s; the deliberations of the Donovan Commission as an aspect of state policy; the role of incomes policies and industrial democracy; and 'In Place of Strife', the IR Act of 1971 and the TULR Acts of 1974 and 1976, and the EP Act of 1975, as key indications of a developing but by no means unambiguous, committed or well founded corporatist strategy on the part of the state. It has been limited not only because it has been connected with other strategies like liberalism, but because it has been opposed by parts of the state outside the executive, e.g. by the paternalism of the judiciary, as well as by groups outside the state. The last and penultimate chapter went into some detail on the institutional changes entailed in these policies and in the attempt to contain industrial conflict, concentrating in particular upon the role of the CIR and its consistent support for strong trade unionism as a mode of social control, and the nature of the more 'interventionist' strategy that this represented when set in the context of the IR Act and when viewed as a transitionary phase between the more liberalistic role of the Ministry of Labour's conciliation and arbitration service and the more corporatist stance of ACAS. In this way it can be seen that the re-structuring of industrial relations entails the re-structuring of the state.

In the analysis of the state my main aim has been to further my explanation of how the state's intervention in industrial relations has been determined. And in this sense it stressed very much how what the state does cannot be reduced either to the systemic logic of capitalism nor to the influence of class struggle rooted primarily in the economy but has also to be seen as the outcome of the specifically political factors of policy conflicts between political groupings and state apparatuses as well as of the institutional structure of the state and the nature of political forms which influence state action. So, for example, it is argued that it can be the case that class interests in state policy are actually constituted and mobilised politically at the level of the state rather than being determined in the economy and then merely reflected or represented in the structure of political conflict. Nor can the state's industrial relations policy be seen as a rational response to the development of capitalism or to class struggle but equally, in any adequate assessment, these factors cannot be seen as being non-existent, or divorced from or irrelevant to the state's actions. What, then, are the general conclusions which I think can be drawn from this study?

It can be suggested, first of all, that a combination of the levels of system and social integration is required for an adequate causal explanation of social processes in sociology: that taking into account the connections between long-term macro-structural developments of the political economy of British capitalism and conjunctural conditions of class and political struggle in the case in question provided a suitable causal context for explaining the problem at hand, why the state started to try to intervene in industrial relations in Britain from the middle 1960s onwards (cf. Lockwood: 1964. Mouzelis: 1974. Godelier: 1972. Giddens: 1976; 124-8). Here as well it is worth while to point out that the nature of the industrial relations 'crisis' has had major explanatory potential in being integral to the causal context but it has to be observed that this crisis has had political and economic aspects which are equally important; for it is not just, say, the crisis of profitability and industrial conflict which have had the most impact but equally influential have been the failure of laissez-faire state mediation, and the immobility of the social democratic state coupled with the need to change state policy and re-organise parts of the state structure. Equally crucial to a sociological understanding of state action is an adequate appreciation of the structure of, and the issues and interests rooted in, class struggles, intra-class struggles and in the conflicts between political factions and agencies of the state. In many ways this is the lynchpin of any structural analysis of state intervention for on the one hand it directly leads into the production of state intervention while on the other hand it is connected with, shapes, and is galvanised by the more long-term and systemic changes in the structure of the political economy of capitalism (see above, especially Chapter 4).

More specifically what must be stressed in this context is the importance of the divisions and even conflicts within the ranks of capital, its splitting into fractions, as a condition for the development of state policy and as a central precondition for the state's autonomy; for it has been shown (see Chapters 8 and 9 above) that the state mediates the class interests of these fractions in attempting to produce an overall and coherent strategy for capital. Although it is difficult to generalise too far, it is probably the normal case for capital to be subjected to economic and political divisions such that explicit class consciousness is as much a problem for capital as it is for the working class. Much sociological writing has pointed to the limitations precluding the working class from developing a clear and indigenous class consciousness and it has almost tacitly assumed that this has not been a problem for capital. I think my discussion of fractions of capital, in particular the accounts of the division between the 'City' and industry and of the role of the CBI in attempting to mobilise capital around what it saw as a distinct set of class interests in state intervention, can serve somewhat to correct this impression. There are certain general interests which mark capital as a class but in view of the divisions noted, how these interests are to be defined and how they are to be pursued strategically can only arise and thus can only be understood in conjunctural terms. If this is so then there can be no general abstract or universal interests of capital by which the state is used. If this is so and if the interests and strategies of capital are fought over under historically specific circumstances then it is difficult to see how the state can be excluded from this conflict. And if the state is imbricated in the conflicts between fractions of capital as well as class and political conflict then what it does cannot result from the demands of the logic of capitalism in a functional manner nor from the interests of capital in an instrumentalist manner but rather the divisions of capital provide for the state an autonomous role with respect to the mediation of class struggle. Since the state is nonetheless subject to (while still influencing) the constraints of the overall structure of capitalism and the demands of capital and labour as they emerge from class conflict this autonomy of the state is only relative. And this point provides a critical corrective to Weberian and pluralist as well as Marxist theories of the state, while indicating, as a consequence, that there is no guarantee that the state will necessarily meet in its policy formation the interests of all capitals or even the very general conjunctural interests of capital as a class, since within the structural limits of capitalism these are always issues of class and political struggle (see above. Chapters 1. 3, 4, 5 and 8).

In this sense it is interesting to note that the notion of fractions of capital allows us to incorporate the valid residue of pluralist political sociology. the fact that modern politics are, in one important respect, about the competition between pressure groups. into our analysis. The fractionalisation of capital, the economic and political divisions and struggles of employers, thus connects their place in the class structure with their role in the state and the politics of policy making, in that the latter are not just about competition between interest groups but also about divisions between class fractions as well as social classes[3] (see above, Chapters 5, 7 and 8).

It has similarly been a major claim of this study that class interests, in particular those of capital, are in an important way politically constituted and they have to be if they are to influence the state's role. This follows on from the argument about fractions of capital and is also directed against reductionist explanations of the state for it suggests that the state and its various agencies do not just mediate class interests but may actually constitute them. So, in view of what has already been said, rather than as a general rule seeing class interests formed elsewhere and then finding their almost automatic expression in politics and in state action, it can be the case that the conjunctural interests of a class or class fraction may be first and most systematically and coherently defined and pursued politically by a state agency or political faction only then, if at all, finding flexible ground for support and further pressure and other formulations within the economic groupings of the class or class fraction. We can see the role of the Conservative lawyers and to a lesser extent the CBI in this light: another example is how the IR Act led to employers in the financial sector setting up staff associations (see Chapters 5 and 7). The initiative here is political and does not correspond to the reflection of interests suggested by many Marxist writers nor to the total autonomy of political interests suggested by Weberian and pluralist models of politics. The interests of classes are thus conditioned economically and politically and it therefore becomes an empirical question as to which is the more important in a specific conjuncture.

I have stressed the central role that the institutional structure of the state plays in channelling, constituting and accommodating class interests and political demands, and how these are constrained to take a certain form and be expressed in a certain way. Here, parliamentarism, the political and ideological conception by class and political actors of parliament as the core of the state and the need to frame demands and policy proposals to suit the constraints of party consensus and adversary bargaining and to see Acts of Parliament as the central focus of political change is one example of this tendency. Another is how a social democratic structuring of the state in, say, the development of quangos allows for the incorporation of trade union leaders. Yet another is how the state has had to be re-structured to allow it to intervene more directly in industrial relations (see above. Chapters 6, 8 and 9).

Related to this is the way in which the law, as I think the study indicates. plays a crucial role in both organising and legitimating state intervention. It forms a particular example of the ideological workings of the state and an analysis of its use shows how it not only serves to legitimate what the state does but also structures what the state does, linking the state to the area in which it intervenes both practically and ideologically. This can apply equally to instances in which the state acts coercively so that coercion of working class organisations will usually have to take a legal form. Thus the state's use of the hegemony of the law is intimately linked to the social control it exercises whether it endeavours to do this in a coercive or a consensual manner. But this argument also calls into question any simplistic division between force and consent as attributes of the state's role for the use of force or coercion needs to be shrouded in the hegemonic consensus of the law while the use of the law needs to be backed up by the use, or the realistic threat, of coercion. As my discussion of industrial relations legislation shows, both consent and coercion are to be found in the state's use of the law because both are fundamental and combined features of the law and the state (see above, Chapters 2, 7 and 8).

Equally important in putting forward a case for taking due account of the specifically political determinants of state action is the articulation and dis-articulation that occurs with respect to the relationships between the various parts of the state. The conflicts I have pointed to in this study between the courts and parliament over trade union rights, between parliament and government over the control of state power, and over the construction of new types of state agency, are sufficient testimony to the explanatory appeal of this factor. This can likewise be seen in the light it throws on the very need to form new state apparatuses to meet new tasks when the limitations of existing ones become apparent. Acknowledging the articulation of state apparatuses and the conflicts between them as a strategic condition for the elaboration of state intervention once again warns against reductionist accounts of the state while emphasising the key influence that the structure of the state itself exercises over what it can and cannot do (see above, Chapters 2, 3 and 9).

As with capital and the state, I need to summarise what I have had to say about the relationship between the working class, the trade union movement and the state. First of all, working class action influences what the state decides to do for the form taken by working class struggle goes a long way towards deciding the character of the state's control of class conflict: we have seen, for example, how the thrust of industrial relations legislation has been towards restoring the authority and control exercised by trade union leaderships over their members in the light of the devolution of bargaining power to shop floor, rank-and-file workers. Thus, a notable element in the relationship between the unions and the state has been the attempt to turn trade unions into agencies of social control. This, however, has met with limited success, not only because of the continued opposition to state policy - until recently at least - of powerful rank-and-file workers, but also because the leading organisations of the trade union movement, the bureaucratic leaderships of the major unions and the TUC, have been caught between, and constrained by, the democratic pressures exerted from below by their rank-and-file memberships and the incorporative pressures exerted from above by the state in general and by certain sections of capital. An interesting way of pin-pointing this contradiction has been to show how the social democratic ideology which tends to characterise the working class as a whole both conforms with but also conflicts with the corporatism that defines the incorporative tendencies that have been fostered by the state. As such, corporatism and social democracy tend to concur if the point is to increase working class and trade union representation and participation within the state but to conflict if the point is to abrogate from unions the strike weapon and undermine their autonomy. And this is contradictory since it is to prevent strikes and to heteronomise trade unions in order to restore capital accumulation and realise state interventionism that corporatism has emerged as a strategy to establish the state's control of industrial relations. Thus, social democratic ideology and practice with their roots in the limits of the labour contract, the separation of politics and economics and the value of the mixed economy tend to keep trade unionism, and by implication at least, the working class within the confines of capitalism. But this still has contradictory consequences for the stability of capitalism since the social democratic emphasis on fundamental trade union rights (especially, the right to strike) and autonomy when set in the context of an economic and political crisis severely limits the options open to the state to resolve such crises. Hence, the study shows that while the working class remains firmly integrated into the structure of contemporary British capitalism this is by no means a consummated and guaranteed process but is subject to persistent and contradictory strains (see above, Chapter 6).

I think that much of what I have had to say in this study helps to place the predictions about the establishment of a corporate state in Britain into some kind of reasoned perspec-

tive. What I have suggested is that corporatism cannot so much
be seen as an inexorable structural feature of the development
of modern capitalism but rather as a specific, conjunctural
strategy pursued by certain fractions of capital and some parts
of the state to constrain class conflict which if successfully
institutionalised would assume a relatively limited and secondary place in the state, co-existing somewhat uneasily with
other forms of state control (cf. Panitch: 1980. Jessop: 1980).
The concept of corporatism thus has use in describing a particular strategy to control class conflict and in defining one
aspect of state intervention but in so far as we might want to
ask 'Why has corporatism emerged at this particular time?' our
real focus becomes the nature of the class conflict to which
corporatism seems to be a suitable response (but only one
amongst others). and the nature of the state for which corporatism forms a suitable strategy. One aim of this study has indeed been to show how and why corporatism has developed as one
possible form of state control of industrial relations, and in
this context its conceptualisation has had a definite and positive analytical use. However, the emergence of corporatism has
been limited by the fact that it has not been favoured by all
the fractions of capital considered in this study; it has not
found wide or consistent support even amongst the trade union
bureaucracies while having for the most part, attracted the
direct opposition of militant shop floor work groups; and its
appearance in the policy of state apparatuses like the executive and some quangos has been more than balanced by the opposition exerted by other state agencies, like the courts, pursuing different strategies for the control of industrial
conflict.

The state, in effect, mediates the class interests and
strategies of distinct fractions of capital in maintaining
capital accumulation and in mediating class conflict and working class demands and struggles and in making state intervention in the economy work. Corporatism has been one leading
contender for managing the state's mediation of industrial
relations which has yet to be effectively established as a
general political response to the crisis of British capitalism.

An important consequence of my argument is the suggestion
that an analysis of the state is possible which is not reductionist, economistic or deterministic in character, and which
does not depend upon the bland and dogmatic presumption of the
autonomy of the state. Equally, I have insisted that it is
possible to have an analysis which takes account of the significance of the economic and political structures of capitalism
and their role in the constitution of class formation, and of
class and political interests and conflicts, and how these in
turn can shape, influence and transform such economic and political structures. If it has achieved nothing else, I hope this
book has at least provided the preliminary indications of the
potential for such an approach to the social analysis of the
state.

NOTES

1. This does not mean that I exclude such things as race or gender – in particular as these and other structures constitute the social relations of civil society – from being determinants of state action. It is rather the case that in this book I have not attempted to unravel the relationship between the state and civil society in any systematic manner. Similarly, it is not my intention to neglect the extent to which my conclusions could be qualified by the use of comparative examples: it has been my aim to present my arguments by means of a case study of a particular society and one obvious point of departure for any subsequent research would be to make full use of both comparative and historical evidence.

2. This raises a major problem I have not confronted in this study which concerns the process of class formation. This involves not only its political aspect as is suggested by the reference to the relationship between the working class and citizenship rights but also how it affects and in turn is affected by technological and economic changes and how these interpenetrate with political formation and other facets of the process of class formation.

3. In making this point I am not suggesting that the pressure group perspective provides an adequate model for analysing the contemporary state. As Offe and Wiesenthal (1979) point out, the very use of the concept of 'interest group' serves to obscure the reality of class inequalities lying behind political struggle by equating groups which cannot be equated in terms of the structure of class power.

BIBLIOGRAPHY

1. GOVERNMENT PUBLICATIONS (when published, and unless otherwise stated, published by HMSO, London)

a) <u>Royal Commission on Trade Unions and Employers' Associations</u>
(Donovan Commission), 1965-1968

i) <u>Published oral and written evidence</u>

<u>Selected Written Evidence</u>, 1968. (Contains written evidence of
     the CBI, TUC, EEF, NFBTE, NALGO and the Law Society)
Ministry of Labour, Minutes of Evidence, <u>Nos. 2 and 3</u>, 1965
Idem, <u>Written Evidence of the Ministry of Labour</u>, 1965
CBI, Minutes of Evidence, <u>Nos. 6, 9, 22 and 69</u>, 1965, 1966 and
     1967. (WE in <u>Selected Written Evidence</u>. See above)
Chief Registrar of Friendly Societies, Minutes of Evidence,
     <u>No. 8</u>, 1965
Idem, <u>Written Evidence of the Chief Registrar of Friendly</u>
     <u>Societies</u>, 1965
NFBTE, Minutes of Evidence, <u>No. 16</u>, 1966. (WE in <u>Selected</u>
     <u>Written Evidence</u>. See above)
National Union of Railwaymen, Minutes of Evidence, <u>No. 17</u>,
     1966 (contains WE 176)
EEF, Minutes of Evidence, <u>No. 20</u>, 1966. (WE in <u>Selected</u>
     <u>Written Evidence</u>. See above)
Motor Industry Employers, Minutes of Evidence, <u>No. 23</u>, 1966
     (contains WE, 200)
AEU, Minutes of Evidence, <u>No. 24</u>, 1966 (contains WE, 111)
Massey-Ferguson (UK) Ltd., Minutes of Evidence, <u>No. 25</u>, 1966
     (contains WE, 103)
NALGO, Minutes of Evidence, <u>No. 26</u>, 1966. (WE in <u>Selected</u>
     <u>Written Evidence</u>. See above)
Philips Industries, Minutes of Evidence, <u>No. 28</u>, 1966
     (contains WE, 102)
USDAW, Minutes of Evidence, <u>No. 29</u>, 1966 (contains WE, 193)
TGWU, Minutes of Evidence, <u>No. 30</u>, 1966 (contains WE, 198)
SIM, Minutes of Evidence, <u>No. 32</u>, 1966 (contains WE, 129)

ICCUS, Minutes of Evidence, No. 35, 1966 (contains WE, 226)
Esso Petroleum Co. Ltd., Minutes of Evidence, No. 39, 1966
    (contains WE, 143)
GMWU, Minutes of Evidence, No. 42, 1966 (contains WE, 277)
Bar Council, Minutes of Evidence, No. 43. 1966 (contains WE,
    295) .
Unilever Ltd., Minutes of Evidence. No. 46, 1966 (contains
    WE, 246)
Shipbuilding Employers' Federation, Minutes of Evidence,
    No. 48, 1966 (contains WE, 311)
Mobil Oil Co. Ltd., Minutes of Evidence, No. 49, 1966
    (contains WE, 270)
NFPI, Minutes of Evidence, No. 51, 1966.
Law Society, Minutes of Evidence, No. 52, 1966. (WE in
    Selected Written Evidence. See above)
ASSET, Minutes of Evidence, No. 53, 1966 (contains WE, 219)
ETU, Minutes of Evidence, No. 57, 1966 (contains WE, 329)
IPC Ltd., Minutes of Evidence, No. 59, 1966 (contains WE, 318)
TUC, Minutes of Evidence, Nos. 61 and 65, 1966 and 1967. (WE
    in Selected Written Evidence. See above)
Kodak Ltd., Minutes of Evidence, No. 67, 1967 (contains WE,
    382)
Sir Halford Reddish, Minutes of Evidence, No. 68, 1967
    (contains WE, 383)

ii) Unpublished written evidence

Employers' organisations
British Federation of Master Printers, WE, 185, 1966
British Iron and Steel Federation, WE, 268, 1966
Cocoa, Chocolate and Confectionery Alliance, WE, 135, 1965
Committee of London Clearing Banks, WE, 130, 1965
EEF (Comment on the evidence of Henry Wiggin and Co. Ltd.),
    WE, 390, 1967
National Association of British Manufacturers, WE, 1, 1964
Newspaper Proprietors' Association, WE, 216, 1965
Soap, Candle and Edible Fat Trades Employers' Federation,
    WE, 239, 1966

Companies and other employers
Dunlop Rubber Co. Ltd., WE, 281, 1966
Esso Petroleum Co. Ltd. (Letter on 'Fawley'), WE, 143, 1965
Kodak Ltd. (Comments on evidence of ACTT), WE, 382, 1967
Lloyds Bank Ltd., WE, 88, 1965
National Provincial Bank Ltd., WE, 44, 1965
Henry Wiggin and Co. Ltd., WE, 390, 1967

Trade unions and other labour organisations
ACTT, WE, 391, 1967
National Provincial Bank Staff Association, WE, 87, 1965
NUBE, WE, 118, 1965

National Union of Seamen, WE, 334. 1966

iii) <u>Research papers published by the Royal Commission</u>

No. 1. The Role of Shop Stewards in British Industrial
        Relations, by W.E.J. McCarthy, 1966
No. 2. (Part 1) Disputes Procedures in British Industry,
        by A.I. Marsh, 1966
        (Part 2) Disputes Procedures in Britain, by A.I. Marsh
        and W.E.J. McCarthy, 1968
No. 6. Trade Union Growth and Recognition, by George Sayers
        Bain, 1967
No. 7. Employers' Associations: The Results of Two Studies:
        1. The Functions and Organisation of Employers'
        Associations in Selected Industries, by V.G. Munns.
        2. A Survey of Employers' Association Officials, by
        W.E.J. McCarthy, 1967
No. 9. Overtime Working in Britain, by E.G. Whybrew, 1968
No.10. Shop Stewards and Workshop Relations, by W.E.J.
        McCarthy and S.R. Parker, 1968
<u>Royal Commission on Trade Unions and Employers' Associations,
    1965-1968: Report</u> (Donovan Report), Cmnd. 3623, 1968

b) <u>Commission on Industrial Relations</u>

Report Nos. 1-3: 1969. 4-13: 1970. 14-24: 1971. 25-33: 1972.
    34-56: 1973. 57-90: 1974

c) <u>Advisory, Conciliation and Arbitration Service (ACAS)</u>

Annual Reports 1975-1979
The role of ACAS, 1978

d) <u>Acts of Parliament</u>

Industrial Relations Act, 1971
Trade Union and Labour Relations Act, 1974
Employment Protection Act, 1975
Trade Union and Labour Relations (Amendment) Act, 1976

e) <u>White Papers and other Command Papers</u>

<u>In Place of Strife</u>, Cmnd. 3888, 1969
<u>Report of the Committee of Inquiry on Small Firms</u>, Chairman,
    J.E. Bolton (Bolton Report), Cmnd. 4811, 1971
<u>The Regeneration of British Industry</u>, Cmnd. 5710, 1974
<u>The Attack on Inflation</u>, Cmnd. 6151, 1975
<u>An Approach to Industrial Strategy</u>, Cmnd. 6315, 1975
<u>Public Expenditure to 1979-80</u>, Cmnd. 6393, 1976
<u>Report of the Committee of Inquiry on Industrial Democracy</u>,
    Chairman, Lord Bullock (Bullock Report), Cmnd.6706, 1977

The Attack on Inflation after 31st July 1977, Cmnd.6882, 1977
Report of a Court of Inquiry under Lord Scarman into a dispute
     between Grunwick Processing Laboratories Ltd., and members
     of the Association of Professional, Executive, Clerical
     and Computer Staff (Scarman Report), Cmnd. 6922, 1977
A Review of Monopolies and Mergers Policy: A Consultative
     Document, Cmnd. 7198, 1978
Industrial Democracy, Cmnd. 7231, 1978
Winning the Battle Against Inflation. Cmnd. 7293. 1978

f) Other Government Publications

Bank of England Quarterly Bulletin, December 1978 and March
     1979
Central Statistical Office, Annual Digest of Statistics,
     various years
Central Statistical Office, United Kingdom Balance of Payments,
     various years
Department of Employment Gazette, June 1975, February 1976,
     November 1976, February 1977, January, March, May and
     November 1978
DOE, British Labour Statistics: Historical Abstract, 1971
DOE, Labour Statistics Yearbook, various years
DOE, Code of Industrial Relations Practice, 1972
DOE, The Reform of Collective Bargaining at Plant and Company
     Level, Manpower papers No. 5, 1971
Report of the Commission of Inquiry into Industrial and
     Commercial Representation, Chairman, Lord Devlin (Devlin
     Report), published by ABCC/CBI for the Commission, London,
     1972
National Economic Development Office (NEDO), Financial
     performance and inflation, London, NEDO, 1975
Joint Statement by the TUC and the Government, The Economy,
     the Government and Trade Union Responsibilities, 1979

2. PUBLICATIONS OF EMPLOYERS' ORGANISATIONS, TRADE UNIONS AND
OTHER BODIES

i) Employers' Organisations

ABCC, Budget Representations to the Chancellor of the
     Exchequer, London, ABCC, 1971
ABCC, Towards National Prosperity, London, ABCC, 1975
ABCC, Employee Participation, London, ABCC, November 1975
AIB, Memorandum to the Committee of Inquiry on Industrial
     Democracy, London, AIB, March 1976
British Insurance Association, Memorandum to the Government
     Committee on Industrial Democracy - 'Employee Participa-
     tion' and Insurance Companies, unpublished mimeo March
     1976
British Insurance Association, Report of Bullock Committee on

Industrial Democracy, unpublished mimeo, April 1977

City Company Law Committee, A Reply to Bullock, unpublished, 1977

Committee of London Clearing Banks, Submission to the Committee of Inquiry on Industrial Democracy, unpublished mimeo, March 1976

Committee of London Clearing Banks, Evidence by the Committee of London Clearing Banks to the Committee to Review the Functioning of Financial Institutions, London, Committee of London Clearing Banks/Longman Group Ltd., November 1978

Confederation of British Industry (CBI) (All published by CBI, London)

CBI, Annual Reports, 1965-1979

CBI, Budget Representations to the Chancellor of the Exchequer, 1966-1978

CBI, Productivity Bargaining, 1968

CBI, Small Firms: their vital role in the economy, 1968

CBI (Economic Directorate), The Short-Term Outlook for Company Profitability, Cash Flow and Investment, 1974

CBI, Industry and Government, 1974

CBI, Let Industry Work, 1974

CBI, The Road to Recovery, October 1976

CBI, Enterprise into the Eighties: a CBI Smaller Firms Council discussion document, October 1977

CBI, Britain means Business, 1977a

CBI, Britain means Business: Programme for Action, January 1978

CBI, Britain means Business, September 1978a

CBI, Challenge to Business, 1979a

CBI Special Publications

Conferences

CBI, The full proceedings of the CBI First National Conference, Brighton, 13-15 November 1977b (Published February 1978)

CBI, National Conference, Brighton, 5-7 November 1978b (cassette tape)

CBI, National Conference, Birmingham, 4-6 November 1979b (cassette tape)

Industrial Democracy

CBI, The Full Text of the CBI's Evidence to the Bullock Committee of Inquiry into Industrial Democracy, March 1976

CBI, Involving People: CBI proposals for employee participation, May 1976

CBI, In Place of Bullock, May 1977

Pay

CBI, The Future of Pay Determination, June 1977

CBI, Pay: the choice ahead — CBI proposals for reforming pay determination, February 1979

EEF, The Donovan Report: An Assessment, London, EEF, 1969

EEF, Statement of Evidence to the Bullock Committee of Inquiry on Industrial Democracy, unpublished mimeo. March 1976

EEF, Response to White Paper Cmnd. 7231: Industrial Democracy, London, EEF, August 1978

The Stock Exchange, Committee on Industrial Democracy: Submissions of the Stock Exchange. unpublished mimeo, March 1976

ii) Trade Unions

EETPU, Evidence to the Committee of Inquiry on Industrial Democracy, unpublished mimeo, no date

GMWU, Industrial Democracy in the light of Bullock, London, GMWU, June 1977

GMWU, The GMWU, the Bullock Report and Industrial Democracy, London, GMWU, August 1977

Trades Union Congress (TUC) (All published by TUC, London)

TUC, Annual Reports and Congress Proceedings, 1960-1979

TUC, Action on Donovan, 1968

TUC, Programme for Action, 1969

TUC, Reason: The case against the Government's proposals on Industrial Relations, 1971a

TUC, The Industrial Relations Bill: Report of Special Congress, 1971b

TUC, The Chequers and Downing Street Talks, July to November 1972, Report by the TUC, 1972

TUC, Economic Policy and Collective Bargaining in 1973: Report of Special Congress, 1973

TUC, Trade Unions and the Industrial Relations Act. 1973a

TUC, Collective Bargaining and the Social Contract, 1974

TUC, The Development of the Social Contract, 1975

TUC, The Social Contract 1976-77: Report of the Special Trades Union Congress, 16th June 1976, 1976

TUC, Industrial Democracy, January 1977. (1st edition published July 1974)

TUC and CBI, Investigation of Strikes, London, CBI/TUC, 1968

iii) Other Bodies

Conservative Central Office, Fair Deal Takes Shape, London, Idem, 1970.

Conservative Political Centre, Fair Deal at Work, London, Idem, 1968

ICCUS, A Giant's Strength: Some Thoughts on the Constitutional and Legal Position of Trade Unions in England, London, ICCUS and Christopher Johnson Publishers Ltd., 1958

Industrial Relations Review and Report (IRRR), No. 188, November 1978 and No. 212, November 1979

Open University, The Conservative Decision to Legislate on Industrial Relations, Audio Tape, D203/4, 1973

State Research, 'The Economic League', State Research Bulletin, No. 7, August-September 1978

TUC-Labour Party Liaison Committee, Economic Policy and the Cost of Living, London, Labour Party, 1973

3. BOOKS AND ARTICLES

S. Aaronovitch, The Ruling Class, London, Lawrence and Wishart, 1961

S. Aaronovitch and M. Sawyer, Big Business, London, Macmillan, 1975

M. Abramovitz and V. Eliasberg, The Growth of Public Employment in Great Britain, Princeton, Princeton University Press, 1957

P. Addison, The Road to 1945, London, Jonathan Cape, 1975

V. Allen, Trade Unions and Government, London, Longmans, 1960

V. Allen, 'The Origins of Industrial Conciliation and Arbitration', International Review of Social History, Volume 9, 1964

V. Allen, Militant Trade Unionism, London, Merlin Press, 1966

V. Allen, 'The Centenary of the British Trades Union Congress, 1868-1968', Socialist Register, 1968

E. Altvater, 'Notes on Some Problems of State Interventionism', Kapitalistate, Nos. 1 and 2, 1973

P. Anderson, 'Origins of the Present Crisis', in Idem and R. Blackburn (eds.), Towards Socialism, London, Fontana, 1965

P. Anderson, 'The Limits and Possibilities of Trade Union Action', in R. Blackburn and A. Cockburn (eds.), The Incompatibles, Harmondsworth, Penguin, 1967

R. Aron, 18 Lectures on Industrial Society, London, Weidenfeld and Nicolson, 1967

A. Aspinall, The Early English Trade Unions, London, Batchworth Press, 1949

P. Bachrach and M. Baratz, Power and Poverty, New York, Oxford University Press, 1970

R. Bacon and W. Eltis, Britain's Economic Problem: Too Few Producers, London, Macmillan, 1978 (2nd Edition)

P. Bagwell, Industrial Relations, Dublin, Irish University Press, 1974

G. Bain, The Growth of White-Collar Unionism, London, Oxford University Press, 1970

G. Bain and R. Price, Profiles of Union Growth, Oxford, Basil Blackwell, 1980

J. A. Banks, Marxist Sociology in Action, London, Faber and Faber, 1970

A. Barnett, 'Class Struggle and the Heath Government', New Left Review, No. 77, 1973

M. Barratt-Brown, 'The Welfare State in Britain', Socialist Register, 1971

M. Barratt-Brown, From Labourism to Socialism, London, Spokesman Books, 1972

E. Batstone, 'Deference and the Ethos of Small-town Capitalism', in M. Bulmer (ed.), Working-Class Images of Society, London, Routledge and Kegan Paul, 1975

E. Batstone et al., Shop Stewards in Action, Oxford, Basil Blackwell, 1977

E. Batstone et al., The Social Organisation of Strikes, Oxford, Basil Blackwell, 1978

F. Bealey and H. Pelling, Labour and Politics, 1900-1906, London, Macmillan, 1958

F. Bechhofer and B. Elliott, 'Persistence and Change: the petit bourgeoisie in industrial society', European Journal of Sociology, Vol. 17, 1976

F. Bechhofer and B. Elliott, 'The voice of small business and the politics of survival', Sociological Review, Vol. 26, No. 1, February 1978

F. Bechhofer et al., 'Structure, consciousness and action: a sociological profile of the British middle class', British Journal of Sociology, Vol. 49, No. 4, December 1978

S. Beer, Modern British Politics, London, Faber and Faber, 1965

S. Beer, British Politics in the Collectivist Age, New York, Random, 1967

D. Beetham, Max Weber and the Theory of Modern Politics, London, Allen and Unwin, 1974

P. Bell, 'Marxist Theory, Class Struggle and the Crisis of Capitalism', in J. Schwartz (ed.), The Subtle Anatomy of Capitalism, Santa Monica, California, Goodyear, 1977

R. Bendix, Nation Building and Citizenship, New York, Anchor Books, 1969

H. Benyon, Working for Ford, London, EP Publishing, 1975

H. Benyon and H. Wainwright, The Workers' Report on Vickers, London, Pluto Press, 1979

S. Blank, Industry and Government in Britain, Farnborough, Saxon House, 1973

S. Blank, 'Britain: the Problem of Pluralistic Stagnation', International Organisation, Vol. 31, No. 4, Fall 1977

F. Block, 'The Ruling Class does not Rule: Notes on the Marxist Theory of the State', Socialist Revolution, May-June 1977

F. Block, 'Beyond Relative Autonomy: State Managers as Historical Subjects', Socialist Register, 1980

I. Boraston et al., Workplace and Union, London, Heinemann, 1975

G. Bowen, Survey of Fringe Bodies, Whitehall, London, Civil Service Department, 1978

S. Box, Deviance, Reality and Society, London, Holt, Rinehart and Winston, 1971

H. Braverman, Labour and Monopoly Capital, New York, Monthly Review Press, 1974

J. Brebner, 'Laissez-Faire and State Intervention in Nineteenth century Britain', in E. Carus-Wilson (ed.), Essays in Economic History, Vol. 3, London, Edward Arnold, 1962

M. Brenner, 'Functional Representation and Interest Group Theory', Comparative Politics, Vol. 2, No. 1, 1969

S. Brittan, Steering the Economy, Harmondsworth, Penguin, 1971

C. Brown and T. Sheriff, 'De-Industrialization: a background paper', in F. Blackaby (ed.), De-Industrialization, London, Heinemann, 1979

R. Brown, 'From Donovan to where?: Interpretations of Industrial Relations in Britain since 1968', British Journal of Sociology, Vol. 29, No. 4, December 1978

W. Brown and M. Terry, 'The future of collective bargaining', New Society, 23 March 1978

W. Brown et al., 'Factors shaping Shop Steward Organisation in Britain', British Journal of Industrial Relations, Vol. 16, No. 2, 1978

A. Budd, The Politics of Economic Planning, London, Fontana, 1978

T. Bunyan, The Political Police in Britain, London, Quartet Books, 1977

L. Carpenter, 'Corporatism in Britain, 1930-45', Journal of Contemporary History, Vol. 11, 1976

R. Caves et al., Britain's Economic Prospects, Washington, Brookings Institute, 1968

R. Caves and L. Krause, Britain's Economic Performance, Washington, Brookings Institute, 1980

D. Channon, The Strategy and Structure of British Enterprise, London, Macmillan, 1973

R. Charles, The Development of Industrial Relations in Britain, London, Hutchinson, 1973

D. Chester and F. Willson, The Organization of British Central Government, 1914-1964, London, Allen and Unwin, 1968 (2nd ed.)

N. Citrine, Trade Union Law, London, Stevens, 1967

W. Clarke, The City in the World Economy, Harmondsworth, Penguin, 1967

H. Clegg, The System of Industrial Relations in Great Britain, Oxford, Basil Blackwell, 1972

H. Clegg, Trade Unionism under Collective Bargaining, Oxford, Basil Blackwell, 1976

H. Clegg et al., A History of British Trade Unionism since 1888: Volume 1, 1888-1910, Oxford, Clarendon Press, 1964

J. Clifton, 'Competition and the evolution of the capitalist mode of production', Cambridge Journal of Economics, Vol. 1, No. 2, 1977

D. Coates, Labour in Power?, London, Longman, 1980

K. Coates and T. Topham, The Shop Steward's Guide to the Bullock Report, Nottingham, Institute for Workers' Control, 1977

B. Cohen, The Future of Sterling as an International Currency, London, Macmillan, 1971

221

E. Coker, 'Local negotiations', in W. McCarthy (ed.), Industrial Relations in Britain, London, Lyon, Grant and Green, 1969

G. Cole, A Short History of the British Working-Class Movement, 1789-1947, London, Allen and Unwin, 1948

G. Cole, 'Some notes on British Trade Unionism in the third quarter of the Nineteenth Century', in E. Carus-Wilson (ed.), Essays in Economic History, Vol. 3, London, Edward Arnold, 1962

R. Collins, 'Trends in Productivity Bargaining', in K. Coates et al. (eds.), Trade Union Register, London, Merlin Press, 1970

J. Corina, 'Planning and the British Labour Market', in J. Hayward and M. Watson (eds.), Planning, Politics and Public Policy, Cambridge, Cambridge University Press, 1975

C. Crouch, Class Conflict and the Industrial Relations Crisis, London, Heinemann, 1977

C. Crouch, 'The Intensification of Industrial Conflict in the United Kingdom', in Idem and A. Pizzorno (eds.), The Resurgence of Class Conflict in Western Europe since 1968, Volume 1, London, Macmillan, 1978

C. Crouch, The Politics of Industrial Relations, London, Fontana, 1979

J. Curran and J. Stanworth, 'Some reasons why small is not always beautiful', New Society, 14 December 1978

J. Curran and J. Stanworth, 'Worker Involvement and Social Relations in the Small Firm', Sociological Review, Vol. 27, No. 2, May 1979

N. Cuthbert and K. Hawkins, Company Industrial Relations Policies, London, Longmans, 1973

A. Cutler, 'Fascism and Political Theory', Theoretical Practice, No. 2, 1971

R. Dahl, A Preface to Democratic Theory, Chicago, Chicago University Press, 1956

R. Dahl, 'A Critique of the Ruling Elite Model', American Political Science Review, Vol. 52, 1958

R. Dahl, Who Governs?, New Haven, Yale University Press, 1961

R. Dahl et al., Social Science Research on Business, New York, Columbia University Press, 1959

R. Dahrendorf, Class and Class Conflict in Industrial Society, London, Routledge and Kegan Paul, 1959

W. W. Daniel, Wage Determination in Industry, London, Political and Economic Planning, 1976

P. Davies et al., Industrial Relations Law and the Conservative Government, London, NCLC Publishing Society (Fabian pamphlet), 1979

E. Denison, 'Economic Growth', in R. Caves et al., op. cit., 1968

G. Denton et al., Economic Planning and Policies in Britain, France and Germany, London, Allen and Unwin, 1968

222

A. Dicey, Law and Public Opinion in England during the Nine-
    teenth Century, London, Macmillan, 1962 (originally pub-
    lished 1905)
M. Dobb, Studies in the Development of Capitalism, London,
    Routledge and Kegan Paul, 1963 (Revised edition)
C. Dobson, Masters and Journeymen, London, Croom Helm, 1980
G. Dorfman, Wage Politics in Britain, 1945-1967, Ames, Iowa,
    Iowa State University Press, 1973
J. Dow, The Management of the British Economy, 1945-1960,
    London, Cambridge University Press, 1964
J. Dromey and G. Taylor, Grunwick: the Workers' Story, London,
    Lawrence and Wishart, 1978
P. Dubois, 'New Forms of Industrial Conflict', in C. Crouch
    and A. Pizzorno (eds.), The Resurgence of Class Conflict
    in Western Europe since 1968, Volume 2, London, Macmillan,
    1978
J. Dunning, United States Industry in Britain, London,
    Financial Times, 1972
D. Easton, The Political System, New York, Knopf, 1953
D. Easton, 'An Approach to the Analysis of Political Systems',
    World Politics, Vol. 9, 1957
D. Easton, A Framework for Political Analysis, Englewood
    Cliffs, N.J., Prentice-Hall, 1965
D. Easton, A System Analysis of Political Life, New York,
    Wiley, 1965
B. Edelman, 'The legalisation of the working class', Economy
    and Society, Vol. 9, No. 1, 1980
J. Elliott, Conflict or Co-operation: the growth of industrial
    democracy, London, Kogan Page, 1978
R. Elliott and R. Steele, 'The Importance of National Wage
    Agreements', British Journal of Industrial Relations,
    Vol. 14, 1976
J. Elster, Logic and Society, New York, Wiley, 1978
F. Engels, The Condition of the Working Class in England in
    1844, in K. Marx and F. Engels, On Britain, Moscow,
    Foreign Languages Publishing House, 1953
F. Engels, 'The Constitutional Question in Germany', in
    K. Marx and F. Engels, Collected Works, Vol. 6, London,
    Lawrence and Wishart, 1976
G. Esping-Anderson et al., 'Modes of Class Struggle and the
    Capitalist State', Kapitalistate, No. 4-5, Summer 1976
C. Farman, The General Strike, London, Panther, 1974
H. Feis, Europe: The World's Banker, 1870-1914, New York,
    Kelley, 1961
P. Ferris, The New Militants: Crisis in the Trade Unions,
    Harmondsworth, Penguin, 1972
B. Fine and L. Harris, 'State Expenditure in Advanced
    Capitalism: a critique', New Left Review, No. 98, 1976
A. Flanders, The Fawley Productivity Agreements, London,
    Faber and Faber, 1964

A. Flanders and A. Fox, 'Collective Bargaining: From Donovan
to Durkheim', in A. Flanders, Management and Unions,
London, Faber and Faber, 1970

J. Foster, Class Struggle and the Industrial Revolution,
London, Weidenfeld and Nicolson, 1974

J. Foster, 'The State and the Ruling Class during the General
Strike', Marxism Today, Vol. 20, No. 5, May 1976

A. Fox, Socialism and Shop Floor Power, London, Fabian Society
Research Series 338, October 1978

B. Frankel, 'On the State of the State: Marxist Theories of
the State after Leninism', Theory and Society, Vol. 7,
Nos. 1-2, 1979

A. Friedman, Industry and Labour, London, Macmillan, 1978

W. Friedmann, Law in a Changing Society, Harmondsworth,
Penguin, 1964

A. Gamble, The Conservative Nation, London, Routledge and
Kegan Paul, 1974

A. Gamble and P. Walton, Capitalism in Crisis, London,
Macmillan, 1976

W. Garside, 'Management and Men: Aspects of British Industrial
Relations in the Inter-War Period', in B. Supple (ed.),
Essays in British Business History, Oxford, Clarendon
Press, 1977

J. Gennard, Multinational Corporations and British Labour: a
Review of Attitudes and Responses, London, British North
American Committee, 1972

J. Gennard et al., 'The Content of British Closed Shop Agreements', Department of Employment Gazette, November 1979

J. Gennard et al., 'The Extent of Closed Shop Arrangements in
British Industry', Department of Employment Gazette,
January 1980

A. Giddens. Politics and Sociology in the Thought of Max Weber,
London, Macmillan, 1972

A. Giddens. The Class Structure of the Advanced Societies,
London, Hutchinson, 1973

A. Giddens, New Rules of Sociological Method, London,
Hutchinson, 1976

A. Giddens, Studies in Social and Political Theory, London,
Hutchinson, 1977

A. Giddens, A Contemporary Critique of Historical Materialism,
London, Macmillan, 1981

A. Glyn and B. Sutcliffe, British Capitalism, Workers and the
Profits Squeeze, Harmondsworth, Penguin, 1972

D. Glynn, 'The last 14 years of Incomes Policy - a CBI
Perspective', National Westminster Bank Quarterly Review,
November 1978

M. Godelier, 'Structure and Contradiction in Capital', in
R. Blackburn (ed.), Ideology in Social Science, London,
Fontana, 1972

C. Golby and G. Johns, Attitude and Motivation, Committee of
Inquiry on Small Firms, Research Report No. 7, London,
HMSO, 1971

D. Gold et al., 'Recent Developments in Marxist Theories of
the Capitalist State', Monthly Review, Vol. 27, 1975

J. H. Goldthorpe, 'Industrial Relations in Great Britain: a
Critique of Reformism', in T. Clarke and L. Clements
(eds.), Trade Unions under Capitalism, London, Fontana,
1977

J. H. Goldthorpe, 'The Current Inflation: Towards a Socio-
logical Account', in F. Hirsch and J.H. Goldthorpe (eds.),
The Political Economy of Inflation, London, Martin
Robertson, 1978

J. Goodman and T. Whittingham, Shop Stewards in British
Industry, London, McGraw-Hill, 1969

C. Goodrich, The Frontier of Control, London, Pluto Press,
1975 (originally published 1920)

I. Gough, 'State Expenditure in Advanced Capitalism', New Left
Review, No. 92, 1975

A. Gramsci, Selections from the Prison Notebooks, London,
Lawrence and Wishart, 1971

W. Grant and D. Marsh, The Confederation of British Industry,
London, Hodder and Stoughton, 1977

J. Habermas, Legitimation Crisis, London, Heinemann, 1976

S. Hall, 'The "Political" and the "Economic" in Marx's Theory
of Classes', in A. Hunt (ed.), Class and Class Structure,
London, Lawrence and Wishart, 1977

L. Hannah, The Rise of the Corporate Economy, London,
Macmillan, 1976

L. Harris, 'The Balance of Payments and the International
Economic System', in F. Green and P. Nore (eds.),
Economics: an Anti-Text, London, Macmillan, 1977

L. Harris, 'The State and the Economy: some theoretical
problems', Socialist Register, 1980

N. Harris, Competition and the Corporate Society, London,
Methuen, 1972

R. Harrison, 'Labour Government: Then and Now', Political
Quarterly, Vol. 41, No. 1, 1970

M. Hart, 'Why bosses love the closed shop', New Society,
15 February 1979

J. Hayward, 'Employer Associations and the State in France
and Britain', in S. Warnecke and E. Suleiman (eds.),
Industrial Policies in Western Europe, New York, Praeger,
1975

R. Hedges and A. Winterbottom, The Legal History of Trade
Unionism, London, Longman, 1930

D. Held, Introduction to Critical Theory, London, Hutchinson,
1980

A. Henderson, Trade Unions and the Law, London, Ernest Benn,
1927

J. Hinton, The First Shop Stewards' Movement, London, Allen
and Unwin, 1973

J. Hirsch, 'Scientific-Technical Progress and the Political
System', German Political Studies, Vol. 1, 1974

J. Hirsch, 'The State Apparatus and Social Reproduction:
Elements of a Theory of the Bourgeois State', in
J. Holloway and S. Picciotto, op. cit., 1978

P. Hirst, 'Economic Classes and Politics', in A. Hunt (ed.),
Class and Class Structure, London, Lawrence and Wishart,
1977

E. J. Hobsbawm, Labouring Men, London, Weidenfeld and Nicolson,
1964

E. J. Hobsbawm, Industry and Empire, Harmondsworth, Penguin,
1968

E. J. Hobsbawm, Labour's Turning Point, 1880-1900, Hassocks,
Sussex, Harvester Press, 1974 (2nd edition)

S. Holland, The Socialist Challenge, London, Quartet Books,
1975

J. Holloway and S. Picciotto, 'Capital, Crisis and the State',
Capital and Class, No. 2, 1977

J. Holloway and S. Picciotto (eds.), State and Capital: A
Marxist Debate, London, Edward Arnold, 1978

B. Holton, British Syndicalism, London, Pluto Press, 1976

R. Hyman, Marxism and the Sociology of Trade Unionism, London,
Pluto Press, 1971

R. Hyman, Strikes, London, Fontana, 1972 (Second revised
edition published 1977)

R. Hyman, 'Industrial Conflict and the Political Economy',
Socialist Register, 1973

R. Hyman, 'Comment', British Journal of Sociology, Vol. 29,
No. 4, December 1978

R. Hyman, 'The Politics of Workplace Trade Unionism', Capital
and Class, No. 8, Summer 1979

G. Ingham, Size of Industrial Organisation and Worker Behaviour,
London, Cambridge University Press, 1970

G. Ingham, Strikes and Industrial Conflict, London, Macmillan,
1974

D. Jackson et al., Do Trade Unions cause Inflation?, London,
Cambridge University Press, 1975 (2nd edition)

P. Jackson and K. Sisson, 'Employers' Confederations in Sweden
and the UK and the Significance of Industrial Infra-
structure', British Journal of Industrial Relations,
Vol. 14, 1976

B. James, 'Third Party Intervention in Recognition Disputes:
the role of the Commission on Industrial Relations',
Industrial Relations Journal, Vol. 8, No. 2, 1979

E. Jenks, A Short History of English Law, London, Methuen,
1934

P. Jenkins, The Battle of Downing Street, London, Charles
Knight, 1970

B. Jessop, 'Recent Theories of the Capitalist State', Cambridge
Journal of Economics, Vol. 1, No. 4, December 1977

B. Jessop, 'Capitalism and Democracy: The Best Possible
Political Shell', in G. Littlejohn et al. (eds.), Power
and the State, London, Croom Helm, 1978

B. Jessop, 'Corporatism, Fascism and Social Democracy', in
   P. Schmitter and G. Lehmbruch (eds.), Trends Towards
   Corporatist Intermediation, London and Beverley Hills,
   Sage Publications, 1979
B. Jessop, 'The Transformation of the State in Post-War
   Britain', in R. Scase (ed.), The State in Western Europe,
   London, Croom Helm, 1980
C. Johnson, Anatomy of UK Finance, 1970-1975, London, The
   Financial Times, n.d. (1976?)
O. Kahn-Freund and B. Hepple, Law against Strikes, London,
   Fabian Society (Fabian Research Series 305), 1972
M. Kalecki, Selected Essays on the Dynamics of the Capitalist
   Economy, Cambridge, Cambridge University Press, 1971
M. Kidron, Western Capitalism since the War, Harmondsworth,
   Penguin, 1970 (revised edition)
K. Knowles, Strikes - a study in Industrial Conflict, Oxford,
   Basil Blackwell, 1952
W. Kornhauser, The Politics of Mass Society, London, Routledge
   and Kegan Paul, 1960
E. Laclau, 'The Specificity of the Political: The Poulantzas-
   Miliband Debate', Economy and Society, Vol. 4, No. 1,
   1975
R. Leigh-Pemberton, 'Public Participation in Business',
   National Westminster Bank Quarterly Review, February 1978
   (Text of speech given in 1977)
V. I. Lenin, 'The State', in Idem et al., Soviet Legal
   Philosophy, Cambridge, Mass., Harvard University Press,
   1951 (Originally published 1919)
J. Leruez, Economic Planning and Politics in Britain, London,
   Martin Robertson, 1975
R. Lewis, 'The Historical Development of Labour Law', British
   Journal of Industrial Relations, Vol. 14, 1976
L. Lindberg et al. (eds.), Stress and Contradiction in Modern
   Capitalism, Lexington, Mass., Lexington Books, 1975
S. Lipset, Political Man, London, Heinemann, 1960
D. Lockwood, The Blackcoated Worker, London, Allen and Unwin,
   1958
D. Lockwood, 'Social Integration and System Integration', in
   C. Zollschan and W. Hirsch (eds.), Explorations in Social
   Change, London, Routledge and Kegan Paul, 1964
F. Longstreth, 'The State and National Economic Planning in a
   Capitalist Society', BSA Conference Paper, Sheffield
   University, 1977
F. Longstreth, 'The City, Industry and the State', in
   C. Crouch (ed.), State and Economy in Contemporary
   Capitalism, London, Croom Helm, 1979
S. Lukes, Power: a Radical View, London, Macmillan, 1974
D. MacDonald, The State and the Trade Unions, London,
   Macmillan, 1960
C. B. MacPherson, 'Do We Need a Theory of the State?',
   European Journal of Sociology, Vol. 18, No. 2, 1977

227

E. Mandel, The Marxist Theory of the State, New York,
    Pathfinder Press, 1971
E. Mandel, Late Capitalism, London, New Left Books, 1975
M. Mann, 'The Social Cohesion of Liberal Democracy', American
    Sociological Review, Vol. 35, No. 3, 1970
M. Mann, Consciousness and Action among the Western Working
    Class, London, Macmillan, 1974
A. Marsh, 1966   ) (See Donovan Commission
A. Marsh and W. McCarthy, 1968)   Research Papers)
A. Marsh et al., Work place Industrial Relations in Engineering,
    London, Kogan Page, 1971
D. Marsh, 'On Joining Interest Groups: An Empirical Considera-
    tion of the work of Mancur Olson Jr.', British Journal
    of Political Science, Vol. 6, Part 3, 1976
R. Martin, 'The Effects of Recent Changes in Industrial
    Conflict on the Internal Politics of Trade Unions:
    Britain and Germany', in C. Crouch and A. Pizzorno (eds.),
    The Resurgence of Class Conflict in Western Europe since
    1968, Vol. 2, London, Macmillan, 1978
K. Marx, 'The Eighteenth Brumaire of Louis Bonaparte', in
    Idem, Surveys from Exile: Political Writings, Volume 2,
    Harmondsworth, Penguin, 1973
K. Marx, 'The Civil War in France', in Idem, The First Inter-
    national and After: Political Writings, Volume 3,
    Harmondsworth, Penguin, 1974
K. Marx, Capital, Volume 1, Harmondsworth, Penguin, 1976
K. Marx, The Poverty of Philosophy, Moscow, Foreign Languages
    Publishing House, 1955
K. Marx, Writings of the Young Marx on Philosophy and Society,
    L. Easton and K. Guddat (eds.), New York, Anchor Books,
    1967
K. Marx and F. Engels, 'The Manifesto of the Communist Party',
    in Idem, op. cit., 1968
K. Marx and F. Engels, Selected Works (in 1 Volume), London,
    Lawrence and Wishart, 1968
A. Mason, 'The Government and the General Strike', Inter-
    national Review of Social History, Vol. 14, 1969
P. Mattick, Marx and Keynes: The Limits of the Mixed Economy,
    London, Merlin Press, 1971
W. McCarthy, 1966 (see Donovan Commission Research Papers)
W. McCarthy, 'The Nature of Britain's Strike Problem',
    British Journal of Industrial Relations, Vol. 8, 1970
W. McCarthy, 'The Politics of Incomes Policy', in D. Butler
    and A. Halsey (eds.), Policy and Politics, London,
    Macmillan, 1978
W. McCarthy and N. Ellis, Management by Agreement, London,
    Hutchinson, 1973
W. McCarthy and S. Parker, 1968 (see Donovan Commission
    Research Papers)
G. Meeks and G. Whittington, 'Giant Companies in the United
    Kingdom, 1948-1969', Economic Journal, Vol.85, Dec.1975

K. Middlemas, _Politics in Industrial Society_, London, Andre Deutsch, 1979

R. Miliband, 'Marx and the State'. _Socialist Register_, 1965

R. Miliband, _Parliamentary Socialism_. London, Merlin Press, 1972 (2nd edition)

R. Miliband, _The State in Capitalist Society_. London, Quartet Books, 1973

R. Miliband, 'The Capitalist State: Reply to Nicos Poulantzas', in J. Urry and J. Wakeford (eds.), _Power in Britain_, London, Heinemann, 1973a

R. Miliband, 'Poulantzas and the Capitalist State', _New Left Review_, No. 82, 1973b

R. Miliband, _Marxism and Politics_, Oxford, Oxford University Press, 1977

W. Milne-Bailey (ed.), _Trade Union Documents_, London, George Bell and Sons, 1929

W. Milne-Bailey, _Trade Unions and the State_, London, Allen and Unwin, 1934

M. Moran, _The Politics of Industrial Relations_, London, Macmillan, 1977

J. Mortimer, 'Powers of ACAS: Case for the Status Quo', _Personnel Management_, Vol. 10, No. 2, 1978

N. Mouzelis, 'Social and System Integration', _British Journal of Sociology_, Vol. 25, 1974

W. Muller and C. Neususs, 'The Illusion of State Socialism and the Contradiction between Wage Labour and Capital', _Telos_, No. 25, Fall 1975

V. Munns and W. McCarthy, 1967 (see Donovan Commission Research Papers)

R. Murray, _Multinational Corporations and Nation States_, Nottingham, Spokesman Books, 1975

A. Musson, _British Trade Unions, 1800-1875_, London, Macmillan, 1972

F. Neumann, 'The Change in the Function of Law in Modern Society', in H. Marcuse (ed.), _The Democratic and the Authoritarian State_, Glencoe, Illinois, Free Press, 1957

H. Newby, 'The Deferential Dialectic', _Comparative Studies in Society and History_, Vol. 17, 1975

H. Newby, 'Paternalism and Capitalism', in R. Scase (ed.), _Industrial Society_, London, Allen and Unwin, 1977

T. Nichols, _Ownership, Control and Ideology_, London, Allen and Unwin, 1969

G. Warren Nutter, _Growth of Government in the West_, Washington D.C., American Enterprise Institute for Public Policy Research, 1978

J. O'Connor, _The Fiscal Crisis of the State_, New York, St. Martin's Press, 1973

G. O'Donnell, 'Corporatism and the Question of the State', in J. Malloy (ed.), _Authoritarianism and Corporatism in Latin America_, Pittsburgh, University of Pittsburgh Press, 1977

C. Offe. 'Structural Problems of the Capitalist State'. <u>German Political Studies</u>, Vol. 1. 1974

C. Offe, 'The Theory of the Capitalist State and the Problem of Policy Formation', in L. Lindberg et al. (eds.), <u>op. cit.</u>, 1975

C. Offe, 'Further Comments on Muller and Neususs', <u>Telos</u>, No. 25, Fall 1975a

C. Offe, 'Political Authority and Class Structures', in P. Connerton (ed.), <u>Critical Sociology</u>, Harmondsworth, Penguin, 1976

C. Offe, '"Crises of Crisis Management": Elements of a Political Crisis Theory', <u>International Journal of Politics</u>, Vol. 6, No. 3, Fall 1976a

C. Offe and V. Ronge, 'Theses on the Theory of the State', <u>New German Critique</u>, No. 6, Fall 1975

C. Offe and H. Wisenthal, 'Two Logics of Collective Action: Theoretical Notes on Social Class and Organizational Form', <u>Political Power and Social Theory</u>, Vol. 1, December 1979

B. Ollman, <u>Alienation</u>, Cambridge, Cambridge University Press, 1976 (2nd edition)

R. Pahl and J. Winkler, 'The Coming Corporatism', <u>New Society</u>, 10th October 1974

L. Panitch, <u>Social Democracy and Industrial Militancy</u>, Cambridge, Cambridge University Press, 1976

L. Panitch, 'The Development of Corporatism in Liberal Democracies', <u>Comparative Political Studies</u>, Spring 1977

L. Panitch, 'Profits and Politics: Labour and the Crisis of British Capitalism', <u>Politics and Society</u>, Vol. 7, No. 4, 1977a

L. Panitch, 'Trade Unions and the Capitalist State', <u>New Left Review</u>, No. 125, 1981

F. Parkin, <u>Marxism and Class Theory</u>, London, Tavistock, 1979

B. Passingham and D. Connor, <u>Ford Shop Stewards on Industrial Democracy</u>, Nottingham, Institute for Workers' Control, 1977

T. Parsons, 'On the Concept of Political Power', in R. Bendix and S. Lipset (eds.), <u>Class, Status and Power</u>, London, Routledge and Kegan Paul, 1967 (2nd edition)

A. Peacock and J. Wiseman, <u>The Growth of Public Expenditure in the United Kingdom</u>, London, Allen and Unwin, 1967 (2nd edition)

H. Pelling, <u>A History of British Trade Unionism</u>, Harmondsworth, Penguin, 1971

H. Pelling, <u>Popular Politics and Society in Late Victorian Britain</u>, London, Macmillan, 1979 (2nd edition)

E. H. Phelps-Brown, <u>The Growth of British Industrial Relations</u>, London, Macmillan, 1959

E. H. Phelps-Brown, 'New Wine in Old Bottles', <u>British Journal of Industrial Relations</u>, Vol. 11, 1973

J. Plamenatz, <u>German Marxism and Russian Communism</u>, London, Longman, 1954

230

G. Poggi, The Development of the Modern State, London, Hutchinson, 1978

K. Polanyi, The Great Transformation, Boston, Beacon Press, 1957

N. Polsby, Community Power and Political Theory, New Haven, Yale University Press, 1963

S. Pollard, The Development of the British Economy, London, Edward Arnold, 1969 (2nd edition)

M. Poole, Workers' Participation in Industry, London, Routledge and Kegan Paul, 1978 (revised edition)

N. Poulantzas, Political Power and Social Classes, London, New Left Books, 1973

N. Poulantzas, 'The Problem of the Capitalist State', in J. Urry and J. Wakeford (eds.), Power in Britain, London, Heinemann, 1973a

N. Poulantzas, Classes in Contemporary Capitalism, London, New Left Books, 1975

N. Poulantzas, 'The Capitalist State: a reply to Miliband and Laclau', New Left Review, No. 95, 1976

N. Poulantzas, State, Power, Socialism, London, New Left Books, 1978

S. Prais, The Evolution of Giant Firms in Britain, London, Cambridge University Press, 1976

S. Prais, 'The Strike-proneness of Large Plants in Britain', Journal of the Royal Statistical Society, Series A, Vol. 141, Part 3, 1978

A. Prest and D. Coppack (eds.), The UK Economy, London, Weidenfeld and Nicolson, 1978 (7th edition)

R. Price and G. Bain, 'Union Growth Revisited: 1948-1974 in Perspective', British Journal of Industrial Relations, Vol. 14, 1976

A. Przeworski, 'Proletariat into Class', Politics and Society, Vol. 7, No. 4, 1977

J. Purcell, 'The Lessons of the Commission on Industrial Relations attempts to reform Work place Industrial Relations', Industrial Relations Journal, Vol. 10, No. 2, Summer 1979

H. Ramsay, 'Cycles of Control: Worker Participation in Sociological and Historical Perspective', Sociology, Vol. 11, No. 3, 1977

H. Ramsay, 'Participation: its Pattern and Significance', in T. Nichols (ed.), Capital and Labour, London, Fontana, 1980

W. Reader, 'Imperial Chemical Industries and the State, 1926-1945', in B. Supple (ed.), Essays in British Business History, Oxford, Clarendon Press, 1977

D. Roberts, Victorian Origins of the British Welfare State, Yale, Archon Books, 1969

J. Rogaly, Grunwick, Harmondsworth, Penguin, 1977

A. A. Rogow, The Labour Government and British Industry 1945-1951, Oxford, Basil Blackwell, 1955

R. Rowthorn, 'Imperialism in the Seventies - Unity or Rivalry?',
   New Left Review, No. 69, 1971
R. Rowthorn, International Big Business, 1957-1967, Cambridge,
   Cambridge University Press, 1971a
R. Rowthorn, 'Late Capitalism', New Left Review, No. 98, 1976
R. Rowthorn, 'Conflict, Inflation and Money', Cambridge
   Journal of Economics, Vol. 1, No. 3, 1977
W. Rubinstein, 'Wealth, Elites and the Class Structure of
   Modern Britain', Past and Present, No. 76, 1977
S. Sardei-Biermann et al., 'Class Domination and the Political
   System: a critical interpretation of Recent Contributions
   by Claus Offe', Kapitalistate, No. 2, 1973
J. Sargent, 'Productivity and Profits in UK Manufacturing',
   Midland Bank Review, Autumn 1979
J. Saville, 'Trade Unions and Free Labour', in A. Briggs and
   J. Saville (eds.), Essays in Labour History, London,
   Macmillan, 1967
A. Scargill, 'The Case for Free Collective Bargaining',
   Personnel Management, Vol. 9, No. 10, October 1977
R. Scase and R. Coffee, The Real World of the Small Business
   Owner, London, Croom Helm, 1980
P. Schmitter, 'Still the Century of Corporatism', The Review
   of Politics, Vol. 36, No. 1, 1974
P. Schmitter and G. Lehmbruch (eds.), Trends Towards
   Corporatist Intermediation, London, Sage Publications
   1979
J. Scott, Corporations, Classes and Capitalism, London,
   Hutchinson, 1979
M. Shalev (formerly Silver), 'Recent British Strike Trends:
   A Factual Analysis', British Journal of Industrial
   Relations, Vol. 11, 1973
A. Shonfield, Modern Capitalism, New York, Oxford University
   Press, 1965
F. Silberman, 'The 1969 Ford's Strike', in K. Coates et al.
   (eds.), Trade Union Register, London, Merlin Press, 1970
D. Simon, 'Master and Servant', in J. Saville (ed.), Democracy
   and the Labour Movement, London, Lawrence and Wishart,
   1954
P. Sinclair, 'Economic Debates', in C. Cook and J. Ramsden
   (eds.), Trends in British Politics since 1945, London,
   Macmillan, 1978
T. Smith, 'The United Kingdom', in R. Vernon (ed.), op. cit.,
   1974
T. Smith, 'Industrial Planning in Britain', in J. Hayward and
   M. Watson (eds.), op. cit., 1975
M. Spencer, 'History and Sociology: an Analysis of Weber's
   "The City"', Sociology, Vol. 11, No. 3, 1977
M. Spencer, 'Marx and the State: the Events in France between
   1848-1850', Theory and Society, Vol. 7, Nos.1 and 2, 1979
J. Stanworth and J. Curran, Management Motivation in the
   Smaller Business, Epping, Essex, Gower Press, 1973

G. Stedman-Jones, 'Class Struggle and the Industrial Revolution',
New Left Review, No. 90, 1975

M. Steuer and J. Gennard, 'Industrial Relations, Labour
Disputes and Labour Utilization in Foreign-Owned Firms
in the United Kingdom', in J. Dunning (ed.), The Multi-
national Enterprise, London, Allen and Unwin, 1971

S. Strange, Sterling and British Policy, London, Oxford
University Press, 1971

D. Strinati, 'Capitalism, the State and Industrial Relations',
in C. Crouch (ed.), State and Economy in Contemporary
Capitalism, London, Croom Helm, 1979

D. Strinati, 'The Political Economy of Class Conflict',
Economy and Society, Vol. 9, No. 2, 1980

D. Strinati, The Political Organisation of Capital, the State
and Industrial Relations Policy in Britain, 1960-1975,
London University Ph.D. thesis, unpublished, 1981

B. Supple, 'The State and the Industrial Revolution, 1700-1914',
in C. Cipolla (ed.), The Industrial Revolution (Fontana
Economic History of Europe, Volume 3), London, Fontana,
1973

J. Symons, The General Strike, London, Cresset Press, 1957

R. Tarling and F. Wilkinson, 'The Social Contract: Post-War
Incomes Policies and their Inflationary Impact',
Cambridge Journal of Economics, Vol. 1, No. 4, 1977

A. Taylor, Laissez-faire and State Intervention in Nineteenth-
Century Britain, London, Macmillan, 1972

M. Terry, 'The Emergence of a Lay Elite?: Some Recent Changes
in Shop Steward Organisation', Discussion Paper No. 14,
Industrial Relations Research Unit, University of Warwick,
Coventry, November 1978

A. Thomson and S. Engleman, The Industrial Relations Act,
London, Martin Robertson, 1975

E. P. Thompson, 'The Peculiarities of the English', Socialist
Register, 1965

E. P. Thompson, The Making of the English Working Class,
Harmondsworth, Penguin, 1968

G. Thompson, 'The Relationship between the Financial and
Industrial Sectors in the United Kingdom Economy',
Economy and Society, Vol. 6, No. 3, 1977

G. Thompson, 'Capitalist Profit Calculation and Inflation
Accounting', Economy and Society, Vol. 7, No. 4, 1978

H. Turner, Is Britain really Strike-prone?, Cambridge,
Cambridge University Press, 1969

H. Turner et al., Labour Relations in the Motor Industry,
London, Allen and Unwin, 1967

H. Turner et al., Management Characteristics and Labour
Conflict, Cambridge, Cambridge University Press, 1977

L. Ulman, 'Collective Bargaining and Industrial Efficiency',
in R. Caves et al., op. cit., 1968

J. Urry, The Anatomy of Capitalist Societies, London,
Macmillan, 1981

M. Utton, Industrial Concentration, Harmondsworth, Penguin, 1970

R. Vernon, Big Business and the State, London, Macmillan, 1974

B. Warren, 'The Internationalisation of Capital and the Nation State: a Comment', New Left Review, No. 68, 1971

B. Warren, 'Capitalist Planning and the State', New Left Review, No. 72, 1972

S. & B. Webb, Industrial Democracy, London, Longmans, 1911

S. & B. Webb, The History of Trade Unionism, London, Longmans, 1920

M. Weber, The Theory of Social and Economic Organization (ed. T. Parsons), New York, Free Press, 1964

M. Weber, From Max Weber (ed. H. Gerth and C. Wright Mills), London, Routledge and Kegan Paul, 1970

K. Wedderburn, The Worker and the Law, Harmondsworth, Penguin, 1971 (2nd edition)

K. Wedderburn, 'Labour Law and Labour Relations in Britain', British Journal of Industrial Relations, Vol. 10, 1972

K. Wedderburn, 'The New Structure of Labour Law in Britain', Israel Law Review, Vol. 13, No. 4, 1978

B. Weekes et al., Industrial Relations and the Limits of the Law, Oxford, Basil Blackwell, 1975

J. Westergaard and H. Resler, Class in a Capitalist Society, Harmondsworth, Penguin, 1976

J. Allen Whitt, 'Can Capitalists Organize Themselves?', in G.W. Domhoff (ed.), Power Structure Research, London, Sage Publications, 1980

E. Whybrew, 1968 (see Donovan Commission Research Papers)

E. Wigham, The Power to Manage: A History of the Engineering Employers' Federation, London, Macmillan, 1973

J. Winkler, 'Corporatism', European Journal of Sociology, Vol. 17, No. 1, 1976

J. Winkler, 'The Corporate Economy: Theory and Administration', in R. Scase (ed.), Industrial Society, London, Allen and Unwin, 1977

M. Wirth, 'Towards a Critique of the Theory of State Monopoly Capitalism', Economy and Society, Vol. 6, No. 3, 1977

A. Wolfe, 'New Directions in the Marxist Theory of Politics', Politics and Society, Vol. 4, No. 2, 1974

R. Wragg and J. Robertson, 'Britain's Industrial Performance since the War', Department of Employment Gazette, May 1978

E. O. Wright, Class, Crisis and the State, London, New Left Books, 1978

D. Yaffe, 'The Marxian Theory of Crisis, Capital and the State', Economy and Society, Vol. 2, 1973

S. Young and A. Lowe, Intervention in the Mixed Economy, London, Croom Helm, 1974

INDEX

Aaronovitch, S., and
   Sawyer, M. 58-9, 70n
Abramovitch, M., and
   Eliasberg, V. 63
ACAS 99, 142, 165, 171,
   177, 180, 186-7, 195,
   197-9, 205-6
ACTT 123n
Addison, P. 65
Allen, V. 33, 48, 49, 50,
   51, 52, 53
Altvater, E. 29n
Amalgamated Society of
   Railway Servants 37-8
Aron, R. 3
AUEW (AEU) 110, 136-7, 166,
   173, 200n

Bacon, R., and Eltis, W. 74
Bagwell, P. 35
Bain, G. 114-15
Bank of England 78, 89, 121,
   174
Barnett, A. 166, 167
Barratt-Brown, M. 63
Batstone, E. 100
Bealey, F., and Pelling, H.
   55n, 56n
BEC 101, 123n
Bechhofer, F., and Elliott, B.
   98, 100
Beer, S. 69
Beetham, D. 29n
Bell, P. 29n
Bendix, R. 3, 140n
Benyon, H. 75, 84, 110, 140n

Blank, S. 66, 67, 89
Block, F. 15, 29n, 30n
Bolton Committee and Report
   59, 70n, 98, 99, 100,
   101, 193
Bonapartism 6-8, 29n
Boraston, I., et al. 84
Bowen, G. 64-5
Box, S. 41
Brebner, J. 46, 56n
Brenner, M. 23
Brown, W., and Terry, M.
   84, 140n
Brown, W., et al. 61, 84,
   140n
Budd, A. 71n
Bullock Committee and Report
   60, 171-8
Bunyan, T. 50, 51, 56n

Capital 5, 7-8, 10, 13, 16,
   19, 24, 25-7, 30n, 33,
   34, 36-7, 41-2, 44, 48-9,
   53-5, 58-61, 66-70,
   87-122, 129, 130-1, 132,
   142, 151, 153, 158-65,
   168-9, 173-8, 181, 186-7,
   190-9, 201, 204, 207-8
capital accumulation 8-10,
   12-14, 15, 16, 17, 18,
   19, 23, 28, 58-61, 70n,
   78-9, 85, 91-3, 95, 106-7,
   117-19, 163, 167, 178,
   181, 183, 188, 199, 201-4,
   210, 211
   centralisation and concen-

235